Benjamin on Fashion

Walter Benjamin Studies

In this series devoted to the writings of Walter Benjamin each volume will focus on a theme central to contemporary work on Benjamin. The series aims to set new standards of work on Benjamin available in English for students and researchers in Philosophy, Cultural Studies and Literary Studies.

Series Editor: Andrew Benjamin, Anniversary Professor of Philosophy and the Humanities at Kingston University, London and Distinguished Professor of Architectural Theory at the University of Technology, Sydney.

Editorial Board:
Howard Caygill, Kingston University, UK
Rebecca Comay, University of Toronto, Canada
Ilit Ferber, Tel Aviv University, Israel
Werner Hamacher, University of Frankfurt, Germany
Julia Ng, Goldsmiths College, University of London, UK
Gerhard Richter, Brown University, USA

Other titles in the series
Inheriting Walter Benjamin, Gerhard Richter
Modernism Between Benjamin and Goethe, Matthew Charles

Benjamin on Fashion

Philipp Ekardt

BLOOMSBURY ACADEMIC
LONDON • NEW YORK • OXFORD • NEW DELHI • SYDNEY

BLOOMSBURY ACADEMIC
Bloomsbury Publishing Plc
50 Bedford Square, London, WC1B 3DP, UK
1385 Broadway, New York, NY 10018, USA
29 Earlsfort Terrace, Dublin 2, Ireland

BLOOMSBURY, BLOOMSBURY ACADEMIC and the Diana logo are trademarks of
Bloomsbury Publishing Plc

First published in Great Britain 2020
This paperback edition published in 2021

Copyright © Philipp Ekardt, 2020

Philipp Ekardt has asserted his right under the Copyright, Designs and Patents Act, 1988, to be identified as Author of this work.

For legal purposes the Acknowledgements on p. xi constitute an extension of this copyright page.

Series design by Catherine Wood
Cover image: Man Ray – Black Silk Taffeta Gown by Alix Gored
(© Man Ray Trust / VG Bild-Kunst, Bonn 2019)

All rights reserved. No part of this publication may be reproduced or transmitted in any form or by any means, electronic or mechanical, including photocopying, recording, or information storage or retrieval system, without prior permission in writing from the publishers.

Bloomsbury Publishing Plc does not have any control over, or responsibility for, any third-party websites referred to or in this book. All internet addresses given in this book were correct at the time of going to press. The author and publisher regret any inconvenience caused if addresses have changed or sites have ceased to exist, but can accept no responsibility for any such changes.

A catalogue record for this book is available from the British Library.

A catalog record for this book is available from the Library of Congress.

ISBN: HB: 978-1-3500-7599-3
PB: 978-1-3502-6232-4
ePDF: 978-1-3500-7598-6
eBook: 978-1-3500-7600-6

Series: Walter Benjamin Studies

Typeset by RefineCatch Limited, Bungay, Suffolk

To find out more about our authors and books visit www.bloomsbury.com and sign up for our newsletters.

Contents

List of illustrations	viii
Acknowledgments	xi
List of abbreviations	xvii
Fashion-Forward Benjamin: A Brief Introduction	1
– Fashion-forward Benjamin	1
– A qualifying remark: The limits of this study and the positivity of fashion	9
– Textual basis	11

Part One   Time/Fashion Models

1	On Some Systematic Aspects of Benjamin's Fashion Theory	15
	– Has fashion ever been modern?	15
	– Fashion as model and as chronotechnics	18
	– Benjamin's fashion passage	20
	– From phenomena in time to models of time	25
	– Fashion changes little	26
	– Being in fashion, being form (Simmel)	29
	– Differentials of time and deviations of direction	36
	– Any past's contemporary: Fashion as a temporal qualifier (the sentimental education of the discontinuous)	40
	– Yesterday, and the day before (sorting time and what has gone out of style)	43
	– Zeitkern (time kernel)	45
	– The ends of Benjamin's time/fashion model I: Revolution	48
	– The ends of Benjamin's time/fashion model II: Historical apocastasis	52

Part Two Benjamin and the Fashion of his Time

2 The Contingent Primacy of Sex(es) — 59
- A sudden affluence: The view of garments gliding by — 59
- Waists are up, skirts are down (1929/1930) — 64
- An onscreen vignette: L'Herbier, Helm, Louiseboulanger — 67
- Should Benjamin have attended fashion shows? Helen Grund, the expert — 75
- The only contemporaneous fashion thinker — 77
- The contingent primacy of sex — 78
- (Schiaparelli's) Genital millinery — 83
- Fashion, whores, Surrealists (The pitfalls of allegory and the forgetting of labor) — 95
- Beyond the logic of the placeholder. Schiaparelli's (and Dora Benjamin's) fashion work — 98
- Morphology of the silhouette (Benjamin vs. Focillon) — 102

3 In/Elegant Materialisms — 105
- Grund's additional notes on the essence of fashion (an unpublished fragment from the Walter Benjamin-Archiv) — 105
- A theory of elegance: The animation of garments according to Helen Grund — 107
- Theory of modeling — 110
- The immanence of elegance — 113
- Taking it to the industry — 114
- Thing and dress (Schiaparelli, Apollinaire) — 116
- The extraneous temporality of the fashion phenomenon — 128
- The supple and the rigid: Two tendencies in 1930s Paris Couture—Vionnet and the Pavillon de l'Élégance — 134
- Versions of inertia: Persistence of the fashion form — 149
- The non-givenness of material — 151
- Materialism à la mode — 156

4 The Tiger's Leap and the Expression of History — 163
- The charm of the previous century — 163
- Striking a note in fashion history — 174

- Morphology in history: Time as ground 176
- The tiger's leap as expression of the economy (Benjamin's fashion ideology) 180

Notes 187
Bibliography 223
Index 233

List of illustrations

0.0	Man Ray: La folie du moment (1937) © Man Ray Trust / VG Bild-Kunst, Bonn 2019.	xviii
0.1	Wols: Mannequin at the Pavillon de l'Élégance (1937). Kunstbibliothek der Staatlichen Museen zu Berlin. © VG Bild-Kunst, Bonn 2019.	12
2.1	George Hoyningen-Huene: Model Dinarzade in a Jean Patou cardigan and notched-collar knit top with tweed inset matching the skirt; hat by Rose Valois. Vogue (1928). © Condé Nast/Getty Images.	62
2.2	Edward Steichen: Tennis player Suzanne Lenglen in a Jean Patou Sports Costume. Vogue (1926). © Condé Nast/Getty Images.	63
2.3	Edward Steichen: Model Marion Morehouse in a black Patou dress with chiffon tiered bottom. Vogue (1930). © Condé Nast/Getty Images.	64
2.4.a–e	Brigitte Helm in Marcel L'Herbier's "L'Argent," costume by Louiseboulanger with Jacques Manuel (1928), film stills. Cinégraphic / Société des Cinéromans / Universumfilm.	68–70
2.5.a–c	Brigitte Helm in Marcel L'Herbier's "L'Argent," costume by Louiseboulanger with Jacques Manuel (1928), film stills. Cinégraphic / Société des Cinéromans / Universumfilm.	72–73
2.6	Brigitte Helm in a Louiseboulanger negligée; Femina (January 1929). Kunstbibliothek der Staatlichen Museen zu Berlin.	74
2.7	Minotaure No. 3/4 (1933), pagespread. Kunstbibliothek der Staatlichen Museen zu Berlin. Man Ray photographs © Man Ray Trust / VG Bild-Kunst, Bonn 2019.	85
2.8.a–d	Mae West in A. Edward Sutherland's "Every Day's a Holiday," costume by Schiaparelli (1937), film stills. Paramount Pictures.	90–91
2.9	Advertisement for Schiaparelli perfume "Shocking" (1937). Kunstbibliothek der Staatlichen Museen zu Berlin.	93

3.1 Man Ray: Elsa Schiaparelli, head on plaster torso, coiffure by
     Antoine (1933). © Man Ray Trust / VG Bild-Kunst, Bonn 2019.   118
3.2 Horst P. Horst: Mrs. Reginald Fellows with coiffure by Antoine
     and white Mandarin collared Schiaparelli coat. Vogue (1935).
     © Condé Nast/Getty Images.   119
3.3 Maison Schiaparelli, design sketch (collection winter 1937).
     Paris, Musée des Arts décroatifs—collection UFAC. Copyright
     MAD, Paris / Jean Tholance.   121
3.4 Schiaparelli Shoe Hat (collection winter 1937). © Ullstein
     Bild/Getty Images.   122
3.5 Maison Schiaparelli, design sketch (collection winter 1936).
     Paris, Musée des Arts décroatifs—collection UFAC. Copyright
     MAD, Paris / Christophe Delliäre.   122
3.6 a, b Cecil Beaton: Models in Schiaparelli Drawer Suits.
     Vogue (1936). © Condé Nast/Getty Images.   123–124
3.7 Cecil Beaton: Wallis Simpson in a black Schiaparelli
     evening jacket with white trimming and a Schiaparelli dress.
     Vogue (1937). © Condé Nast/Getty Images.   125
3.8 George Hoyningen-Huene: Model Toto Koopman in an
     Augustabernard evening dress. Vogue Paris (1934).
     © Hoyningen-Huene Estate Archives / Horst Estate.   135
3.9 George Hoyningen-Huene: Model Marion Morehouse in a
     Vionnet dress. Vogue (1933). © Condé Nast/Getty Images.   137
3.10 Vogue Paris (June 1937)—page spread. © Condé Nast.   139
3.11 a, b Pavillon de l'Élégance booklet (1938). Bibliothèque
     Nationale de France.   140–141
3.12 Wols: Mannequin at the Pavillon de l'Élégance (1937).
     Kunstbiblitohek der Staatlichen Museen zu Berlin. © VG
     Bild-Kunst, Bonn 2019.   143
3.13 a George Hoyningen-Huene: Model Sonia in Vionnet pale
     crepe romain pajamas. Vogue (1931). © Hoyningen-Huene
     Estate Archives / Horst Estate.   145
3.13 b George Hoyningen-Huene: Model Sonia in Vionnet pale
     crepe romain pajamas. Vogue (1931). © Condé Nast/Getty Images. 145
3.14 Vogue Paris (November 1931)—page spread. © Condé Nast.   146

3.15 a–d Lee Miller in Jean Cocteau's "Le Sang d'un Poète," (1930), prod. Charles de Noialles, filmstills. ... 147–148

3.16 a Maison Vionnet, copyright shot (collection winter 1930, model 4220). Paris, Musée des Arts décroatifs—collection UFAC. Copyright MAD. ... 157

3.16 b Maison Vionnet, copyright shot (collection winter 1930, model 4219). Paris, Musée des Arts décroatifs—collection UFAC. Copyright MAD. ... 158

4.1 Edouard Manet: Berthe Morisot With a Bouquet of Violets (1872), oil on canvas. Wikimedia. ... 164

4.2 François Kollar: Three Models from Elsa Schiaparelli's Spring-Summer 1939 Collection (1939). Kunstbibliothek der Staatlichen Museen zu Berlin. © Mediathèque de l'architecture et du patrimoine, Charenton le Pont. ... 168

4.3 Maison Schiaparelli, design sketch (collection spring-summer 1939). Paris, Musée des Arts décroatifs—collection UFAC. Copyright MAD, Paris / Christophe Delliäre. ... 169

4.4 a–c Zsa Zsa Gabor in John Huston's "Moulin Rouge," costumes by Schiaparelli (1952), filmstills. United Artists / British Lion Films. ... 171–172

4.5 Horst P. Horst: Model in corset by Detoile for Mainbocher (1939). © Condé Nast/Getty Images. ... 173

4.6 Femina (June 1939). Kunstbibliothek der Staatlichen Museen zu Berlin. ... 175

Acknowledgments

My first thanks go to Andrew Benjamin for inviting me to propose a book about Benjamin and the subject of fashion for the series *Walter Benjamin Studies*. The invitation came at the end of a day-long seminar dedicated to the question of *Image and Time* in Benjamin's thought, which Andrew had co-organized with Julia Ng through the *Walter Benjamin London Research Network* at Goldsmiths and the London Graduate School at Kingston. The invitation was as surprising as it was welcome. My surprise resulted from the fact that one of my main points of discussion during the section of the workshop, for which I had served as a panel moderator, lay on a number of instances in which Benjamin's reflections on fashion were quite off, not to say indefensible, when it came to accounting for fashion's actual systematic and aesthetic realities. Andrew responded with great interest and encouragement.

My gratitude to those in whose seminars in Berlin and at Yale I first properly studied Benjamin: I thank Winfried Menninghaus, whose sharply discerning and rigorous analyses of Benjamin's works have long been a model, and with whom I had the privilege of working for several years at the Freie Universität Berlin. He facilitated my first publication about Benjamin – an article about his architectural theory, a topic to which I briefly return in this book, by way of Benjamin's enigmatic formulation that the corset can be considered "the torso's arcade" (*die Passage des Rumpfes*). My deepest thanks to Carol Jacobs who in her teaching steadfastly insisted on the complexities and irreducibilities of reading, and in whose classes and advising, consequentially, Benjamin's texts became the objects of closest scrutiny. And I thank Hella Tiedemann – an important teacher remembered by many, and a co-editor of Benjamin's works, who, when I was fortunate enough to still be able to tell her that I was in the process of writing this monograph about Benjamin and fashion, cheerfully replied: "That's wonderful, you've always had an eye for that." If central sections of this book are dedicated to the question of elegance, I now cannot but also think of the elegance that Hella brought to the classroom – intellectual and beyond.

I also am particularly grateful to those individuals in whose seminars, workshops, discussions and responses there was room for thinking through questions of fashion; to David Joselit, when I was a student at Yale, and more recently on the occasion of an invited talk at the CUNY Graduate Center in New York. And Molly Nesbit – also at Yale – in whose work questions of art and aesthetics draw on and out onto the pages of magazines, encounters with the commodity – into the thicket where also fashionable styles linger. In London I was fortunate to have been greeted as a colleague by two outstanding experts, who freely engaged in dialogue, as well as being forthcoming with important advice: historian and theorist Caroline Evans at Central Saint Martins, whose scholarship about the co-emergence of film and the fashion show is of great importance for my own analyses; and Judith Clark, of the Royal College of Fashion, whose work has opened all new trajectories for showing fashion in the exhibition space. I owe particular gratitude to Barbara Vinken, who in her work has formed a pioneering alliance between literary theory and the understanding of fashion, from the most general systematic questions down to matters as concrete as where a seam sits right and where not. Over the years she has been a wonderful interlocutor in public discussions – an eloquent guest and an impeccable host, at the lectern, in the museum, at the opera, and on paper. She also generously invited me to publish an early sketch of a number of ideas about questions of material and elegance, as they emerge in the intellectual exchange between Benjamin and fashion critic Helen Grund in her volume *Die Blumen der Mode*.

The vast majority of the work for this book was done while I was a member of the international research group *Bilderfahrzeuge. Aby Warburg's Legacy and the Future of Iconology*, based at the University of London's Warburg Institute. Funded by the German Federal Ministry of Education and Research and administered through the Max Weber Stiftung, the project provided – and, in its current, second run still provides – a forum for transdisciplinary reflections pertaining to questions of the migration and circulation of images. At *Bilderfahrzeuge* I have had the fortune of finding a group of colleagues who willingly followed my work on Benjamin, and fashion with great curiosity. I would like to thank in particular Johannes von Müller, the group's coordinator, for many a shared hour of comraderie at the Warburg. And I would like to express my profound gratitude to Andreas Beyer, the group's speaker, and one of its central initiators, who, prior to my London time, also enabled a year as a fellow at the *Centre Allemand d'Histoire de l'Art* in Paris, during which I had the opportunity to visit the archives at the *Musée des Arts décoratifs* for the first time. I, like many others, have profited from the energy and dedication that Andreas has brought to these and other institutions, where he has created many a forum for free spirited debates.

On the very last stretches of work on the book I was lucky to have been situated at eikones, the Center for the Theory and History of the Image at the University of Basel, an institution whose colleagues are as rigorous in their thinking about the question of images, as they are model hosts. It has been my great privilege to spend a year's worth of work at eikones as a NOMIS Foundation Fellow where, prior to taking up my long term stay, I had already profited from the interest, curiosity, and encouragement of the director Ralph Ubl and my colleague Rahel Villinger, who invited me at an earlier stage to lecture about the role of fashion in Benjamin's image theory. The rare intellectual and financial generosity of the NOMIS Foundation, finally, enabled me to conduct a last bout of archival research and acquire reproduction rights for a number of visual documents included in this volume.

The book has received the most valuable feedback from two reviewers at the proposal stage, and the encouragement and criticism of one anonymous reviewer of the full manuscript. I thank them for investing their time and labor in crafting their helpful responses. I especially would like to thank the final reviewer for applying their scholarly acumen to my work, in particular for re-orienting segments of my first chapter dealing with Benjamin's philosophy of time and history. At Bloomsbury Academic's Continental Philosophy section I thank its publisher Liza Thompson, as well as Frankie Mace and Lisa Goodrum for organizing the editorial process; particular thanks to Lucy Russell, who during the manuscript's final stages has been a patient and supportive presence. The staff at the Walter Benjamin Archiv at the Berlin Akademie der Künste, in particular Ursula Marx and Michael Schwarz have never wavered in providing ideal support and a welcoming, collegial atmosphere for the visiting researcher. I would also like to thank Emmanuelle Beuvin at the Centre de documentation of the Musée des arts décoratifs (MAD) in Paris for her assistance in researching the estates of Schiaparelli and Vionnet in the collection of the Union française des arts de costume (UFAC); and Richard J Horst of the Horst Estate and Sir

Andrew Cowan of the George Hoyningen-Huene Estate Archives for graciously granting me permission to reproduce pictures by George von Hoyningen-Huene. I thank Caroline Berton at Vogue Paris for generously allowing me to reproduce pages from its 1930s editions. I thank Johanna Zanon, of the University of Oslo, for allowing me to read and cite her magisterial *thèse pour le diplôme d'archiviste paléographe* on the house of Patou submitted at the *École nationale des chartes*, as well as a pre-print version of her and Véronique Pouillard's article on Patou's short lived line *Jane Paris*; and I thank Maude Bass-Krueger for facilitating this contact. And thanks to Christine Mehring for pointing the way on questions pertaining to the work of Wols.

As anybody familiar with the genesis of scholarly writing knows, it is not just the institutions in which one learns and works, but also those to which one is invited to speak that can matter for the development of one's thought, not to mention the intermittent, yet sustained, long term conversations that one develops with colleagues in one's fields. I thank a number of fellow travelers among the ranks of the *International Walter Benjamin Society (IWBS)*, first of all Mike Jennings, whose passion and keen sense of scholarly and institutional necessities have contributed significantly to creating a lasting forum of exchange and dialogue in which the study of Benjamin's works can unfold, and from which the field has no less profited than from Mike's recent joint undertaking with Howard Eiland of writing a model scholarly biography of Benjamin's life and work. And I thank Ilit Ferber, Julia Ng and Daniel Weidner for a number of important discussions and responses. I presented an early version of the book's final chapter in the framework of an IWBS conference at the University of Oxford, and I thank the participants who gave me feedback on that occasion. I thank Denise Koller for a much earlier invitation – also to Oxford – to lecture at her conference on *Clothing Eros. The Erotic Potentials of Dress*. Robin Schuldenfrei invited me twice to speak about Benjamin and fashion to her seminar at the Courtauld Institute, both profoundly enjoyable visits as were our chats in London and in Berlin. Caroline van Eck gave me the opportunity to present material on the fashion criticism of Helen Grund at the Material Agency Forum which she organized at Leiden University, and at later points facilitated related presentations about textile matters at Cambridge. I also tested a version of the Grund-material at the workshop *The Warburg*

Haus: Apparatus, Inscription, Data, Speculation that was co-organized by my Bilderfahrzeuge-colleagues with Mick Finch of Central Saint Martins and the *Institut de recherche et d'innovation* of the Centre Pompidou. Elena Vogman invited me to participate in a seminar organized by her working group on *Critical Morphology* at the Freie Universität, an occasion for me to sharpen some of my ideas regarding Benjamin's implicit theory of the morphology of the development of fashionable silhouettes. Karine Winkelvoss and Andreas Beyer hosted the conference *Erinnerung an das nie Gesehene. Das Bild als Vergegenwärtigung in Kunst und Literatur* at the *Centre Allemand d'Histoire de l'Art* in Paris where I was able to speak about those aspects of Benjamin's work in which fashion becomes an articulation of the past. And so did I at a panel on Benjamin's thinking in constellations at the American Comparative Literature Association in Toronto organized by Nassima Saroui and Caroline Sauter, as well as at a conference dedicated to Benjamin and Warburg as founding figures of *Kulturwissenschaften* organized by Claudia Wedepohl and Peter Mack, a good while before I set up office on Woburn Square for a number of years.

I, finally, thank a number of individuals and institutions who have over the course of the years invited me to speak and publish about related questions, including the medial and artistic practices of styles and fashion, yet from a more contemporary angle: Mick Finch for repeated invitations to speak at Central Saint Martins; as well as Eliza Bonham-Carter, Dean of the Royal Academy Schools, for subsequently bringing me to her institution to lecture for its students; Willem de Rooij and the MMK Frankfurt/Main; Yilmaz Dziewior and Leonie Radine at Museum Ludwig Cologne; Kathi Hofer and MuMOK/Vienna; my former colleagues at the journal Texte zur Kunst; Mirjam Schaub and Iris Dankemeyer at Burg Giebichenstein.

A very special thanks to Lucy McKenzie and Beca Lipscombe aka Atelier E.B for asking me to write for their Paris *Passer by*-book with Lafayette Anticipations. I have tremendously enjoyed – and profited for my own work – from the depth of their expertise and their passion for questions of style, the makers of garments, and issues of display. In Lucy I have found a fellow aficionado of the *Pavillon de l'Élégance,* and of the truly stunning mannequins of the aptly named Robert Couturier, and of Wols' promotional pictures.

I have always been able to count on the company – personal, and intellectual – of friends near and far, among them Jess Atwood-Gibson, Heike-Karin Foell, Tom Hastings, Florian Klinger, Irene Small, and Maria Zinfert.

And then there is the one, again, with whom I share so much more than a "passion for fashion;" namely, my life: Jan.

Abbreviations

AC   Walter Benjamin. *The Arcades Project*, transl. Howard Eiland, Kevin McLaughlin, On the basis of the German volume edited by Rolf Tiedemann. Cambridge, Mass. and London: The Belknap Press/ Harvard University Press, 1999.

BG   Walter Benjamin. *Werke und Nachlaß. Kritische Gesamtausgabe*, vol. 19. *Über den Begriff der Geschichte*, edited by Gérard Raulet. Berlin: Suhrkamp, 2010.

OCH   Walter Benjamin. 'On the Concept of History', transl. Edmund Jephcott, in idem *Selected Writings* vol. 4, edited by Howard Eiland, Michael Jennings, 389–411. Cambridge, Mass. and London. The Belknap Press/Harvard University Press, 2006.

GS   Walter Benjamin. *Gesammelte Schriften*, edited by Rolf Tiedemann, Hermann Schweppenhäuser et al, vol. i–vii. Frankfurt am Main: Suhrkamp, 1974–1991.

PdM   Georg Simmel. 'Philosophie der Mode', in idem, *Gesamtausgabe* vol. 10, edited by Michael Behr, Volkhard Krech, Gert Schmidt, 7–37. Frankfurt am Main: Suhrkamp, 1995

PoF   Georg Simmel. 'Philosophy of Fashion', transl. David Frisby, Mark Ritter, in *Simmel on Culture. Selected Writings*, edited by David Frisby, Mike Featherstone, 187–206. London, Thousand Oaks: Sage, 1997.

PW   Walter Benjamin. *Das Passagen-Werk*, edited by Rolf Tiedemann. Frankfurt am Main: Suhrkamp, 1983.

SW   Benjamin, Walter. *Selected Writings*, vol 1–4, edited by Howard Eiland, Michael Jennings et al. Cambridge, Mass. and London: The Belknap Press/Harvard University Press, 1996–2005.

Figure 0.0 Man Ray: La folie du moment (1937) © Man Ray Trust / VG Bild-Kunst, Bonn 2019.

Fashion-Forward Benjamin: A Brief Introduction

Fashion-forward Benjamin

The main intention of the present book is easily summarized: to provide a general analysis of Walter Benjamin's ideas about the subject of fashion, in their implications, their productivity, and, to a certain extent, their validity. Its purpose is also to situate Benjamin's thought within the context of the aesthetic, historical, and critical aspects of the fashions out of which his ideas, implicitly, emerged—which is to say, primarily, the fashion discourse and practice of 1930s Paris couture and its various mediations. "Fashion-forward Benjamin" as an emphatic indicative, then, signals the manifest connections that existed between Benjamin's writing and the realm of styles, designs, and fashion criticism, as well as other fashion theories (a number of which will be analyzed in this book), hence positioning Benjamin's thought "within" the field of fashion. "Fashion-forward Benjamin" can also be read as relating an imperative; namely, to advance our understanding of Benjamin's work by employing the forces, arguments, and dynamics that emerge from an investigation of the field and problems of fashion—forces with which Benjamin deliberately engaged, and which he himself knew how to put to use.

After the point of attack is marked so clearly, differentiation and with it a certain degree of necessary complication ensue. For it would be wrong to insinuate that Benjamin provided his readers with a fashion theory in the sense of a finished and focused treatment of this one particular topic. Benjamin produced fully formed studies dedicated to questions such as technological reproducibility and its connection to the study of media and aesthetics, of literary and philosophical genres, such as the German mourning play, the art criticism of the Early Romantics, or of individual works, such as Goethe's novel *Elective Affinities*, and the philosophical problems that emerge from these. By contrast, the most focused treatment of the subject of fashion that we find in Benjamin's writing occurs in the *Arcades Project* (Passagenwerk) in which one of the convolutes of notes and excerpts that make up its body—the convolute labeled "B"—is dedicated to the topic of fashion. If this agglomeration is to be considered Benjamin's "most focused" treatment of the matter, it is clear that beyond this collection we aren't looking at concise or developed treatises. Rather, we find a number of further shorter passages, some them generally grouped with the *Arcades* materials, others forming parts of different convolutes, as well as instances in different texts in which Benjamin turns to the subject of fashion, most centrally among them one passage in the theses *On the Concept of History* (Über den Begriff der Geschichte), which Benjamin varied over the course of the subsequent reworkings of this text. (The interests articulated in the theses recur within the body of the *Arcades Project* in "convolute N—Critique of Epistemology, Theory of Progress" [Erkenntniskritik, Theorie des Forschritts], which also occasionally touches on the problem of fashion.) The present study thus also faces the task of connecting and comparing these distributed passages, in order to trace the lines of an argument that was, by all accounts, and despite its rigor, still in the making. Rather than being located in a definite body of text(s), Benjamin's fashion theory needs to be reconstructed.

One method that is instrumental in the context of this task also answers to the concrete embedding of Benjamin's fashion thought. It consists in establishing comparative readings with a different set of fashion writing(s), which Benjamin was aware of, which he partly quotes in the *Arcades Project*, and which in their similarity and contrast also serve to more clearly determine Benjamin's own argument. In the following, three such positions will be addressed, to varying degrees of attention and extension. These include the sociological fashion philosophy of Georg Simmel (investigated in chapter 1); and to a much smaller extent I will address a morphological argument derived from art historian Henri Focillon's essay "The Life of Forms" (La Vie des Formes), which in Benjamin's work connects with a different, post-Goethean strain of morphological thought (I develop these in sections of chapters 2 and 4 respectively).

The most important points of reference, however, are the criticism and theoretical reflections of fashion critic Helen Grund, with whom Benjamin was acquainted since the years of the Weimar Republic and whose published work and, in part, personal guidance introduced him to the fashion scene of 1930s Paris (this is done most centrally in chapters 2 and 3). While Benjamin does not quote them, a number of pieces of fashion criticism which Grund published in the German magazine *Für die Frau* tie Benjamin's overall argument to the development of fashionable styles of his own moment. Even more important is a systematic essay by Grund titled "On the Essence of Fashion" (Über das Wesen der Mode), which Benjamin excerpts in the *Arcades Project*, and one further document which, to the present author's best knowledge, has remained unpublished until today. This is an eight-page typescript, nowadays kept at the Walter Benjamin-Archiv at the Akademie der Künste in Berlin, which Grund must have handed over to Benjamin. Its exact origin and purpose are unclear (see chapter 3), whereas its subject is not. On these pages Grund develops a small theory of elegance in dress and modeling, which can be read as a counterpart to Benjamin's own reflections on the deployment of temporality and the status of material and matter in fashion.

As we shall see, Benjamin's ideas also communicate with a number of further positions in literature and criticism (Apollinaire, Baudelaire, Tzara), and, if we follow and extend the trajectories indicated by Grund's work, we can also establish connections into the actual production of fashion in the work of couturiers such as Jean Patou. However, the two designers whose work is most important here are Elsa Schiaparelli and Madeleine Vionnet, with a sideglance being cast on creations by Louise Boulanger. The photographic mediation of their designs through protagonists such as Man Ray, Cecil Beaton or George von Hoyningen-Huene, as well as fashion's filmic manifestations in the work of directors such as L'Herbier, or of actresses such as Mae West, occupies an important place, too—the technology and praxis of film being generally of significant importance for the mediation of fashion at the moment under consideration.

Of these latter names, Grund's pertinent writings only indicate one—Patou—and not in the systematic pieces which Benjamin had definitely read. The work of Schiaparelli is implicitly, or through negligence anonymously, present in the *Arcades Project* by way of an argument led by Grund, and hyperbolized by the Surrealists and Benjamin, according to which fashion must be considered an extension of the morphological transformation of bodies along the vectors of sex, desire, and genital intercourse. As we shall see in chapter 2, this is an influential but ultimately contingent position in the explanation of fashion, and we will have to situate Benjamin's participation in it as such. In the subsequent chapters Schiaparelli's designs are also considered in their capacities of articulating what could be called an "obdurate" fashion form, a notion that, while coinciding with Benjamin's fashion aesthetics, through various aesthetic strategies, places garments on a shared tangent with the realm of things; Schiaparelli's work of the late 1930s also serves as an emblematic treatment of fashion's staging of historical recursivity. Vionnet's work, by contrast, is investigated for its capacities to make matter light, to animate what—according to the rules of elegance—may not rest inert. In chapter 3 both Schiaparelli and Vionnet are, finally, set into a relation with the presentation of couture at the 1937 *Pavillon de l'Élégance*, erected on the occasion of that year's Paris World Fair, in which, again an aesthetic of the obdurate, inert fashion form prevailed.

What emerges in the investigation of the mentioned couturiers' work are empirical moments in the history and the aesthetic of fashion—Paris fashion, more precisely—with which Benjamin's work clearly, and at times explicitly, communicates. Three developments are particularly important, and they each occasion one of the chapters that are gathered in the second section of the book, titled "Benjamin and the fashion of his time." First, a shift from the more androgynous cuts of the second half of the 1920s to the gender-dimorphous silhouettes of the 1930s is treated in chapter 2, "The contingent primacy of sex(es)." Chapter 3, "In/Elegant materialisms," analyzes the (re)institution of an ideal of elegance into a position of aesthetic dominance, and the structural formulation of two opposing modes of articulating material and materiality in fashion, namely— associated with the program of elegance—the ideal of an animation and a making light of matter, and an opposing ideal, formulated implicitly by Benjamin, of what could be called an "obdurate" fashion form: hieratic, monumental, fragmentary. Finally, chapter 4 examines the return towards the end of that decade to the styles of the Belle Époque, up to the reintroduction of garments such as the corset, which Benjamin referred to as "the torso's arcade" (AP 492) (die Passage des Rumpfes [PW 614]), providing a strange double to one of Benjamin's central figures of thought, the "tiger's leap into the past," and of the *Arcades Project*'s overall thrust of recuperating the lost formations of nineteenth-century Paris. Each of these chapters also addresses general questions that are either implicitly or explicitly developed in Benjamin's writings—questions of a sexual etiology of fashion and the merely contingent assignment of the gender binary as the prime structuring force of fashionable distinction; notions of material, form, and temporality; and, finally, the preconditions and implications of turning fashion's rearticulation of the past into its central characteristic.

Putting Benjamin's writings in touch with these developments not only helps us realize a more complete and frequently more finely grained picture of Benjamin's ideas about fashion and their implications in his overall thinking; the exchange with the historical and aesthetic reality of fashionable styles is also instrumental in achieving a clearer understanding of the audacity and limitations of Benjamin's intellectual project. This is arguably most acute in relation to the last of the mentioned developments, namely the return to the styles of the late nineteenth century. This specific historico-temporal thrust— to rearticulate the forms and contents of the Belle Époque—parallels Benjamin's own overall intention in the *Arcades Project*, namely to work through the discarded manifestations of said period. As chapter 4 demonstrates, Benjamin explicitly establishes this parallel between his own work and the historical movements of contemporaneous couture himself. No less important is a certain qualification of Benjamin's arguments, which these connections allow for. This concerns, centrally, the figure that stands at the very heart of Benjamin's fashion thought and that serves as one of the prime mediators to his wider philosophy of time and history: the figure of fashion's tiger's leap into the past, by which fashion rearticulates the temporally disconnected manifestations of what has gone out of style. Relating this figure to the systemic and specific historical conditions of fashion in its diversity highlights a certain generalizing tendency in Benjamin's thought: whereas said historico-temporal recursion is a *potential* generally inherent to fashion, not all fashion operates on its *actualization*. Benjamin's thought—like the fashions of the moment in which it was articulated, i.e. the late 1930s however, presents the tiger's leap as *the* constitutive operation of fashion, *tout court*. Even a cursory investigation of the development of Paris couture from the late 1920s to the late 1930s helps us position his thinking—employing Benjamin's own ideas in the *Arcades Project*—in relation to a set of historical circumstances which favored the emergence of this one specific aspect of fashion. Benjamin's theorization of it is not determined or "caused" by these developments but, rather, exemplifies an expression (*Ausdruck*) of these conditions—a type of relation that Benjamin diagnosed himself in the *Arcades Project*, by drawing his interpretation of Goethean morphology into the study of historical time and the economic formations that develop in it. Surprisingly (or not) it becomes clear that this central element of Benjamin's concept of fashion—the tiger's leap—expresses a condition of widespread economic devastation, a harsh state of impoverishment and disenfranchisement of wide sectors of society, while wealth is centralized in a few insular spots (not dissimilar to the conditions we are witnessing in our own present). As will become clear in the last chapter of this book, the exclusive focus on the tiger's leap as the central operation of fashion partakes in this logic of overall impoverishment and the concomitant identification of fashion with a rarefaction of wealth and luxury—a moment which, it could be argued, lays bare an ideological component in Benjamin's thinking about this subject matter

While focusing on Benjamin's treatment of vestimentary fashions, there is, by the way, no reason for modeling a general understanding of "fashion" exclusively on the example of garments; anthropologists such as Marcel Mauss, or their readers in contemporary fashion studies, have expanded the field of analysis, for instance, into the investigation of modes of standing, walking, or gesticulating.[1] And everybody is aware of the fact that, even beyond these matters, all sorts of articulations can be subject to the ebbs and flows of fashion, from gastronomic preferences (avocado toast), to the consumption of artistic subgenres (superhero comic book adaptations in film), to the usage of theoretical vocabularies or interpretative frameworks in scholarly analyses. While the present study does not aim at providing a general theory of fashion, we could perhaps point to a number of basic structural components, such as the temporalized processing of difference in the medium of forms, which travel through a stratum that is to a certain extent coextensive with social fields. And we could speculate that one reason as to why the question of fashion and fashions is most frequently posed in relation to manifestations of clothes could be that these vestimentary transformations are set against the cultural-temporal meta-stable ground of the human body—a stability against which the oscillations of styles à la mode are particularly visible.

The concerns sketched up to this point are developed for the most part in the book's second section, "Benjamin and the fashion of his time", comprising chapters 2 through 4. The book's first section "Time/fashion models," by contrast, comprises a single yet very extensive chapter that operates differently and could stand on its own against the remaining three, in that, while establishing a comparison with Simmel's ideas, it develops a systematic reading of Benjamin's works in which a number of its central *structural* concerns are established. Cutting vastly across the *Arcades Project* and the theses *On the Concept of History* this chapter tracks the intricacies of Benjamin's deployment of fashion as the temporalized processing of difference. Having one of its anchors in Simmel's sociology of the fashion form, Benjamin expands the purview of these ideas considerably, allowing him to develop not only one model of historical time, but also figurations such as the dialectical image or the trans-historical constellation, for which fashion's tiger's leap served as an important model, culminating in its parallel with another Benjaminian intellectual figure, namely the *Zeitkern*—the time kernel of (historical) cognition. This chapter also takes a look at the implications of what Benjamin calls the differentials of time, which fashion makes operative. The chapter further clarifies the specific structures in which Benjamin and Simmel see fashion as implementing temporal recursions and the rearticulations of past (stylistic) contents, hence enabling an understanding of fashion as a temporal qualifier. The chapter also revolves around a fundamental observation regarding the functionality of fashion, and Benjamin's theoretical unfolding of this circumstance. Fashion is a chronotechnics, a collectively articulated mechanism for handling and articulating time. Or, in Benjamin's words, fashion is a *Zeitmass* (PW 997), a "measure of time" (AP 830). This argument occasions the probing of several connections to current models in the post-media archeological and post-actor network-field of cultural techniques, in which such techniques are understood in terms of their operative potentials. The example of fashion counting towards an operationalization of time.

However, rather than merely diagnosing this operationalization of time, Benjamin pushes further and functionalizes fashion for his own wider purposes. Rather than a mere object to be studied for its own sake, in Benjamin's work fashion also becomes an object that allows for the wider production of knowledge. Thinking through fashion allowed Benjamin to formulate certain insights, in our case primarily with regards to his understanding of time and history (cf. fashion's function as an exemplar of and for the dialectical image). In Benjamin's writing we thus face an intriguing dual status of fashion: while clearly embedded in the actuality of historical time, and Benjamin's historical present, and studied by Benjamin as such, there is also a tendency in his thought to remove fashion from its status as a phenomenon in time and realize it as a model of time.

With an eye to these general concerns, this first chapter also positions Benjamin's thought in relation to other systematic approaches to the problem of fashion. One general question is whether or not fashion, as a systemic condition, is datable—i.e., whether there is a point within the history of humankind at which we can locate the beginning of fashion, or whether it is coeval with the state of all systems of human culture (and perhaps already to be found in earlier manifestations of systemic self-organization). With regard to the work of Benjamin in general, and in particular with regard to Benjamin's work on fashion, this question most frequently occurs in the guise of theories of "modernity," understood as a post-traditional point of inception for fashion—a perspective which Benjamin clearly did *not* espouse.[2]

This is a central point at which the analysis presented in this book engages critically with a number of interpretations of Benjamin's work: of these, Susan Buck-Morss's *The Dialectics of Seeing: Walter Benjamin and the Arcades Project* is particularly pertinent. As will become clear throughout chapter 1, my reading, which is based on following the logics of Benjamin's fashion thought, leads us to a position that is critical of a number of Buck-Morss's assumptions. This critique is developed in the spirit of recognition for her achievements. Upon the date of publication of the present book, *The Dialectics of Seeing* marks its 30th anniversary, and it still represents an approach that demands serious engagement. As will become clear in chapter 2, in which I call upon Buck-Morss's feminist critiques of certain tropes in Benjamin's argument, her work is in other parts indeed foundational for the perspective developed in my own work. Other important points of orientation are Werner Hamacher's studies of Benjamin's writings on the philosophy of historical time, as well as Peter Fenves' and Julia Ng's more recent investigations of Benjamin's philosophy of time. And it is safe to say that within the field of fashion studies, while building on a whole body of scholarship, this book relies on at least two examples: one, the work of Barbara Vinken, who pioneered a perspective in which the insights of literary theory and the investigation of the aesthetics of fashion are treated on par; and the foundational historical work of Caroline Evans, whose far-reaching yet detailed studies of the culture, practices, institutions, and mediality of fashion in the age of classical modernity, in particular her work on the history of the fashion show, form one of the pillars for the analysis that is gathered in the present book.

A qualifying remark: The limits of this study and the positivity of fashion

At first sight, the present monograph could be seen as being characterized by a slightly monofocal perspective. Starting out with a reconstruction of a number of systematic aspects of Benjamin's fashion theory, to then move into three main points of intersection between Benjamin's thought and the discourse and practice of the fashion of his own present (the alleged grounding of fashion in sexuality; questions of material; and the de facto historical recursion of the fashions of the moment of his work on the *Arcades Project*), this book provides—to a certain extent—a reading of Benjamin's works through the lens of fashion. If this interrelation is unfolded on the following pages, it is not with the intention of positing fashion as a master-trope for a rereading of Benjamin, *tout court*, and neither is the idea to posit Benjamin's work as the sine qua non of understanding the systemic, temporal, and aesthetic aspects of fashion. The limits of the applicability between these two terms—"Benjamin" and "fashion"—are explored from within rather than from without.

In other words: where, for instance, the specific configuration of fashion and sexuality, or fashion and material, are analyzed, this study only provides comparative and contrasting examples insofar as the nature of the relationship under investigation is concerned. The discussion of the sexual etiology of fashion, a position which Benjamin adhered to, is elucidated through similar and contrasting opinions among his peers, sources, and contemporaries, as well as discussed in relation to general reflections about the potential configuration of the erotic and the modish. It is not contrasted or compared with Benjamin's general theory of sexuality—procreative or not—or with the many other specific ways in which, historically, aesthetically, and discursively, fashionable difference has been interpreted to ultimately run off sexual desire (or if only sparingly so). Similarly, the discussion of the way in which fashion and the material are configured in Benjamin's thought is developed in contrast to the manner in which his contemporary and source, critic Helen Grund, implicitly positioned these terms in her theory of elegance; the work of couturiers such as Vionnet—the master-technician of the elegant animation of textiles—and Schiaparelli—her opponent—is investigated; and relations to Benjamin's theory of camera shot and the editing of filmic material are established, because each of these specific operations furthers our understanding of the structure and content of Benjamin's ideas about fashion and the way in which they are situated within a contemporary panorama of fashion-related ideas and practices (including their general implications beyond their historic specificity). What the present study does not do is systematically situate these analyses, for instance, within an extensive and explicit discussion of the totality of Benjamin's materialism in all its manifold nuances and articulations, or provide a history of elegant styles prior to the moment on which it focuses (the 1930s).

The reasons for these limitations are simple: they result from the combination of the necessary finitude of all analytical endeavors, and the comparatively intense labor that still needed to be done in order to chart the historical and theoretical, discursive and praxis-related aspects of the territory of fashion as it presented itself to Benjamin, and as it framed his reflections.

The precondition for this set-up is, finally, that one conceptualizes fashion in a sober manner, as a systemic, historical, and aesthetic reality; or, along the lines of inquiry that at one point opened the fields of media and discourse archeologies, as a positivity. Adopting this approach does not mean to posit that fashion, as Kittler once famously claimed for media, is "determining our situation"; nor does it mean to presume that its purview could be as vast as that of Foucault's notion of discourse, the knowable at a given point in history; one of the paradigms on which a Kittlerian media archaeology was built.[3] It does, however, entail that, in its modest way, one acknowledges what, to an extent, Benjamin did: that fashion, prior to its potential critiques, is a fact.

Textual basis

The textual basis for references to Benjamin's works in this book are, for the most part, the still valid *Gesammelte Schriften* edition, published under the direction of Rolf Tiedemann with Suhrkamp Verlag, and the standard translations and editions provided in the *Selected Writings* edition, published with Belknap Press under the direction of Michael Jennings and Howard Eiland. Suhrkamp is currently in the process of producing a new critical edition (*Werke und Nachlaß*), which provides a much higher degree of philological and editorial information on Benjamin's texts than its predecessor. As my argument, in particular in segments of chapter 1, is partly based on certain variations in the different versions of *On the Concept of History* (*Über den Begriff der Geschichte*), which only emerge fully in this new edition, I have worked with the relevant volume in this more recent version, which was done by Gérard Raulet. On a number of instances I have slightly modified Howard Eiland's and Edmund Jephcott's existing, highly reliable English translations, to put an emphasis on semantic nuances that are more pertinent to the overarching questions of my inquiry. These modifications are indicated by the abbreviation TM (translation modified). Throughout, English translations are given alongside German quotes, to either allow the proficient reader to track Benjamin's thought in its original language, or, if need be, to verify the translation offered. All other translations are mine, unless indicated differently.

For frequently quoted texts I have used the following abbreviations, which appear in parentheses throughout the text (for complete references, please see the bibliography): the *Arcades Project*, AP; *Das Passagenwerk*, PW; *On the Concept of History*, OCH; *Über den Begriff der Geschichte*, BG. References to other texts by Benjamin appear in the footnotes and are abbreviated *SW*, referring to the *Selected Writings* edition, and *GS*, referring to the *Gesammelte Schriften*. In both cases, numbers indicate the respective volumes. References to Simmel's *Philosophy of Fashion* are abbreviated as *PoF*, and to the German original *Philosophie der Mode* as *PdM*.

Figure 0.1 Wols: Mannequin at the Pavillon de l'Élégance (1937). Kunstbibliothek der Staatlichen Museen zu Berlin. © VG Bild-Kunst, Bonn 2019.

Part One

Time/Fashion Models

1

On Some Systematic Aspects of Benjamin's Fashion Theory

Has fashion ever been modern?

Across a number of smaller and larger divergences, it is possible to recognize in the field of systematic fashion theory a major subdivision that touches on questions of fashion's origin and inceptions. Let us consider two opposite approaches first. One school regards fashion as a feature pervasive to the entirety of human culture and possibly even to pre-human—i.e., animal and evolutionary—formations. Another school operates with a concept of fashion as datable, i.e., as a phenomenon which can be ascribed a more or less distinct point of temporal emergence that lies within the continuum of (human) history. The first school assigns a *systemic origin* to fashion and thus propagates an idea of fashion as responding to basic needs that are coeval with the condition of societal, cultural, or all systemic existence (anthropological, proto-anthropological, animal).[1] The second school assigns a *discrete temporal origin* to the phenomenon of fashion. While the protagonists of this second school usually operate within constricted cultural confines—for the most part an understanding of "Western" societies—there is still a surprisingly high number of suggestions as to when and where to situate the *actual* inception of "fashion," encompassing, in chronological order, the abrogation of common cuts in men's and women's garb through the introduction of tailored, fitted, and—in the case of feminine attire—laced vestments as of the twelfth century; the emergence of the earliest forms of capitalism in the Flemish and Italian city states of the Renaissance; the indeed fundamental overthrowing of aristocratic and stratified social formations in the French Revolution and the concomitant emergence of bourgeois society, with its realignments of the vestimentary codes for men and women; and the beginnings of the couture system in the mid-nineteenth century (i.e., the period of the *mode de cent ans*).[2] While the period since this last system's collapse in the late 1970s—i.e., the ascendancy of the economic formation of prêt-à-porter—is swiftly expanding toward half a century, this transformation hasn't quite been dignified by being recognized as (yet another) starting point of fashion. Given its fundamental significance for an alignment of the tastes, aesthetics, and styles of vast parts of the globe, it eventually might. And there is no doubt that in some future treatise the transition into the digital era will also be recognized as one of those shifts that start fashion (again).

This latter, datable approach to fashion doesn't preclude systematic concerns. The principle of fashion's datability can be reconciled with the idea of passing over a more encompassing historico-systemic cliff edge. This makes for a third approach, espoused in various ideological and epistemological shades, all of which recognize in the advent of fashion the hallmark or symptom of a systemic break, a major rupture, usually seen as correlating with a historico-systemic transformation, some sort of alteration in the basic conditions which triggered, necessitated, or favored the emergence of "fashion." These can be as unspecific as declaring fashion to be coeval with—in blanket terms—"the origin and development of the modern West," or as specific both in terms of theoretical approach and date as locking the incipit of fashion in step with the emergence of a semantics of contingency and the beginning of a transition into what, in sociological systems theory, is referred to as functional differentiation and second-order observation.[3] Unsurprisingly, these approaches tend to consider the systemic preconditions for the existence of fashion as incompatible, if not irreconcilable, with an opposite type of systemic organization usually referred to as "traditional," and as if both were the two sides of a Rubin's vase diagram: one in which the profile of fashion emerges only under the condition of the obfuscation of the vessel of "tradition."[4]

The mentioned model of a meta-historical subdivision—the pitting of a regime of acceleration and rupture against the vision of an "archaic and stable past"—as well as a certain concomitant understanding of "modernity" as a passage from the first into the second stage, have in recent decades been treated with due skepticism and have received their share of criticism. This has been achieved not least by applying the fundamental critique of ethnological models and their mere positing of non-Western (i.e., "traditional") societies as "being without history" to the very Western framework itself.⁵ Yet there remain strong voices to argue for adopting a quasi-Baudelairean perspective and for identifying the time span of the historical existence of *la mode* with the age of modernity, of aesthetic modernism in particular, and, if you will, to declare the famous enumeration from *Le peintre de la vie moderne*, "l'époque, la mode, la morale, la passion," to be the headline for an assumed joint life span of the modish and the modern; and be it only because the scholarly and theoretical study of the subject under consideration here (fashion) would respond to the semantics with which a number of its most eminent thinkers, protagonists, and observers did describe its formations *à l'époque*.⁶

Whereas such a framing plays off the affinity between *la mode* and modernity, etymology actually suggests a different kinship. The *Grand Robert* informs its readers that the first usages of the French term *la mode* occurred in the late fourteenth century (pointing to a documented instance about a century later in 1485), when it simply translated the Latin *modus*—i.e., "manner" or "measure"—from which sprang those usages of the term which nowadays are more commonly associated with fashion. In 1549 there is a documentation for *mode* as referring generally to manifestations of collective taste, passing manners of living, thinking, or feeling, as well as conforming with what is socially considered *bon ton*. In 1480 (i.e., even earlier) *mode* is also employed to specifically describe collective habits and passing manners of dress.⁷ *Mode*, however, is etymologically unrelated to the adjective *moderne*, which is first documented in 1361 and translates the Latin *modo* (not *modus*), meaning "recent."⁸ The alleged linguistic originary proximity of *mode* and *modernity* is thus a classical "false friend." The situation is—albeit slightly—complicated by the fact that the current French term for the mode in which something occurs or presents itself (i.e., the manner or the *modus*) does not share the same grammatical gender with the word that is employed when referring to fashion. Whereas the latter (fashion) is *la mode*, the former (manner/*modus*) is *le mode*. The reason for this divergence may lie in an early attempt to set the reputable business of intellectual inquiry apart from the mundane realm of circulating tastes and fashions: only by the early seventeenth century (by way of imitating the original Latin gender of *modus*) was the gender for the philosophical usage of this term changed to masculine, hence referring to, for instance, a "mode of being" (modus essendi) as *un mode*–not, or more precisely no longer, as *une mode*.⁹ (One entertaining consequence of this kinship is that, in contemporary French, the noun *modiste* can either refer to a vendor of fashions, a hatmaker (Coco Chanel's first profession), or the medieval grammarian philosophers (such as Thomas von Erfurt) who founded the theory of universal modes.)¹⁰ (See also later in this chapter the section "Being in fashion, being form"; and sections "On the non-givenness of material" and "Materialism à la mode" in chapter 3).

Fashion as model and as chronotechnics

To open this first chapter of a book about Walter Benjamin "on fashion" with such a (necessarily less than detailed) overview of a few basic tendencies in scholarly accounts of the subject of fashion is not just to begin the endeavor of situating Benjamin's writing on this provisional map of critical literature. Rather, while retaining an awareness for the historical and systemic specificity and concreteness of fashion as an object of study that fascinated Benjamin, the key question of this present book is in equal parts to analyze the arguments, tropes of thought, and so on that make up Benjamin's ideas about fashion, and to inquire as *to what end* Benjamin engaged with questions of fashion—i.e., what theorizing fashion enabled him to think. Or, to put it slightly differently: the answer to the question "To what end does one study Benjamin on fashion?" is in parts coextensive with the answer to the question "To what end did Benjamin study fashion?", implying that while Benjamin of course had an interest in the object of fashion itself, fashion was also a means, a test case, a model, the theorization of which allowed him to access and perspectivize other questions.¹¹

One of the basic assumptions that is crucial to the argument is that fashion can be considered a *chronotechnics*—i.e., a distributed, collectively actualized, and perpetually reactualized technique for operationalizing time.¹² Returning to the previous summary of positions in fashion theory, it will be obvious that only very few of them place the question of time center stage, at least not explicitly. The implicit, and in most cases unreflected, address of temporality occurs either through the mentioned unquestioned subscription to the idea of a historico-systemic *passage* from which fashion springs, or through the always available semantics of the transitory—i.e., the fleeting moment that is readily ascribed to fashion phenomena.[13] One exception here is Luhmannian sociologist Elena Esposito's *The Reliability of the Transient: Paradoxes of Fashion* (Die Verbindlichkeit des Vorübergehenden. Paradoxien der Mode); she presents the systems theorist's view of modernization, that with the passage into a functionally differentiated state of society and the concomitant dissolution of a stable (i.e., extra-temporal) ontological fundament for communication, contingency is felt in all temporal acuity. Under these temporalized conditions, fashion acquires a specific functionality, in part precisely through its essentially temporalized character.[14] We find another in literary scholar and fashion theorist Barbara Vinken's work, who, through a meticulous analysis of individual fashion poetics of garments produced at the moment she terms "post-fashion," reveals that these designs frequently articulate the temporal dimensions of their making and existence, and which, in a retroactive perspective, demonstrate the historically preceding formation of haute couture to be largely concerned with a negation of temporality and its effects. In this fine-grained and complicating approach, which deciphers designs and looks as negotiations of such historical ruptures, dresses thus become the medium for a working through, for displacements, shifts, and reorderings of fashion's temporal articulations.[15]

That the question of time was one aspect of this topic that interested Benjamin is clear when he refers to fashion as a "measure of time" (AP 830) (Zeitmaß [PW 997]). In Benjamin scholarship this has received surprisingly little attention; the work of Andrew Benjamin marks one notable example, in which he—while examining the role of fashion within Benjamin's concept of *historical* time—has spoken of fashion as a "register of time."[16] The other, no less notable case is, again, the work of Vinken, who points to the harnessing of the categories of the ephemeral and the eternal into a characteristic contradiction (and stylistic opposition), which Benjamin derives from his interpretation of Baudelaire's sonnet "À une passante."[17] (For a detailed account of Benjamin's post-Baudelairean fashion poetics, see chapter 3.) A covert (i.e., unacknowledging) acknowledgment finally pre-dates these in Adorno's *Aesthetic Theory*, in which the Frankfurt philosopher, tacitly appropriating the Benjaminian concept of the *Zeitkern* (the "time kernel"), dialectically positions fashion as an agent which—through its often ignored yet manifest implication with the contested realm of aesthetic autonomy—articulates what the defenders of an idealist conception of art need to deny: that the ephemeral and the temporalized are inscribed into the very arcane regions of the aesthetic, that the sanctum of art is always eaten away at by real, historical time.[18] (Regarding the concept of the time kernel, see the eponymous section below.)

Benjamin's fashion passage

Benjamin has at a prominent point in scholarship been described as the exponent of a theory of fashion bound to the idea of a systemic passage. While these are not her own words, they still serve to paraphrase the position espoused by Susan Buck-Morss in *The Dialectics of Seeing: Walter Benjamin and the Arcades Project,* where she writes ambiguously that "Benjamin opened up to [sic] philosophical understanding the phenomenon of fashion that is specific to capitalist modernity."[19] It is not quite clear from this formulation whether Buck-Morss here means a concept of fashion that is specific to capitalist modernity—i.e., an understanding of the coming and going of styles that could only have emerged under the conditions of capitalist modernity—hence marking Benjamin's thought as an exemplar of a still to be more clearly determined epistemology in the age of modern capitalism; or if Benjamin cast fashion as a phenomenon of capitalist modernity, hence marking him (in Buck-Morss's reading and that reading, too) as a proponent of the mentioned earlier theories that date the emergence and development of fashion in relation to the "systemic break" of "modernization" (which in Buck-Morss's account is coeval with capitalism).

That at least Buck-Morss holds this conviction is, however, implicitly indicated where she quotes Benjamin's already mentioned formulation, from the *Arcades Project,* that fashion is to be considered as "the modern 'measure of time.'"[20] The modernity in question, as the setting of quotation marks within her quote demonstrates, is her interpolation. In the original quote, Benjamin, in the style of an aphorism, playing on the vocabulary and imagery of the sweeping infrastructural reorganizations of the nineteenth century with their implementation of grand train terminals into city structures, juxtaposes "Death, the dialectical central station, fashion, measure of time" (AP 830) (Der Tod, die dialektische Zentralstation: die Mode das Zeitmaß [PW 997]). While it could be argued that the imagery here—railway construction—points to the period of industrialization that is usually associated with "modernization," it is still worth noting that on a conceptual level Benjamin makes no express mention of "modernity" at all.

This fact—that the Benjaminian understanding of fashion as a chronotechnics is not necessarily inherently bound to the temporal trope of modernity—is also suggested by the sweeping extempore on the topical allegorical encounter of death and fashion, with its two main literary sources in the fashion convolute: Leopardi's *Dialogue between Fashion and Death*, from which Benjamin culls one brief citation to form one half of the convolute's incipit, "Fashion: Sir Death, Sir Death!" (AP 62, TM) (Mode: Herr Tod, Herr Tod! [PW 110]); and Rilke's fifth "Duino Elegy," with its evocation of the figure *die Modistin*, the "Modiste" Madame Lamort, the milliner or dressmaker Madame Lamort (PW 111, AP 63).[21] In this quote, a Benjaminian para-literary confection of sorts, death is cast as fashion's "tall and loutish" clerk (AP 63) (langer flegelhafter Kommis [PW 111]), and it is he, not fashion, that provides temporal measurement, albeit according to a unit that is intricately bound up with the manufacturing of garments: he "measures the century by the yard" (AP 63) (mißt das Jahrhundert nach der Elle [PW 111]), employing a unit of measurement, *Elle*, that was initially derived from the length of a forearm, between hand and elbow, and that standardized lengths in the textile trade. Benjamin models their interaction as a long-term game of catch, in which fashion, over centuries, mocks death:

> That is why fashion changes so quickly; she titillates death and is already something different, something new, as he casts about to crush her. For hundreds of years she holds her own against him.
>
> AP 63 TM

> *Darum wechselt sie so geschwinde; kitzelt den Tod und ist schon wieder eine andere, neue, wenn er nach ihr sich umsieht, um sie zu schlagen. Sie ist ihm Jahrhunderte nichts schuldig geblieben.*
>
> PW 111

Again, the time measurement in question is not modeled here on the scale of "modernity"; rather, it is a question of allegorically pitting two types of transience against each other—the limited temporal existence of fashions, and the *vanitas* aspect of the finitude of a human lifetime. There is, finally, a passage from a letter to Hofmannsthal, dated March 17, 1928, which Buck-Morss also refers to, in which Benjamin describes fashion as the "natural and entirely irrational temporal scale of the course of history" (natürlichen und ganz irrationalen Zeitmassstab des Geschichtsverlauf [PW 1084]). Again, fashion is cast as a chronotechnics, but its scale is not "modernity"—rather, it is all of history and its course (Geschichtsverlauf).²²

These Benjaminian formulations notwithstanding, Buck-Morss in *The Dialectics of Seeing* paraphrases the historical deployment of fashion—with an eye to analyzing Benjamin's take on it—as follows:

> Now clothing is quite literally at the borderline between ... the individual and the cosmos. Its positioning surely accounts for is emblematic significance throughout history. In the Middle Ages, the 'proper' attire was that which bore the imprint of the social order: Cosmetics were a reflection of a divinely ordered cosmos, and a sign of one's position within it. Of course, class position was then as static as the nature in which human beings saw their life reflected: Accident of birth determined one's social situation; the latter, in turn, determined one's probabilities of death.... [S]tyles in clothing reinforced the social hierarchy by reiterating it. Against this background, the positive moment of modern fashion stands out clearly. Its constant striving for 'novelty,' for separation from the given, identifies generational cohorts, whose dress symbolizes an end to the dependency and natural determinacy of childhood, and entry into their own collective role as historical actors. Interpreted affirmatively, modern fashion is irreverent toward tradition, celebratory of youth rather than social class, and thus emblematic of social change.²³

While the single cited reference in Buck-Morss's account of fashion's historical implementation is, slightly oddly, Fletcher's *Theory of Allegory* (an absolutely canonical title in the study of literary figuration, but perhaps not the most central interpretation of social and vestimentary stylistics), the basic temporal trope of her account is, of course, familiar enough. It is a nearly perfect execution of the scheme of fashion as a datable systemic passage.

We could at this point indicate a number of further instances in which Benjamin's work does not follow the trope of fashion as a systemic passage, at least as identified with the period of "modernity," which Buck-Morss claims to recognize in it. In the fashion convolute, he asks, "Were there fashions in antiquity? Or did the 'authority of the frame' preclude them?" (AP 99) (*Gab es in der Antike Moden? Oder hat die "Gewalt des Rahmens" sie untersagt?* [PW 115]); he symmetrically closes this speculation by writing on a later occasion: "Does fashion perhaps die (as in Russia, for example) because it can no longer keep up the tempo—at least in certain fields?" (AP 71, TM) (Stirbt die Mode vielleicht—in Rußland z.B.—daran, daß sie das Tempo nicht mehr mitmachen kann—auf gewissen Gebieten zumindest? [PW 120]). Had Benjamin chosen to develop these ideas into a coherent account, he would have ended up with a historical model in which fashion would have marked the period between antiquity and socialism/communism. The first would have interdicted fashions through an appeal to the *aptum*; the latter would have outrun its pace through accelerated development. As implausible as such a model would seem, it would definitely not have tied the existence of fashion to the moment of "modernity"; rather, in an echo of the grandest historical schemata of Marx, it would have declared antiquity as the alleged precursor, and the communist state as the alleged overcoming of history proper as potential moments before and after the age of fashion, i.e., history. If paradise (antiquity or ur-communism) is lost and fallen into the state of fashion, paradise regained would in this scenario be the fashion-free communist utopia.

On a different occasion, Benjamin goes on to complicate these ideas by introducing the idea of multiple speeds and varying zones and degrees of fashion's dominance:

> Does fashion die because it can no longer keep up the tempo—at least in certain fields? While, on the other hand, there are fields in which it can follow the tempo, and even dictate it?
>
> AP 859

> *Stirbt die Mode vielleicht daran, dass sie das Tempo nicht mehr mitmachen kann—auf gewissen Gebieten zumindest? Während es andererseits Gebiete gibt, auf denen sie dem Tempo folgen, ja es vorschreiben kann?*
>
> PW 1029

In line with this more nuanced, more complicated, and ultimately more convincing reflection, Benjamin also asks, with a view to long-term developments, "In what measure of time did changes of fashion erstwhile take place?" (AP 837, TM) (In welchem Zeitmass vollzog sich früher der Wechsel der Mode? [PW 1005])—the implicit motif behind the question being that the seemingly readily available answer, "slower," cannot have satisfied him. This demonstrates that not only did Benjamin not tie the emergence of fashion to the passage into modernity, he also didn't subscribe to problematic accelerationist or dromological models, which operate with the idea of linear acceleration, and which predicate the ultimate annihilation of fashion at the moment at which its temporal processing is trumped by the sheer speed of advanced transmissions. The case that such determinist thinking is inherently flawed has recently—again—been sufficiently demonstrated: rather than abolishing fashion, digitization has, if anything, led to a consolidation of a number of its subsectors, industries, establishing new circuits and fora— sometimes at the cost of extant ones.

The overall irrelevance of a unilaterally techno-determinist approach for Benjamin's fashion thought, according to which increased speed and clarity of transmission would minimize the transmission span of new styles and ultimately cancel fashion altogether, is also illustrated by a related note from the materials that belong to the context of the *Arcades Project*. Here, Benjamin explores misunderstanding ([d]as Missverständnis) as a "constitutive element in the development of fashion": "No sooner is a new fashion at a slight remove from its origin and point of departure than it is turned about and misunderstood" (AP 867) (Die neue Mode wird schon in winziger Entfernung von ihrem Ausgangs- und Entstehungsort umgebogen und missverstanden [PW 1037]). Benjamin here clearly evinces insight into the genuinely differential character of fashion, which, if taken as seriously as it ought to be, would preclude the easy discrediting of fashion on the grounds of it requiring "slavish adoption" or "uniformity" from those who execute it. Even if one grants that imitation *is* a central operation in the spread of fashions, it would defy basic logic to assume that imitation in fashion requires exact copying. Rather, the production of difference is already inherent in it. Or, to translate this into vestimentary terms and to return to Benjamin: fashion is neither the distortion nor the delay of a signal that would run through an imperfect medium; nor is it the identical adoption of a style, manner, look, or aesthetic by a group. Rather, these would be basic examples for what Benjamin termed the "contrast between fashion and uniform" (AP 865) (Gegensatz von Mode und Uniform [PW 1036]), one implementing difference and transformation, the other identity.

From phenomena in time to models of time

On yet another level, Benjamin's thought is also surprisingly far from the routinely assumed figure of modernization, beginning first with a conceptualization of "modernity's" counter-term, namely tradition, and implying second, and perhaps even more consequentially, a shift away from merely investigating manifestations in time, toward the modeling of time. Both have implications for Benjamin's fashion theory. There is, first, a rather surprising note from the materials for the theses *On the Concept of History*, in which he opens a "fundamental aporia" (Grundlegende Aporie):

> Tradition as the discontinuum of what has been in contrast to history as the continuum of events. It may be the case that the continuity of tradition is semblance (*Schein*). But then the persistence of this semblance creates the persistence of tradition within it.
>
> *Die Tradition als das Diskontinuum des Gewesenen im Gegensatz zur Historie als dem Kontinuum der Ereignisse.—Mag sein daß die Kontinuität der Tradition Schein ist. Aber dann stiftet eben die Beständigkeit dieses Scheins di/ er Beständigkeit die Kontinuität in ihr.*
>
> BG 123

If compared to the fashion historical tropes of "modernization," we clearly recognize a first divergence here. Whereas these approaches cast "tradition" as the historical stratum of continuity, against which fashion operates a principle of perpetual rupture, Benjamin here, in an at first counterintuitive operation, casts tradition as the *discontinuum* of "what has been." Rather than embodying the principle of steadfast continuity (and absence of transformation), tradition is here already understood as that which is discontinuous, or that which forms a paradoxically interrupted "space" which is not a continuum. In a dialectical turn, Benjamin then does allow for an idea of tradition as continuous, but goes on to specify that this continuity amounts to semblance, and, even further, that semblance grounds the persistence of this very continuity. Rather than propping up tradition as the bedrock of continuity (to be shattered, for instance, in the moment of "modernization," including one of its main alleged manifestations, namely the emergence of fashion), Benjamin presents this very idea of the continuity of tradition as a dissimulation.[24]

For our understanding of this note, for Benjamin's understanding of "tradition" in it, and ultimately for our understanding of Benjamin's fashion theory, it is instructive to attend even more closely to Benjamin's argument here: he clearly juxtaposes the *discontinuum of tradition* with the idea of *history as a continuum of events*. In other words, in Benjamin's system, or at least in this one instantiation of his thought, the categories of continuity and discontinuity do not function as coattributes of the opposition of tradition and "modernity." Rather, they refer to different modes of conceptualizing the temporality of the past—one discontinuous, and here associated with the term "tradition"; the other continuous, and here associated with the idea of history as a continuum of events. At a later point we shall see that Benjamin indeed harnesses the temporality of fashion for reasons and effects not dissimilar to those for which he here turns to "tradition"—namely, in order to model temporality as discontinuous (see the section in this chapter, "Any past's contemporary"). What matters more at present is the following: when correlated with the question of continuity vs. discontinuity, the Benjaminian idea of tradition does not refer to a historical facticity, a positivity in the temporal field of history, an empirical fundament against which to profile the fluctuations of fashion (as modern). Rather, for Benjamin, the idea of continuity, in relation to matters of tradition and the past, refers to a model of time. Not a phenomenon in time—it is a matter of an epistemology of temporality and history, not of a phenomenology of temporal stages within the history of culture. It follows that the idea that Benjamin would have positioned fashion as a modern "rupture" against "continuous tradition" is problematic.[25]

Fashion changes little

There is, finally, another related point at which Benjamin's fashion thinking diverges from what common sense, *idées reçues*, and also Buck-Morss's interpretation may suggest. As we saw above, a model in which fashion is cast as the end and opposite of an alleged continuity of tradition is also predicated on the concept of a major incision, a rupturing of "present" and "past," in which fashion acts as the continuous and iterated implementation of a rupture with the past. One of the central figures in which this concept is couched is the idea of "the new," an ongoing revision. In the words of Buck-Morss: "when newness became a fetish, history itself became a manifestation of the commodity form."[26] This is also found in other fashion theories, for instance, in Gilles Lipovetsky's contention that "the taste for novelty" and "the passion for what is 'modern'" are to be understood as "a consistent and regular principle" and "as an autonomous cultural requirement," as the psychological engine of a sociocultural state in which fashion, allegedly, dominates.[27] In this "systematic reign of the ephemeral, of frequent evanescent fluctuations," Lipovetsky claims, "an essentially modern system" is instituted which is "freed from the grip of the past."[28] A "devaluing of the ancestral heritage" is met by "a tendency to dignify the norms of the social present."[29]

In this model, the idea of fashion's specific version of newness is tied to a vision of a regime of inconsistency. In Buck-Morss's framework, this entails both a neutering of "actual" transformations and a streamlined pressure for a persistent and complete overhaul of the stock of aesthetic options: "Reified in commodities, the utopian promise of fashion's transitoriness undergoes a dialectical reversal: The living, human capacity for change and infinite variation becomes alienated, and is affirmed only as a quality of the inorganic object. In contrast, the ideal for human subjects (urged into rigorous conformity to fashion's dictates) becomes the biological rigor mortis of eternal youth."[30]

Now there clearly are passages in which Benjamin remarks on the character of the ideology of the new, and the character of *nouveauté* in nineteenth-century department stores. This is, for instance, the case when he speaks of fashion as the "indefatigable agent" of "false consciousness" whose "quintessence" is "newness" (AP 11) (nimmermüde Agentin des falschen Bewusstsein, dessen Quintessenz das Neue ist [PW 55]). These passages from an early exposé for the *Arcades* clearly adopt the vocabulary of the critique of ideology. However, it is far less clear what relation between fashion and the new Benjamin actually has in mind here. Let us note that he connects the concept of the new to the category of false consciousness. Fashion, he suggests, is its agent, rather than its direct implementation.[31] It would of course be ridiculous if one were to deny the implication of fashion and commodity, or of fashion and capitalism, and it would be no less laughable if one were to deny that Benjamin had thought about this implication. However, such an implication does not suggest a straightforward identification of fashion with the commodity. Both with regard to historical and empirical reality, and with regard to Benjamin's theory, it is important to state that while fashion—like nearly all other manifestations of Western and modern-day global societies—is capitalistically warped, it is still not identical with the laws of capital. And, by implication, that the market-driven cycles of wholesale stock liquidations—perceived as implementations of "the new"—are not the rhythms of fashion.

Even within the logics of fashion itself, such implementations of "the new" may register as incisive in their respective temporal situatedness (where their function, as we shall see, is in part to *qualify* temporal relationality); yet their actual empirical realization also still differs markedly from the disposition that they are being assigned by those who view fashion as the harbinger and effect of the "break with tradition" that is "modernity." Compare Benjamin's remark that it is fashion's movement of life (Lebensbewegung) to "change *little*" (AP 862, TM) (weniges ändern [PW 1032]).[32] Benjamin's observation is correct on more than one level. It firstly accurately describes the empirical reality of fashion development in which the vast majority of implemented changes are actually minimal, slight transformations, minor modifications, and where the actualization of major modifications, the instantiations of a "new look," is rare enough to get duly noted. (We shall see in the following chapters that Benjamin's writing implicitly responds to at least three such significant transformations, but that these transformations did not occur in the nineteenth century, i.e., within the historical field parsed in the Arcades Project: the re-emergence of a clearly signposted gendering in silhouettes and cuts after a moment in which more androgynous models had dominated; the institution of an ideal of elegance and refinement; and the return to cuts of the Belle Époque. All three of which are contemporary to Benjamin's theoretical work on the problem of fashion.)

What counts as fashion, counts in relation to its aesthetic surroundings, and if these operate under the premise of comparative restraint, a quantitatively small difference can have the exact same fashion impact as quantitatively "large" differences in other settings. In other words, fashion is relational and it is differential, not substantial. For an aesthetic and formal manifestation to take on the character of fashion, the (accelerated) rapidity of its implementation and revocation, or its inherent "bigness," its in-your-faceness, are irrelevant. While these speeds and quanta can of course be productively studied, they do not touch on the basic differential character of fashion.

Being in fashion, being form (Simmel)

Fashions are lacking in constancy. The field of fashion is a medium for an ongoing process of self-differentiation where formal solutions ("fashions") that were acceptable or even groundbreaking yesterday are up for permanent re-evaluation and reassessment. The only permanence fashion offers is change, a fact which sociologist and philosopher Georg Simmel captured in his 1905 *Philosophie der Mode* (Philosophy of Fashion)—one, if not *the* most central theoretical account of the subject quoted by Benjamin in the *Arcades Project*, and a piece to rival the impact of Benjamin's own work in this field. In the fashion convolute, Benjamin, for instance, quotes Simmel on the subject of fashion's "rapid changes" (AP 77) (rasche Wechsel [PW 126]).[33] In *Philosophy of Fashion*, Simmel emphasizes "that change itself does not change" (PoF 204) (daß der Wechsel nicht wechselt [PdM 34]), fully recognizing the slipperiness of the subject.

> A fashion always exists and it is therefore, as a general concept, as a fact of fashion as such, indeed immortal; and this seems to reflect in some manner or other upon each of its manifestations, although the essence of each individual fashion is precisely that of not being immortal.
>
> PoF 203–204

> *Es gibt immer eine Mode, und sie ist deshalb als allgemeiner Begriff, als Faktum der Mode überhaupt, in der Tat unsterblich, und dies scheint auf jede einzelne ihrer Ausgestaltungen zu reflektieren, obgleich das Wesen jeder einzelnen grade ist, nicht unvergänglich zu sein.*
>
> PdM 34

Strictly speaking, the relationship between fashion as a general phenomenon on the one hand, and fashion as its particular instantiations on the other, verges on the paradoxical. Whereas these individual instantiations are marked by their ephemeral or transient status, the structural phenomenon seems pervasive and constant: "the fact that change itself does not change" proved reassuring enough for Simmel to write his *Philosophie*, which provides an analysis of fashion as a constitutive structural feature of society. In it, Simmel models fashion as a systemic phenomenon—if not as a strict paradox, then at least as a contradiction—and he demonstrates its pertinence to a number of fashion's structural features, one of them being, centrally, fashion's temporality.

Besides the mentioned chiasma between the transience of fashions and the permanence of fashion, the object's contradictory temporality can also be located in fashion's specific way of becoming: "The essence of fashion consists in the fact that it should always be exercised by only a part of a given group, while the entirety is merely on the road to adopting it" (PoF 192, TM) (Das Wesen der Mode besteht darin, daß immer nur ein Teil der Gruppe sie übt, die Gesamtheit aber sich erst auf dem Wege zu ihr befindet [PdM 16]). This amounts to the insight that the totality of fashion is relegated to a strictly structural level. Fashion's actualizations, on the contrary, are limited to a state of permanent becoming: "As soon as a group is fully permeated, that is, as soon as anything that was originally done by a few has really come to be practised by all ... we no longer characterize it as fashion" (PoF 192, TM) (Sobald sie völlig durchdrungen ist, d.h. sobald einmal dasjenige, was ursprünglich nur einige taten, wirklich von allen ausgeübt wird, ... so bezeichnet man es nicht mehr als Mode. [PdM 16]). Once a particular fashion has reached full expansion, it disappears: "Every growth of fashion drives it to its doom, because it thereby cancels out its distinctiveness" (PoF 192) (Jedes Wachstum treibt sie ihrem Ende zu, weil sie dadurch die Unterschiedlichkeit aufhebt [PdM 16]). Fashions grow toward their destruction: once they reach their maximum spread, they annihilate the constitutive difference which triggered them.

In the *Arcades Project*, Benjamin raises related ideas, but through quoting a different author, namely nineteenth-century legal philosopher Rudolph Jhering, who in his 1883 *Der Zweck im Recht* (The Purpose of Law) develops an approach that parallels Simmel's, while adding an—at first sight plausible, on reflection problematic—proto-accelerationist view:

> The lifetime of a fashion is inversely proportional to the swiftness of its diffusion, the ephemerality of fashions has increased in our day as the means for their diffusion have expanded via our perfected means of communication.
>
> AP 75 TM
>
> *Die Lebensdauer der Mode bestimmt sich im entgegengesetzten Verhältnis zur Raschheit ihrer Verbreitung; ihre Kurzlebigkeit hat sich in unserer Zeit in*

dem Mass gesteigert, als die Mittel zu ihrer Verbreitung durch unserer vervollkommneten Communicationsmittel gewachsen sind.

PW 125

The valid insight here lies in the correlation of fashion's existence with the "means of communication," hence pointing to the mutual implication of fashion and media. The error lies in the determinist assumption that the spread and existence of fashions should be predicated by the perfection of media *technologies*: while it is clear that fashion travels through media, the speed (or clarity) of transmission does not necessarily determine the life span or stability of a given style. These would, for instance, also correlate with the measure of the saturation of a field, and the borders, visibilities, and obfuscations on such an (informational) terrain are not identical with media-*technological* penetration. Fashions also rely on publics, counter-publics, the openness or secrecy of channels, etc. In other words, fashion is not informational; a fashion is not a signal. What is clear, however, to Simmel, Benjamin, and us, is that fashion implies media and mediation.

The two temporal and structural differences that Simmel locates as engines of the fashion phenomenon translate into a peculiar experiential signature: by way of the aesthetic, fashion produces an emphatic experience of presence that plays becoming against disappearance, and thus permanently revokes and renews itself. Simmel's *Philosophie* recognizes in fashion the point at which the phenomenon of a being that at once *is* and *is not* shifts from a problem of semblance to a question of time and difference:

> The question of fashion is not 'to be or not to be'; but rather, it is simultaneously being and non-being, it always stands on the watershed of the past and future and, as a result, conveys to us, at least while it is at its height, a stronger sense of the present than do most other phenomena.
>
> PoF 192, TM

> *Ihre* [fashion's] *Frage ist nicht Sein oder Nichtsein, sondern sie ist zugleich Sein und Nichtsein, sie steht immer auf der Wasserscheide von Vergangenheit und Zukunft und gibt uns so, solange sie auf ihrer Höhe ist, ein so starkes Gegenwartsgefühl, wie wenige andere Erscheinungen.*
>
> PdM 17

Being—i.e., becoming and vanishing—in fashion means to partake in a socio-temporal building up and tearing down which plays out in the field of aesthetics: "Life according to fashion consists of a mixture of destruction and construction" (PoF 195) (Das Leben gemäß der Mode ist . . . eine Mischung von Zerstörung und Aufbauen [PdM 29]). Benjamin shares in this insight when he includes Simmel's observation regarding a shift of the "accent of attractions" (Akzent der Reize) from their "substantial center to their inception and their end" (substanziellen Zentrum auf ihren Anfang und ihr Ende), emphasizing the "force of the formal attraction of the boundary" (Stärke des formalen Reizes der Grenze) (AP 77, PW 127). What Simmel describes as a cross-fade of becoming and vanishing is another example for this charm of boundaries, or demarcations: the superimposition of an end and a beginning through which runs the dividing line of what was in, what will be, thus marking what is "in".

Benjamin's excerpt entails three important points: first, an acknowledgment of Simmel's standpoint according to which fashion must be understood in relation to the category of *form*. This is to say that forms are not just the object of fashion (cuts of dresses, color choices, manners of speaking, tastes in art, etc); rather, fashion as a systemic activity can be understood according to formal concepts (here the form of the boundary, or the limit), because in total fashion *is* a form: "a form of the social" (Sozialform) whose "marvelous expediency" (PoF 200, PdM 28) Simmel explored, charting its "formal social" "motivation" (PoF 190, PdM 13). For Simmel, fashion permeates all kinds of "social forms" (gesellschaftlichen Formen [ibid.]), because, reciprocally, fashion is one of the central forms *of* the social. (Also because the social *is* a form.)[34] Simmel recognizes (temporally processed) contradiction as a key to the fashion form's social productivity which underlies its "significance for the form of the social process" (PoF 189) (Bedeutung für die Form des gesellschaftlichen Prozesses [PdM 12]). According to Simmel, fashion performs the "double function" (Doppelfunktion) of combining, "in a unified act," "the tendency towards social equalization with the tendency toward individual differentiation and variation" (PoF 189) (die Tendenz nach sozialer Egalisierung mit der nach individueller Unterschiedenheit in einem einheitlichen Tun [PdM 11]).

The second aspect of such an appreciation of the "charm of boundaries" as form relates to fashion's temporal and experiential structure. It is clear that the particular intensity afforded by fashion is tied to what Simmel here calls demarcation, or boundary, which relates both to the marking of in and out as stylistic "territories" or "zones," as well as their emergence and vanishing:

> If the momentary concentration of social consciousness upon the point which fashion signifies is also the one in which the seeds of its own death and its determined fate to be superseded already lie, so this transitoriness does not degrade it totally, but actually adds a new attraction to its existing ones.
>
> PoF 192–193

> *Wenn in der momentanen Aufgipfelung des sozialen Bewusstseins auf den Punkt, den sie bezeichnet, auch schon ihr Todeskeim liegt, ihre Bestimmung zum Abgelöst-werden, so deklassiert diese Vergänglichkeit sie im ganzen nicht, sondern fügt ihren Reizen einen neuen hinzu.*
>
> PdM 17

The intensity of the fashion moment is thus inherently bound to a temporalized differential structure. It is not immanent.

It also relates—and this is the third aspect—to fashion's peculiar ontological signature, which Simmel traced by twisting Hamlet's famous line: the fashion question is not "to be or not to be"; rather it is "to be and not to be at once," and the intensity of experiencing something *as fashion* relates to the temporal unfolding of this strange double state of non/being into actual processes. Something emerges while it is already about to vanish, a cross-fade of appearance and disappearance, of sliding into and out of existence—as a temporal event. Given Simmel's formalist approach, we could call this an exploration of fashion as a form of (temporalized) being. We could, of course, think of parallel cases for such a peculiar ontology: one example for an entity which, in the moment of its appearance already vanishes, would be the technologically temporalized image, as least as it manifests itself for its viewers. Another parallel case, in which something at once *is* and *is not*, would be fiction—not just literary or generally narrative fiction, but also mythical and religious belief systems.[35] However, none of these share fashion's peculiar character of a collectively produced and implemented, temporalized (aesthetic) form that spreads and vanishes in and through medium, which is partly coextensive with the social.

We could recognize here a strange partial anticipation of what nowadays is being discussed under the concept of operative ontologies. Associated with the research program of cultural techniques, this position assumes that ontological differences (for instance, form and matter, image and object, thing and process, figure and ground, etc) are the product of what in this framework is referred to as "ontic operations," meaning assemblages of practices, operations, and media which amount to "collectives of accidents," collectives of modifiers of being, rather than stable substances.[36] Devised in the wake of actor-network theory and media archeology, this approach inquires into "materialities of ontologization," understanding what *is* to result from a stratum of *being* defined by the material, the technological, etc.[37] Departing from Simmel's elegant analysis, we could see his theory of fashion as partially anticipating these concerns, provided that we understand by fashions the strangely transient manifestations of something that is but also—just like a fiction—isn't (fashion's question is how to be and not to be at once), while emerging in and through complex assemblages of media, materials, collectives, etc: collective, time-based fictions, if one wants.[38] We could even identify a certain cultural-technical functionality of fashion: it operationalizes time and thus would, for instance, comply with the demand not to think of time as existing independently, but rather in relation to "cultural techniques of time measurement."[39] Just as Benjamin writes: fashion can be considered a *Zeitmass*, a measure of time. Another way of looking at fashion from this perspective would finally connect Simmel's analysis to the already mentioned observation that the emergence of the notion of *la mode* is historically coemergent with the reworking of a notion of ontological modes.[40] Rather than mapping our understanding of fashion point by point onto the grid of the mentioned theoretical discourses, we would still be warranted to say that fashion indeed could provide a nearly categorical example for constructing an instance of being from the perspective of modalities, i.e., accidents rather than essences. And not just because, as Esposito points out, fashion responds efficiently to the demands of contingency and its broad implementation, shunning any necessary and essential deductions. And neither in the sense that contingency marks one of the central categories of modal logic. Rather, the argument could be based on the fact that, in addition to these qualities, fashion is in the business of modalities to begin with. Rather than introducing and processing "substantive" additions, fashions tend to *modify* existing forms—a new way of walking, a new twist of phrase, a new way to cut or color an item, etc. Up to fully formulated stylistic programs, fashions are filters onto what is, and what exists in and through them.

One way in which Simmel conceives of fashion in terms of its operationality is through a comparison with the function of a picture frame (PoF 189) (wie der Rahmen eines Bildes [PdM 12]), and the parallels extend to a short essay he penned on the very same subject, i.e., the picture frame. There Simmel speaks about a

> closure which exercises indifference towards and defence against the exterior and a unifying integration with respect to the interior in a single act. What the frame achieves for the work of art is to symbolize and strengthen this double function of its boundary.
>
> *Abschluß, der die Gleichgültigkeit und Abwehr von außen und den vereinheitlichende Zusammenschluß nach innen in einem Akte ausübt. Was der Rahmen des Kunstwerks leistet, ist, daß er diese Doppelfunktion seiner Grenze symbolisiert und verstärkt.*[41]

And yet, Simmel's theory of the picture frame also serves as a ground against which to profile the specificity and, we might say, the advantages, of his rethinking of the problem of liminality in his fashion theory. One distinction pertains to what could be called a difference that is, again, located on the ontological level: the border of the picture frame divides (and binds) that which is an image and that which is not an image, that which is art and that which is not art.

Fashion also operates such divisions: it allows for simultaneous social integration and differentiation—"holding a given social circle together and at the same time closing it off from others" (PoF 189) (einen Kreis in sich zusammen und ihn zugleich von anderen abzuschliessen [PdM 12]), it has a "double effect, both inwards and outwards" (PoF 189) (Doppelwirkung nach innen und nach aussen [PdM 12]). In this double function, Simmel argues, lies its functionality: it calibrates the tendency toward the particular with the movement toward homogeneity in a way that produces a non-linear process of social self-organization:

> Fashion is the imitation of a given pattern and thus satisfies the need for social belonging, it leads the individual onto the path that everyone travels, it furnishes a general condition that resolves the conduct of every individual into

a mere example. At the same time, and to no less a degree, it satisfies the need for distinction, the tendency toward differentiation, change, and standing out.

PoF 188–189 TM

Mode ... ist die Nachahmung eines gegebenen Musters und genügt damit dem Bedürfnis nach sozialer Anlehnung, sie führt den einzelnen auf die Bahn, die Alle gehen, sie gibt ein Allgemeines, das das Verhalten jedes Einzelnen zu einem bloßen Beispiel macht. Nicht weniger aber befriedigt sie das Unterschiedsbedürfnis, die Tendenz auf Differenzierung, Abwechslung, Sich-abheben.

PdM 11

But what fashion divides in such a manner are not two ontological states, as extra-temporal entities. The fashion division of literally "in" and "out" is time-based, and it is genuinely differential. To effect a change in its particular "mode of existence" does not require an alteration on a level of ontic operations, a rearrangement of the configuration of media, technologies, and processes that facilitated its emergence in the first place (although such a rearrangement may result in fashion transformations). Rather, as Simmel puts it: "Connection and differentiation are the two fundamental functions which are here inseparably united" (PoF 189) (Verbinden und Unterscheiden sind die beiden Grundfunktionen, die sich hier vereinigen [PdM 12]). Fashion thus figures as the meta-distinction of difference and homogeneity that keeps these two elements structurally separate *and* bound together, while permanently processing them through varying actualizations in the socio-aesthetic field where difference is produced and consumed ad infinitum.

Differentials of time and deviations of direction

Whereas Simmel's sociological approach tracks short-term processings of emerging and vanishing differences, Benjamin probes temporal depth, exploring the steeper views that open from the vantage point of the philosophy of history. By introducing the problem of fashion into the field of historical inquiry, Benjamin advances on two fronts: he extends sociological thought into historical depth; but he also complicates a certain way of conceptualizing history. Both moments are brought together in a brief methodological self-assessment from the *Passagenwerk*: "On the differentials of time (which, for others, disturb the grand lines of inquiry), I base my calculation" (AP 456, TM) (Auf den Differentialen der Zeit, die für die anderen die "großen Linien" der Untersuchung stören, baue ich meine Rechnung auf [PW 570]). Nothing but the broached topics of time and temporality might indicate at first sight that this sentence eventually gives access to central elements of Benjamin's theory of fashion. In order to begin to understand Benjamin's contribution, we first need to embark on a short detour of close analyses. A number of passages from Benjamin's texts are thematically grouped around our quote, and we shall look at some of them now.

Both Benjamin's famous notion of the dialectical image and his elaborations of the temporal mechanisms of fashion allow for a more palpable understanding of what such a time differential might be. A well-known definition of the dialectical image from the *Arcades Project* states:

> image is that wherein *what has been* comes together in a flash with the now to form a constellation.... For while the relationship of the present to the past is a purely temporal, continuous one, the relationship of *what-has-been* to the *now* is ... not progression, but image, like a leap.
>
> AP 462 TM[42]

> [D]as Bild ist dasjenige, worin das Gewesene mit dem Jetzt blitzhaft in Konstellation zusammentritt. ... Denn während die Beziehung der Gegenwart zur Vergangenheit eine rein zeitliche, kontinuierliche ist, ist die des Gewesenen zum Jetzt ... nicht Verlauf, sondern Bild <,> sprunghaft.
>
> PW 576–577

The "temporal, continuous" (zeitliche, kontinuierliche) relation of present (Gegenwart) and past (Vergangenheit) conceptualizes history as a continuous line in the space of time: an uninterrupted vector leads from past to present. The relation of present and past exemplified by the *Bild*, by contrast, occurs first of all in a flash and not a progression ("blitzhaft" and "nicht Verlauf")—i.e., it is not the product of a linear, even development. It is also *sprunghaft* (like a leap, erratic), which is to say not belonging to the formations described by the homogeneous space of time. This discontinuity of the relation between past and present exemplified by the Benjaminian image finally finds its correlate in the "tiger's leap into the past" (OCH 365) (Tigersprung ins Vergangene [BG 102]), and the model for this tiger's leap is *fashion*. The trigger for fashion's leap into the past is the generation of the current: "Fashion has a nose for the current where it stirs in the thickets of once" (OCH 365, TM) (Die Mode hat die Witterung für das Aktuelle, wo es sich im Dickicht des Einst bewegt [BG 102]). Like a predator, fashion leaps into the thicket of once, in order to reintroduce its catch—that which has been temporally disconnected and forgotten—into a current context where it sparks fresh fashionable difference.

Before we turn to the intricacies of this model, it should be noted that in Benjamin's work, one central aspect of this turn to fashion is precisely that it offers an alternative to a progressist, linear model of history, a fact which helps us understand in an even more precise manner the specific determination of Benjamin's interest in the temporality of fashion at this point (see above, the section "From phenomena in time to models of time").

As Peter Fenves puts it in a comment on the passage in the *Arcades Project* under consideration here: "A differential of time in this case is precisely not its direction but, on the contrary, its deviation from the very direction that [other] ... modes of historiography are trying not so much to discover as to enforce, in conflict with compasses that always only point elsewhere."[43] Fenves's and Julia Ng's recent scholarship give us a more accurate idea of how Benjamin might have thought about such deviations. Working with materials discovered by Ng at the Scholem Archive in Jerusalem, both reconstruct an early exchange between Benjamin and Scholem regarding the philosophy of Herman Cohen, in particular his philosophy of mathematics, as well as their discussions about how to conceptualize time. These reflections start out from a conversation between the two friends—reported by Scholem—in which the idea is laid out that time may have an *Ablauf* (a progression, a run) yet no direction (Richtung).[44] Translated into the register of mathematical functions, this would, as Ng explains, amount to the question of "whether or not time necessarily has a 'tangent' or determinable direction."[45] In this framework, Fenves sets out, this would mark a difference between the categories of time and history. There exists a tension between "the nondirectionality of time and the unidirectionality of history."[46] To model the non-directionality of time, Benjamin and Scholem would have turned to the so-called Weierstraß function, a function that is "continuous yet nowhere differentiable": "A curve corresponding to this function is unimaginable in the exact sense of the term: every point consists in a sharp turn."[47] There could indeed be a connection between this figure of the turn, which in Benjamin's and Scholem's early conversations would have plotted the non-directional character of time, and his later elaborations of the nexus between fashion and temporality. "What for others are deviations are, for me, the data which determine my course" (AP 456) (Was für die anderen Abweichungen sind, das sind für mich die Daten, die meinen Kurs bestimmen [PW 570]), as Benjamin put it in the context of the note in which he mentions the differentials of time.[48]

The idea of time as a non-directional progression, which stands in tension to the unidirectionality of history, indeed might prefigure the later modeling of historical time through the model of fashion, in which the linear and unidirectional motion of progressing time is interspersed with the turns and deviations manifest in fashion's recursions. Fashion allows here to remodel temporality. While a powerful factor, it comes into effect, once again, less as a phenomenon in time than as a model of time. We might even say that in his later work, Benjamin turned to fashion in order to put time back into history, because the models of historical time which he encountered weren't sufficiently temporalized.

One of the notes grouped with the *Arcades* materials allows for yet another approach to Benjamin's ideas. It is worth quoting at length:

> On the dialectical image. In it lies time. Already with Hegel, time enters into the dialectic. But the Hegelian dialectic knows time solely as properly historical, if not psychological, time of thinking. The time differential in which alone the dialectical image is real is still unknown to him. Attempt to demonstrate it in fashion. Real time enters the dialectical image not in natural magnitude—let alone psychologically—but in its smallest form.
>
> AP 867, TM

> *Zum dialektischen Bilde. In ihm steckt die Zeit. Sie steckt schon bei Hegel in der Dialektik. Diese Hegelsche Dialektik kennt aber die Zeit nur als eigentlich historische, wenn nicht psychologische, Denkzeit. Das Zeitdifferential, in dem allein das dialektische Bild wirklich ist, ist ihm noch nicht bekannt. Versuch, es an der Mode aufzuzeigen. Die reale Zeit geht in das dialektische Bild nicht in natürlicher Grösse—geschweige den psychologisch—sondern in ihrer kleinsten Gestalt ein.*
>
> PW 1037/38

This note is instructive not only because it provides at least an approximate clarification of the relation between the Benjaminian dialectical image and the

Hegelian dialectic, at least as Benjamin saw it—in contrast to the idealist philosopher, Benjamin sought to deploy a type of dialectic whose temporality was neither historical nor psychological (not *Denkzeit* [thought-time]). Rather, Benjamin claimed, the issue was "real time" (reale Zeit), and this real time not only "enters" the dialectical image (geht . . . ein), hence qualifying it as existing or hiding within it (steckt in ihm); reciprocally, the dialectical image only acquires reality if it is cast in a particular temporal form, namely as the differential of time (in dem das dialektische Bild wirklich ist). Fashion—and its operationalizations of real time—provided Benjamin with one opportunity to model these circumstances.

Any past's contemporary: Fashion as a temporal qualifier (the sentimental education of the discontinuous)

Through its specific orientation toward the past, Benjamin's concept of fashion both gains and loses. The gains lie in the extension of fashion's temporal reach into the dimension of history, in particular as contrasted with the short-term processes which Simmel's approach allows for, where the temporal processings of fashionable difference that are immanent to the social field play out on a synchronic plane, and where the temporal relief extends to the mere moment beforehand.[49] On the other hand, this particular specification—the orientation toward the past—also entails a loss on the part of Benjamin's concept of fashion, namely exactly where fashion's practices are not concerned with working the historical dimension. At the present point of our argument it is sufficient to point out that where Benjamin's concept of fashion extends into the positive articulation of its subject—i.e., where it matches, or doesn't match up with the whole historico-empirical field of styles, design practices, couture codes, etc—it is rather limited in that it so unilaterally focuses on what Benjamin termed "the tiger's leap"—i.e., the recuperation of past fashionable contents, looks, etc. To put it slightly more boldly: from Benjamin's perspective, nearly all of fashion tends toward "retro," an assumption manifest in his dictum that "[t]he stream gradient of every fashion-current . . . originates from what is forgotten" (AP 393, TM) (Jede Strömung der Mode . . . hat ihr Gefälle vom Vergessenen her [PW 496/7]), as well as in his definition of fashion as "contemporary with any past" (AP 894) (jeder Vergangenheit Zeitgenossin [PW 1229]). We shall have a look at the (fashion-)historical and even economico-historical preconditions for this narrowing down at a later point (see chapter 4).

Benjamin specifies the way in which he sees fashion as engendering such relations with the past as follows: "Each time, what sets the tone is … the newest, but only where it emerges in the medium of the oldest, the *longest past* [*Gewesenste*], the *most familiar* [*Gewohnteste*]" (AP 64, TM) (Tonangebend ist nur das Neueste, aber doch nur wo es im Medium des Ältesten, Gewesensten, Gewohntesten auftaucht [PW 112]). Fashion thus converts the (temporally) disconnected and forgotten into the newest, the most recent. The mechanism of this sudden, jump-like—erratic—conversion is dialectics: "This spectacle, the formation of the newest in the medium of what has been, makes for the true dialectical spectacle of fashion" (AP 64, TM) (Dieses Schauspiel wie das jeweils Allerneueste im Medium des Gewesenen sich bildet, macht das eigentliche dialektische Schauspiel der Mode [PW 113]).

There are at least two implications to this construction that we need to attend to. First, concerning its mechanics, so to speak—namely the way in which it serves as a counter-model to an idea of historical time as progressing, and, by implication, the degree to which Benjamin's model must be understood *as such a modification or revision of another temporal model*. In this sense, Benjamin here deepens the concept of the differential of time, as the structure of this dialectical temporal relation defies a linearly progressive concept of time in a double way: first of all because the transformation of forgotten/latent into current occurs abruptly; instead of a stretched out, even development, there is a sudden dialectical switch of out-of-fashion into in-fashion. Second, because this re-entry of the latent and forgotten presupposes a qualitative break which has previously separated now and once: it is precisely its disconnection from the current that qualifies the *démodé* as possible material for the generation of the *Allerneueste*, because it has dropped out of sight, as it were. The *démodé*'s repository is "the heart of things abolished" (AP 212) (Herz der abgeschafften Dinge [PW 281])—i.e., an accumulation of elements which the course of time has eliminated.

The second implication concerns a different aspect, which becomes apparent when attending closely to Benjamin's language here, which, beyond mapping a temporal relation that stands at the center of fashion, also *qualifies* this relation; or, rather, that casts this relation in qualitative terms, and which finds another articulation in the sentence "the antiquated—which includes, however, *the most recent past*" (AP 4, TM) (das Veraltete—das heisst aber das Jüngstvergangene [PW 47]). Its central concepts are the above quoted "the longest past," the "most familiar," which Benjamin's original German gives as *das Gewesenste* and *das Gewohnteste*. The positions of the "newest" and the "oldest" could still be understood as marking locations on a chronological scale which merely measures or indicates quantitative distance, in which case "the newest" would simply mean "the most recent," and "the oldest" would refer to those occurrences which have taken place at the furthest temporal remoteness. However, Benjamin's subsequent veering into an enumeration of *das Gewesenste* and *das Gewohnteste* points to the fact that such a quantitative distancing is not intended here. Both terms—*das Gewesenste* and *das Gewohnteste*—are, first, Benjaminian neologisms and they stretch the linguistic form of the conceptual vocabulary of fashion beyond the borders of what at first sight would be considered logical: *Das Gewesenste* is obviously derived from the German term *das Gewesene*, a substantive version of the past participle *gewesen* (has been) and indicating "what has been." *Das Gewesenste* thus translates as "the most past," "that which is more past than any other comparable instance"—the "pastest," if you will—and *das Gewohnteste* follows a parallel logic, describing a state in which something is more habitual or common than in all other comparable instances, the "most habituated," or "the commonest." In other words, in grammatically correct form, none of these terms exist as the superlatives in which they are presented here (and it may come as a relief to the Anglophone reader that in this case even the celebrated— or notorious—capacity of the German language to give word form to recently invented concepts by simply coining a new substantive falls short: both terms are linguistically "wrong").

What connects both terms and also stands behind Benjamin's linguistic violation is that they are not gradable, a grammatical fact that—to a certain extent—corresponds to the basic logic disposition of these two adjectives: while we could speculate about rising degrees of habituation, the past does not allow for shadings of its pastness. Benjamin's transposition of both terms into the, strictly speaking, agrammatical states of the superlative, however, can be read as a linguistic marker of an intensification of the qualities that are under consideration: the "pastest" and the "commonest," then, are neither merely wrong or inapplicable forms for, for instance, the temporally most remote, or what has reached a maximum spread. Rather, both are cast here as particularly intense states of the qualities they each name. They relate to moments in which something figures as particularly old or overly common. In this pairing they indeed already suggest the very quality that is under consideration here, namely what is outdated or "out of fashion."

Such a relegation of a given style, taste, look, etc to the realm of the *démodé* (i.e., the generation of the outmoded) is as much a product of fashion as is the resuscitation of the obsolete (under the right conditions). Fashion not only produces *both*, in and out; both are also two sides of a similar operation, namely the *qualification* of a temporal relationship with aesthetic and formal manifestations (about to be) situated in the past. Fashion, in this sense, is a qualifier. Partly due to this quality of fashion, and its operationalization of time, this could provide Benjamin with a counter-model to the spatial medium of empty and homogeneous time in which progressist and positivist vectors are deployed. This is one of the core aspects of fashion's temporal agency, and of its differentiating potential, which Benjamin recognized. Fashion is not the great evacuator, the big voider, whose correlate among temporal models would be the "homogenous and empty" time of progressist and positivist historical thinking, the adherence to what Werner Hamacher has called "the transcendental conformism of the continuum of time and history," requiring the price of the deadening of temporal affect.[50] Fashion, by contrast, is a school of discontinuity, and one of the lessons it provides is the sentimental education of the discontinuous.

Yesterday, and the day before (sorting time and what has gone out of style)

And it is in the context of this differentiating operation that it is possible to, again, and even more clearly, discern the actual medium in which Benjamin epistemologically embeds fashion. Much rather than a negotiation of the problem of modernity, fashion is a model for rethinking history in its temporal articulation. And this is also the basic difference that separates Benjamin's thinking from Simmel's. Both see fashion as intricately connected to temporality. But for Simmel it is the time of "society," for Benjamin the time of "history," if such sweeping generalizations are permitted for the moment.

Their respective models are supported by different views (we could call them rhythmizations in their own right) of the way in which fashions engage with (and re/produce) the styles of the past. It is instructive here to consider the way in which Simmel describes the reappropriation of styles gone by in fashion developments. For, like Benjamin, Simmel actually does acknowledge that current fashions can return to, rearticulate, and modify what has once gone out of fashion. But the contrast between his and Benjamin's approaches is telling. Simmel considers the outmoded to be forgotten and, in this voided capacity, a potential reservoir for the formation of stylistic options that register as new in relation to a given current fashion panorama (cf. PdM 34; PoF 204). But unlike Benjamin, he does not treat the outmoded as entering new styles *as démodé*. In Simmel's scenario, what has gone out of fashion is only retained as a back-up, but is no longer qualitatively related to the fashion present—it has become disarticulated from the now. This has to do with Simmel's particular modeling of the temporal structure of fashion, in which the production of current difference is, firstly, synchronously related to the shared plane of the present (in which any given difference is characterized through its narrower or wider spread, and hence its propensity to guarantee a marking against the rest of the field—or its failure to do so); and, secondly, where difference is set off against the immediately preceding past which it—through its ongoing formation, transformation, growth, and vanishing—produces continuously.[51] Bracketing its immanent forward drift (which is coextensive with its continuous production of the outmoded), the temporal signature of Simmel's fashion theory is binomic. The present is profiled against the past, which serves as its backdrop or ground.[52]

Not so Benjamin, for whom the *démodé* is situated at a constitutive remove from the present. Hence the concept of the temporal caesura, which has to be bridged when reactualizing past styles. However, although structurally separated from the fashion present—i.e., not immediately preceding it, as Simmel holds—Benjamin, in contrast to Simmel, contends that this outdated past maintains a qualitatively determinate relationship with the fashion present. Hence its capacity to function and figure as more than mere material for new fashions. For Simmel, all temporally and geographically remote styles are equally suitable as material for new fashions; for Benjamin, the relation to the past is articulated throughout and constitutes the main axis of fashion work. This relation is at the heart of Benjamin's genuinely dialectical and not just polar or dualist temporal model.

Putting things schematically, we could say that, for Simmel, fashion plays out in a continuous alteration and re/production of today vs. yesterday, whereas Benjamin models fashion as temporal work that extends from today over the hiatus that is yesterday to the day before yesterday. History only begins at the day before yesterday. In this manner, Simmel and Benjamin anticipate one of our own contemporary theoretical stances, which holds that it is not the times that make the sorting, but rather the sorting that makes the times[53]—in this case, sorting out fashion/s.

Zeitkern *(time kernel)*

Within the range of systemic features discussed up to this point, one core aspect of Benjamin's elaborations of the subject of fashion is: time. To say that Benjamin assigned time a "core" position is actually not much more than to paraphrase his own formulations. As much is indicated, firstly, by a parallel between two versions of a familiar passage in *On the Concept of History*. Both begin with a nearly identical, already quoted sentence: "History is the object of a construction whose site is not homogenous, empty time, but time filled full by now-time" (COH 395) (Die Geschichte ist Gegenstand einer Konstruktion, deren Ort nicht die homogene und leere Zeit sondern die von Jetztzeit erfüllte bildet [BG 24–25]). The first version develops this predication into a reflection on the French Revolution, its return to ancient Rome, and its analogy to the temporal recourses of fashion:

> Thus, to Robespierre, ancient Rome was a past charged with now-time, a past which he blasted out of the continuum of history. The French Revolution viewed itself as Rome reincarnate. It cited ancient Rome exactly the way fashion cites a bygone mode of dress. Fashion has a nose for the current. No matter where it stirs in the thickets of once; it is the tiger's leap into the past.
> OCH 395, TM

> *So war für Robespierre das antike Rom eine mit Jetztzeit geladene Vergangenheit, die er aus dem Kontinuum der Geschichte heraussprengte. Die französische Revolution verstand sich als ein wiedergekehrtes Rom. Sie zitiert das alte Rom genauso wie die Mode eine vergangene Tracht zitiert. Die Mode hat ... die Witterung furs Aktuelle, [[das sie [welches sie] aufzustöbern nicht müde wird.]] wo immer es sich [im Dickicht des einst bewegt] (...) Sie ist der Tigersprung ins Vergangene.*
>
> BG 24

The alternative to this first version proceeds differently; namely, apart from substituting the expression "medium" for "site" by veering into heuristic reflections:

> History is the object of a construction whose medium is not homogenous, empty time, but time filled full by now-time. Where the past is charged with this explosive matter, (historical materialism)/materialist research puts a fuse to the homogenous and empty continuum of history. With this method it envisages to blast the epoch from it.
>
> *Die Geschichte ist Gegenstand einer Konstruktion, deren Medium nicht die homogene und leere Zeit sondern die von 'Jetztzeit' erfüllte bildet. Wo die Vergangenheit mit diesem Explosivstoff geladen ist, legt (der historische Materialismus)/die materialistische Forschung an das homogene und leere Kontinuum der Geschichte die Zündschnur an. Bei diesem Verfahren schwebt ihr vor, die Epoche aus ihm herauszusprengen.*
>
> BG 25

The crucial parallel to the first version of the thesis that is of interest here, however, occurs after Benjamin has laid out the disjunctive mechanics of historico-temporal analysis. The formulation in question is: "The nourishing fruit of what is historically understood contains in its interior time as a precious, but tasteless seed" (COH 396) (Die nahrhafte Frucht des geschichtlich Begriffenen hat die Zeit als den kostbaren aber des Geschmacks entratenden Samen in ihrem Innern [BG 25]).[54] This image closes the alternative version of thesis, occupying an equivalent position to that of the tiger's leap in the previous one. While maintaining the described difference in registers—version one addressing a case of historical circumstantiality, and, with the figure of the tiger's leap, the manifestation of a temporal operation in history; version two addressing questions of historical epistemology—the comparison between both versions leaves us with the conjunction between the reactualization of the temporally disjunct at a given present (fashion's tiger's leap), and the image of time as the seed of the fruits of historical cognition.

In further versions and notes of the theses, there are slight yet instructive variations of what Benjamin here calls the "seed of time." In the French version, which has the formulation in thesis XVII, "the nourishing fruits of the tree of knowledge" (fruits nourrisants de l'arbre de la connaissance) are said to carry "enclosed in their pulp" (enfermé dans leur pulpe) like a "precious seed" (une semence précieuse), "historical time" (le Temps historique) (BG 57); that is not just *time*, but *historical time*. In a draft version, Benjamin speaks of a *Kern*, the kernel, instead of the *Samen*, the seed (BG 111). In the latter form—i.e., as the figure of a *Zeitkern*—the idea also entered the *Arcades Project*, where, in convolute N, on epistemology, Benjamin again establishes a parallel to the subject of fashion:

> Resolute refusal of the concept of 'timeless truth' is in order.... [T]ruth is not ... a merely contingent function of knowing, but is bound to a kernel of time, lying hidden in the knower and the known at once. This is so true that the eternal, in any case, is far more the ruffle on a dress than some idea.
>
> AC 463, TM

> *Entschiedne Abkehr vom Begriffe der 'zeitlosen Wahrheit' ist am Platz. ... Wahrheit ist nicht ... nur eine zeitliche Form des Erkennens sondern an einen Zeitkern, welcher im Erkannten und Erkennenden zugleich steckt, gebunden. Das ist so wahr, daß das Ewige jedenfalls eher eine Rüsche am Kleid ist als eine Idee.*
>
> PW 578

This latter sentence reoccurs, in the mode of self-quotation, again in the fashion convolute: "In my formulation: 'The eternal is in any case far more the ruffle on a dress than some idea' dialectical image" (AP 69) (Ich formulierte, "daß das Ewige jedenfalls eher eine Rüsche am Kleid ist, als eine Idee" Dialektisches Bild [PW 118]).

This collated panorama of interrelated passages from the *Arcades Project* and *On the Concept of History* now allows us a number of observations regarding the (quite literally) "core" function that time occupies in Benjamin's fashion theory. We are now in the position to more precisely understand the concept of the *time kernel* in relation to fashion. Apart from the mentioned double structure of relating both to phenomena within the actuality of historical time and to questions of an epistemology of history, or historical time, respectively, it is also clear that what Benjamin here refers to as a "core" or "kernel" should not be taken as indicating the immanence of a moment, a self-centered instant, or a transient yet isolated (fashion) manifestation. It is also unrelated to an idea of aesthetic ephemerality, a romantically revered or reactionarily decried notion of fashion's "passing" character.[55] Rather, the Benjaminian notion of the time kernel—which in its historico-epistemological form is said to exist in what is recognized (Erkanntes) and in the position of she or he who recognizes (Erkennenden), which in its implementation in history indicates a distribution over discrete and disconnected instants—is thus structurally coextensive with the figure of the constellation. Or, even if at first counterintuitive, the time kernel is an analog figure to (fashion's) tiger's leap. While immanent to history, the time kernel is not a figure of (momentary) immanence; rather, it is a figure of temporal relationality—like the constellation, the dialectical image, or fashion's tiger's leap (which in themselves are again subject to temporalization). It is, in Werner Hamacher's words, the "nucleus of a differential time": the time of history, and its cognition, for which fashion served as a model.[56]

The ends of Benjamin's time/fashion model I: Revolution

Like all analogies, Benjamin's time/fashion model is not without limits. On some of these limitations Benjamin comments explicitly; others are implicit in his writing. There are two larger complexes where these ends become particularly palpable: the subjects of revolution and apocatastasis, i.e., the idea derived from early Christian theology of a restitution of all lost souls and things to the integrity of creation after the end of times. What these terms have in common is not just a certain gravitas, not to say grandeur (let alone their not at all evident connection with the subject of fashion to begin with); they also serve to demonstrate that Benjamin's understanding of fashion is particularly contentious and also problematic where it touches on negotiating issues of systematicity *in toto*. More concretely put, the limits of the Benjaminian fashion model frequently lie where he attempts to extend its applicability from particular instantiations, such as the constellational rearticulation of past material to questions that arise when thinking of systemic totality, such as the beginnings and endings of the overall layout of history, or the radical break by which one political system is suspended, overthrown, and a new system is instituted.

This epistemic finitude may well in part be the effect of the very topic under consideration: fashion's individual instantiations and operations may be easily circumscribed and analyzed, while its systemic aspect (for instance, the question of its overall beginnings) is elusive—more a general, ongoing, distributed, temporalized activity, the processing of difference, than a set system that enables such processing. Benjamin could thus be lauded for taking fashion to its limits, or to the limits of its compossibility and compatibility with questions of systematicity. On the other hand, his approach lacks the suppleness of, for instance, Simmel's arguably more narrow view, in which the differentiating and transformational aspect of fashion is located at the very core of fashion itself, and change is seen as the foundational (im)permanence of the fashion game. Benjamin's thought is not as smooth. In his work, the contact zones between the fashion question and the thinking of the entirety of a system are friction points, and where these issues rub against each other there occurs the occasional yet discernible screeching sound. It would be unwise to ignore these noises.

That Benjamin considered the relation of fashion and revolution to extend beyond his central but potentially contingent example of the French Revolution's return to ancient Rome as a concrete correlate to the structural operation of fashion's tiger's leap into the past, is indicated by his occasional referring to the relevant thesis XIV by the title of "Fashion and Revolution" (Mode und Revolution) (BG 59). That he also considered the interrelation between these terms to be at least not entirely evident becomes clear from a somewhat opaque sketch which occurs twice in Benjamin's work: once among the notes for *On the Concept of History* and another time, in a slightly more extensive form, in the notes for the 1935 text *Paris, Capital of the 19th Century* (Paris, Hauptstadt des 19. Jahrhunderts). Both versions comprise the sentence, "Fashion always places its fig leaf on the spot where the revolutionary nakedness of society may be found" (AP 909) (Die Mode setzt ihr Feigenblatt immer an der Stelle auf, wo sich die revolutionäre Blöße der Gesellschaft befindet [BG 130, PW 1215]). In the *Arcades* notes, Benjamin fragmentarily expands this observation by adding: "A slight adjustment and ... But why is this adjustment fruitful only when it is carried out on the body of the recent past?" (AP 909) (Eine kleine Verschiebung, und ... Aber wieso ist diese Verschiebung fruchtbar nur wo sie am Körper des Jüngstvergangenen vollzogen wird? [PW 1215]). The difficulty in pinpointing the content of Benjamin's pronunciation here lies in ascertaining what he means by "revolutionary nakedness," and in relation to it, what function fashion is assigned here. It is much easier, if not to answer, then at least to understand his question as to why the small displacements become fertile only where they are operated on the body of what has just passed. These terms are in line with other observations in the *Arcades Project*, namely that fashion tends to operate with small, not large, shifts (see the section in this chapter, "Fashion changes little"), and that one of fashion's central chronotechnical operations is to qualify the (affective-aesthetic) relation to the recent past (see the section in this chapter, "Any past's contemporary"). The compatibility of the insight into fashion's small or minor transformational register and the arguably very major transformational powers of revolution could be resolved by pointing to other moments in Benjamin's thought in which he did combine the idea of a radical alteration of the status quo with a concept of minor interventions, perhaps most prominently in the paradoxical formulation of "weak messianic power" (OCH 390) (schwache messianische Kraft [BG 17]). But what exactly is the relation between fashion and revolution that is indicated by the figure of the "fig leaf"? Is revolutionary nakedness that instance on which societies have failed to achieve revolution? And is fashion its cover up? Are fashion's transformations here seen as both mirrorings and bad compensations for the lack of achievement of a societal, historical revolution? Given the incomplete state of Benjamin's notes, it is impossible to answer these questions.

Let us thus turn to another instance on which Benjamin establishes a nexus between fashion and revolution, and see if this pithy yet more complete argument also retroactively allows us to weigh in on our previous question. Benjamin ends thesis XIV with the following addendum to the image of the tiger's leap:

Fashion has a nose for the current, no matter where it stirs in the thicket of once; it is the tiger's leap into the past. Such a leap, however, takes place in an arena where the ruling class gives commands. The same leap under the open skies of history is the dialectical leap Marx understood as revolution.

OCH 395, TM

Die Mode hat die Witterung für das Aktuelle, wo immer es sich im Dickicht des Einst bewegt. Sie ist der Tigersprung ins Vergangene. Nur findet er in einer Arena statt, in der die herrschende Klasse kommandiert. Derselbe Sprung unter dem freien Himmel der Geschichte ist der dialektische als den Marx die Revolution begriffen hat.

BG 79

The presets of the argument at first seem clear enough: the situation ("arena") in which Benjamin observes fashion's tiger's leap is one in which "the ruling class" commands. And we could thus be led to assume that once the revolution has taken place and "the ruling class" has either abdicated or been "dealt with," the operation that we have come to appreciate as fashion's trans-temporal maneuvers could finally take place in a state of "freedom" (or at least under "open skies"). Yet to espouse such an idea of conditions freed from power and fashion would not just be naïve; we would also be misunderstanding Benjamin, whose argument is more counterintuitive, and more perplexing. For the analogy does not suggest that the revolution institutes a state of freedom from power (and social stratification), in which what used to be a fashion operation could then be exercised under circumstances in which the ruling class has let go of the reins, hence no longer necessitating the petty game of *ersatz* upward mobility and pseudo-participation in which fashion is cast in trickle-down theories. Rather, what Benjamin proposes is that the dialectical leap of fashion "under open skies" *is* the very leap of revolution (as Marx understood it). That is, revolution here doesn't clear the terrain for classless and fashionless society, and the "open skies" aren't free from power. Instead, the open skies are those of *history* (Geschichte), and as transposed into this setting, the leap that we are familiar with from fashion becomes the leap *of* revolution. As challenging as the thought may be, it is clearly Benjamin's idea here that the historical upheaval of revolution can be thought of as being akin to the operation with which what was "out" is reintroduced and becomes "in" again. Revolution does not clear out the conditions that enable and engender fashion; instead, one specific fashion operation turns out to model the event and operation of revolution. The crucial difference being that revolution occurs in the realm of history, whereas fashion occurs under a temporality that isn't quite historical yet. Apart from the remarkable epistemological trust that Benjamin invests in the fashion model, we can remark, once again, that the key difference here is one between modes and models of temporality, not between phenomena in time.

The ends of Benjamin's time/fashion model II: historical apocatastasis

There is, finally, yet another way in which Benjamin's thinking, at least implicitly, correlates the fashion question with issues of systemic totality, and among the examples discussed here this arguably proceeds by way of the most obscure reference. Its keyword is the ancient Greek term *apocatastasis*, used by Benjamin in what he calls a "modest methodological proposal" (AP 459) (Kleiner methodischer Vorschlag [PW 573]), by which he vises the possibility of a process in which "the entire past is brought into the present in a historical apocatastasis" (AP 459) (die ganze Vergangenheit in einer historischen Apokatastasis in die Gegenwart eingebracht ist [PW 573]).

If we subtract the element of history for a moment, the figure is easier to understand, and its origins and outlines have been described on several occasions in Benjamin scholarship: Irving Wohlfahrt mentions first a passage in Benjamin's essay "The Storyteller" (Der Erzähler), in which the writings of the antique Greek theologian and Church Father Origen, and in particular his concept of *apocatastasis* are referred to—that is, the idea that eventually all souls will enter paradise.[57] Citing Hans Blumenberg's *Die Lesbarkeit der Welt*, (The Readability of the World), which in tracing an intellectual line from Origen to a Leibnizian fragment on *apocatastasis* casts this as a counter-figure to the orthodox biblical model of a linear eschatology, Josef Fürnkäs emphasizes in particular Blumenberg's view that the model of *apocatastasis* implies the concept of an iterability of the history of the world—the *Wiedholbarkeit des Weltlaufs*—which he connects to the "cosmological idea of an integral keeping (*Aufbewahrung*) and palingenetic recreation of the original state of paradise, as well as the return of all the dead and forgotten."[58] Finally, Michael Jennings has recently traced the source from which Benjamin appropriated this concept—the writings of Protestant theologian Adolf von Harnack—as well as describing the broader conceptual frame of such an idea of *restitutio in integrum*, or "the restoration of all things after the end of times," namely a basic apocalyptic trait.[59]

While it is, of course, well known that Benjamin's late thinking, and in particular the theses *On the Concept of History*, are in close dialogue with theology (Jewish and Christian), it is helpful to ask here how exactly the peculiarly hopeful and inclusive apocalypticism of *apocatastasis* (after all, this is a model by which the end of times, by way of the dire straits of the cosmos's ending, promises a happy ending for all and everything) is transposed onto the terrain of history (and ultimately to parse its relation to the fashion question). In his methodological proposal, Benjamin sketches the following mechanism:

> It is very easy to draw divisions, according to determinate points of view, within the various 'fields' of any epoch, such that on one side lies the 'productive,' 'forward-looking,' 'lively,' 'positive' part of the epoch, and on the other the abortive, retrograde and withered.
>
> AP 459, TM

> *Es ist sehr leicht, für jede Epoche auf ihren verschiedenen 'Gebieten' Zweiteilungen nach bestimmten Gesichtspunkten vorzunehmen, dergestalt daß auf der einen Seite eine 'fruchtbare', 'zukunftsvolle', 'lebendig', 'positive', auf der andern der vergebliche, rückständige, abgestorbene Teil dieser Epoche liegt.*
>
> PW 573

Benjamin then proceeds to probe the relation between the two elements which result from this division, and to assess their respective valuation:

> The very contours of the positive element will appear distinctly only insofar as this element is set off against the negative. On the other hand, every negation has its value solely as background for the contours of the lively, the positive.
>
> AP 459, TM

> *Man wird sogar die Konturen dieses positiven Teils nur deutlich zum Vorschein bringen, wenn man ihn gegen den negativen profiliert. Aber jede Negation hat ihren Wert andererseits nur als Fonds für die Umrisse des Lebendigen, Positiven.*
>
> PW 573

The positively valued elements are thus put into relief through being profiled against the background of those elements set aside as negatively valued, whose valuation (resulting in their *Wert*) as negative—i.e., their negation—receives its character *as value* only in relation to the positive which they contour. However, rather than fixating the result of this sorting into positive and negative, Benjamin envisions a continuation of this process with regards to those elements marked as negative:

> It is therefore of decisive importance that a new partition be applied to this initially excluded, negative component so that, by a displacement of the angle of vision (but not of the criteria) a positive element emerges anew in it too—something different from that previously signified.
>
> AP 459

> *Daher ist es von entscheidender Wichtigkeit, diesem, vorab ausgeschiednen negative Teile von neuem eine Teilung zu applizieren, derart, daß, mit einer Verschiebung des Gesichtswinkels (nicht aber der Maßstäbe!) auch in ihm von neuem ein Positives und ein anderes zu Tage tritt als das vorher bezeichnete.*
>
> PW 573

The valuating, separating, and discerning labor thus continues, and what was previously signified as "negative" is again split, in order to produce the distinction between positive and negative anew. This is the process that Benjamin calls *historical apocatastasis*, and it needs to continue ad infinitum—in infinity—until "the entire past is brought into the present" (die ganze Vergangenheit ... in die Gegenwart eingebracht ist [AP 459; PW 573]).

At this point, the otherwise rather improbable parallels between a theory of fashion and a philosophy of history that takes its cue from the work of an ancient sectarian eschatological thinker begin to emerge. There is, first, the subdivision into positively and negatively valued elements that echoes the qualifying operations by which fashion, at any given moment, generates what will go forward and what will be left behind, the *démodé*. Benjamin specifies the relation of negative to positive elements as follows: the negative *fonds* (ground) to the figure of the positive correlates with the outmoded, against which what is in fashion stands out. What makes for an even fuller parallel, however, is the correlation between what Benjamin here calls the *Einbringen* (introduction, entering, bringing in) of the past into the present, by which parts of what had previously been cast out as negative pasts are recuperated for the present. The construction of this reactualization of what had previously been cast aside *as and in the present* clearly parallels the operation of fashion's tiger's leap, in which the outmoded is reintroduced to generate present fashion value.

Even if the note in which the concept of historical apocatastasis is introduced is but a self-declared "small methodological proposal," its basic logic still allows us not only to chart the parallels to Benjamin's fashion theory, but also to map another, final, limit to the reach of Benjamin's fashion model. The crucial difference here lies in the meaning of the formulation "in infinitum." Within the mechanism laid out in the methodological proposal, this unending process must be understood as an infinite approach, the ever-ongoing approximation toward a limit that, qua definition, can never be met. For if the process by which the past is quite literally "sorted out" relies on the principle of division (into positive and negative), it is clear that this method will never achieve an exhaustive working through: what is found positive is marked as such through its profiling against its ground, the negative, which will, in turn, become the terrain for the next division. There will always exist a remainder, and be it the smallest, in which positive and negative have not been split. Yet while this quasi-fractal progressing into ever more minute segments of the past is without end, the overall movement of the operation has a clear direction. It strives toward the defined and determinate horizon of history in its totality. What in the theological model of apocatastasis would amount to the eschaton—i.e., the end of time—is here transposed into the immanence of history, which, through this folding of a transcendental operation into its body, is paradoxically determined as finite: although categorically beyond reach, the end of history has been set, and history has turned into "History."

The conceptualization of time that can be derived from fashion's chronotechnical operations is different, in that it proposes a different mode of handling the non-finite element. As we saw, fashion's temporalized processing of difference also results in an unending implementation of ever-new differentiation. But the driver here is not the pull of a horizon that is set but can never be reached. Rather, it is the fact that difference, in its spread, loses its differentiating quality and in the moment of its vanishing requires a different implementation. Whereas the model of historical apocatastasis treats difference and its articulation as an operation and a phenomenon that occurs within historical time (until that time reaches its unattainable limit), fashion proposes a model in which difference itself "is" in time, in which difference is temporalized, and in which its only limit is the vanishing of difference. To be more precise, in which the ever-recurring and ever-revoked limit is the vanishing of one particular type of difference and the emergence of another type; in which one difference is replaced by another, in order for the unending articulation of difference to take place. In this model, fashion's tiger's leap into the past is central and instrumental, but it is not unique; whereas in Benjamin's framework of historical apocatastasis, the tiger's leap is the unique operation by which what in the past has been found to be "good" is introduced into the present. It is a means to an end, the end of history, whereas in fashion it is but one means among many: the means of fashion.

Part Two

Benjamin and the Fashion of his Time

2

The Contingent Primacy of Sex(es)

A sudden affluence: The view of garments gliding by

In 1929, German fashion journalist Helen Grund authored a series of dispatches informing her readers about a significant shift that was unfolding in the parades of designs presented that very year in the fashion showrooms of her adopted hometown of Paris. Grund's articles and reviews appeared, like most of her texts, in the monthly magazine supplement *Für die Frau* (For Women) which, addressing issues of "fashion and society" (Mode und Gesellschaft), accompanied the venerable *Frankfurter Zeitung*, Germany's leading liberal newspaper, whose culture pages—the famed *Feuilleton*—counted Siegfried Kracauer as one of their leading editors, and which also published shorter texts and essays by Benjamin. Grund had moved to Paris in 1924 after spending years in the Berlin sociable networks of bourgeois bohemians and as a frequent visitor to France, and after she had already begun publishing occasionally—for instance, her *Mentor for the Nouveaux Riches*.[1] In Paris, Grund took the position of a fashion correspondent for the *Frankfurter Zeitung*, marking *Für die Frau* as the terrain of her Paris reports as soon as the magazine supplement was launched in 1926, for which she became the fashion editor.[2]

In February 1929, reviewing that year's upcoming spring collections, Grund observed what she referred to as an "architectonic" effect, meaning an intervention in the overall constructive layout of the presented designs, a moment of outline and cut: an attempt "to clearly define woman's shape from the hips, from the middle" (die Gestalt der Frau von der Hüfte her, von der Mitte her deutlich zu bestimmen).[3] The formulation is at first slightly ambiguous, leaving doubts as to why such an observation would merit reporting. The hips had, after all, been one of the main points of orientation in women's fashion for a good deal of the decade that was about to draw to a close. Along with the shoulder line, they had served as the two shorter imaginary parallels of the approximate rectangle as which designers had been projecting the female body. Referred to as the "flapper," the *garçonne*, or the *Neue Frau*, her outfits had, either as dresses or costumes, cast the torso as a flat plane, dropping straight down from the shoulders, ideally along two lines that hung as perpendiculars to the imaginary horizontal of the ground on which woman stood. The touchpoints below the shoulders for these vectors were the hips, below which the dress or a short skirt would drop until ideally just below the knees. Arms and legs—preferably skinny—attached to or protruded from this geometrical slab like sticks, avoiding all volumetric shaping, or suppressing as much visual information as possible that would have indicated extensions into the third dimension (Fig. 2.1).

What Grund observed, and what she meant by the definition of a woman's form from its middle, becomes clearer in a short paragraph in which she focuses on a black crêpe romaine afternoon dress, designed by Jean Patou:

> The new summer fashion delivers straight lines of cut for dresses and coats. Ever more frequently we see diagonally positioned groups of pleats that are crossed by vertical stripes. An afternoon dress in black crêpe romaine has a double hem and gives us a bell shape. The associated coat has a straight line in front, while on the back the orthogonal stripes widen into a bell.
>
> *Die neue Sommermode bringt gerade Schnittlinien der Kleider und Mäntel. Immer häufiger sieht man quergestellte Faltengruppen, die von glatten vertikalen Streifen überschnitten werden. Das Nachmittagskleid aus schwarzem Crêpe Romain fällt in einem doppelten Saum glockig aus. Der associierte Mantel hat vorn eine gerade Linie, rückwärts verbreitern sich die Längsstreifen zur Glocke.*[4]

The diagonally positioned pleats are one element that markedly contradicts the parallel layout of the styles of dress that had been favored before; and that Patou was a, if not *the* designer to watch at this point became increasingly obvious to Grund. In the April issue, she declared the considerably elongated pleated skirt and the increasingly steep plunge of the base of dresses observed in his models to be characteristic for the spring fashion of 1929.[5] Grund also noted the break with what had become fashion common sense in the 1920s. Patou attempted and suggested "to pick up certain prewar traditions and adapt them to our modern ideas" (gewisse Vorkriegs-Traditionen wieder aufzunehmen und sie unseren modernen Ideen anzupassen).[6] As the year progressed, and with it the development of fashion, and in particular Patou's (who was also granted growing significance on the pages of *Für die Frau*—photographs and drawings of his models increasingly outnumbering those of the publication's previous apparent favorite, Lucien Lelong), Grund zeroed in on the transformations which, in spring, had become palpable. In July she observed that "in the current season" the "waistline" (Taillenlinie) was "clearly moving upward" (in deutlicher Aufwärtsbewegung).[7] The September issue—putting a Patou-model on the cover—condensed the development even further in several isolated observations. A sweater was singled out, "short and belted around the waist" (kurz und in der Taille gegürtet), but the main vestimentary media for a new definition of the fashionable appearance in women's wardrobes—"Woman appears tall, young and slim, but distinctly feminine" (Die Frau erscheint groß, jung, schlank, aber entschieden weiblich)—were skirts and dresses. Under the headline "What is New in Winter Fashions" (Das Neue der Wintermode), Grund mentioned that the "the waist is positioned where woman is most slender. It is emphasized by the beginning of the skirt or a belt. Frequently also through the shape of the dress" (Taille liegt dort, wo die Frau am schmalsten ist. Sie wird durch den Rockansatz oder einen Gürtel markiert. Oft auch durch den modellierenden Schnitt des Kleids).[8] In November 1929 these indications and premonitions had condensed into a genuine shift, and Grund felt confident enough to present her readers with the following diagnosis of a potential watershed moment:

> Apparently, fashion is about to introduce a new set of norms, not just through playfully shifting proportions against one another. The attempt to display the waist, where the female body is the most flexible, has been a resolute success. This shape would seem to become obligatory again. Until now the hip-line, woman's most exterior measure, has been the point of departure from which all fashionable proportions were calculated and perceived. If the waist is indeed fixated anew, only the long dress will be worth spending our attention on. In the meantime also the more bold and more hesitant transitions aren't without interest, not without charm.
>
> *Offenbar steht die Mode im Begriff, neue Normen einzuführen, nicht nur in spielerischer Weise die Maße gegeneinander zu verschieben. Entscheidend ist der Versuch geglückt, die Taille dort evident zu machen, wo die Gestalt der Frau am biegsamsten ist. Diese Form wird von neuem verantwortlich in Erscheinung treten. Bisher war die Hüftlinie, dieses äußerste Maß der Frau, der Ausgangspunkt aller errechneten und empfundenen Proportionen der Mode.*

Gelingt es, die Taille neu zu fixieren, so wird allein das lange Kleid es sein, dem unsere Aufmerksamkeit zu schenken sich lohnen wird. Inzwischen sind auch die kühneren und zögernden Übergänge nicht uninterressant, nicht ohne Reiz.[9]

Another way in which Grund sought to grasp the contrast to the looks that had dominated Parisian and, by extension, international fashion was by observing that the "notion of 'sport' as a blanket term disappears from the vocabulary of fashion" (Der Begriff "sport" als eine Sammelbezeichnung verschwindet immer mehr aus dem Vokabularium der Mode)[10]—indicating that, whereas in particular during the second half of the 1920s a certain athleticism had prevailed, also in womenswear—for instance in form of the many "sportif" beach outfits for Deauville and the Côte d'Azur—now, with the

Figure 2.1 George Hoyningen-Huene: Model Dinarzade in a Jean Patou cardigan and notched-collar knit top with tweed inset matching the skirt; hat by Rose Valois. *Vogue* (1928). © Condé Nast/Getty Images.

Figure 2.2 Edward Steichen: Tennis player Suzanne Lenglen in a Jean Patou Sports Costume. *Vogue* (1926). © Condé Nast/Getty Images.

lengthening of the skirts, the direction went more into the interior realm of social occasions, soirees, etc. (Fig. 2.2; 2.3).[11]

In a piece also written for *Für die Frau*, Helen Grund's husband, the author Franz Hessel, condensed the development, in absence of the more technical details and expertise his wife was privy to, into an overall impression. In the appropriately titled, shortish article *Mitgenommen in eine Modenschau* (Company for a Fashion Show), he described the feeling as follows:

> And there is a surprise. Something has changed! Suddenly there is affluence, a flood of too much, a charming wastefulness, a gentle splendor. In recent years actual or pretended boyish rigor and sparseness have impressed us very much in feminine appearance, and, like all fashions, these responded to a certain male desire.... Now we may enjoy ... the view of long sliding garments.

> *Und da gibt es eine Überraschung. Da ist etwas anders geworden! Mit einmal ist Überfluß da, ein flutendes Zuviel, eine reizende Verschwendung, eine sanfte Pracht. In den letzten Jahren waren uns wahre oder falsche Knabenstrenge und*

Figure 2.3 Edward Steichen: Model Marion Morehouse in a black Patou dress with chiffon tiered bottom. *Vogue* (1930). © Condé Nast/Getty Images.

Knappheit der Frauenerscheinung ein großer Eindruck gewesen und hat, wie alle Mode, einer Mannessehnsucht entsprochen. ... Genießen ... können wir nun ... den Anblick lang gleitender Gewänder.[12]

Waists are up, skirts are down (1929/1930)

Helen Grund's observations were written for the not necessarily quantitatively, yet fashion-culturally comparatively marginal German sphere, which wasn't as closely interwoven with the Paris production scenery as Great Britain or, in particular, the United States. Yet the aptness of her analysis puts Grund's texts on par with those of her colleagues writing for international flagship publications, such as the various *Vogues* or *Harper's Bazaar*, whose judgment echoed those of their German colleague. Baron de Meyer, reporting on the winter 1930 collections for *Harper's* also considered Patou's designs, for the very transformation that Grund had described, to be noteworthy: "The Patou silhouette is new, significant and bound to exert a widespread influence. His evening gowns, the most salient feature of his presentation, combine extreme length of skirt with fullness. Result—elongated height."[13] And in the same issue, under the headline "Paris Proposes," Marjorie Howard declared that not for years had winter collections "been so sensational, so upsetting,"[14] detecting a first hint of the "princess silhouette" (again) and declaring the transformation that played out before her eyes as the "movement of 1930," a "sartorial revolution" that was at Patou's "more complete than at almost any other house."[15] In a sketch for the English *Vogue*, a publication which declared that after "a revolution in fashion" a "new period costume" had "made its début—the Mode of 1930," Cecil Beaton similarly drew the dividing line between the winter of 1929 and that of 1930. In a double illustration, placed on opposite pages of the magazine, he depicts three ladies each: on the left, a trio titled "Ladies in the Winter of 1929," one comfortably seated on a stool, the two others leaning on the sill of a fireplace, all three dressed in short flapper outfits, their arms and their legs down from the knees bared, forming an image of easy casualness and snappiness. On the right, the reader of *Vogue* sees another group, titled "Ladies in the Winter of 1930," whose attire and stance couldn't be more different: as if a princess-commando had requested a stiffening up, all three are a picture of poise, holding their torsos and backs perfectly upright, while their dresses, in comparison to their predecessor from a season ago, have considerably gained in length, layers, and frilliness. Garlands, ruffles, volants, flounces, and trains play around a silhouette both more attenuated and sinuous. It is as if the short, practical dress had, in the time span of a single season, grown into an artfully frazzled yet figure-hugging gown.[16] Beaton's "Ladies in the Winter of 1929" and "Ladies in the Winter of 1930" distribute across two frames the shift in silhouettes that had taken hold—as the magazine called it, the "revival of moulded curves."[17]

In *Harper's Bazaar*, Marjorie Howard resorted to the same anatomical and body-morphological terms that Grund had used to capture the impact of this shift in the silhouette: "We have been accustomed for a long time to take care of the hips and let the waists take care of themselves, but the designers have changed all that."[18] Pondering the implications which the new directive "where there's a waist, there's a way" (or, in the words of her colleague Martine Rénier, editor in chief of *Femina*, "la taille … revenue à sa place") had for those customers who had, under the sheets of the flapper dress, banked on shoulders and hips, Howard summarized the sartorial shift by describing the exact same displacements that Grund had also noted: "Waists are UP, skirts are DOWN, and many of us are wondering what we are going to do about it."[19] There seems to have been a consensus in the fashion press at the time, firstly, that this "change in proportion," through a new return to sartorial virtuosity ("never has there been so much cut," *Vogue UK* exclaimed), had to be regarded as "the first dramatic change in dress" to occur "since the *garçonne* mode came in."[20] And, just as Grund pointed out to her German readers, Patou's house was the place where it was first seen: "Patou's is the first collection visited. It is the time when buyers from the world over are in Paris. They line the broad stairs at Patou, standing two by two until a *vendeuse* shall 'pass' each one."[21] Apart from the pioneering quality of this aesthetic move to drop the hems, and to begin to hug waistline and hips more closely in an attempt to sculpt the characteristically curved yet elongated form that dominated for the following decade, producing what Rénier termed *le corps moulé*, Patou's body of work might have been a particularly suitable terrain on which to exemplify this transformation.[22] His previous reputation had, after all, been earned by capitalizing on the lithe, athletic woman for whom he designed outfits that were compatible with sports. Tennis player Suzanne Lenglen had been his celebrity customer, and, together with Coco Chanel, he was seen as putting in place a "healthy" and "hygienic" appeal of the female body (Fig. 2.2).[23] The most pronounced publicity stunt to cement this image was probably his meticulously broadcast and reported 1924 trip on an ocean liner to the United States, where in New York he cast a group of American girls—in the European perception exemplars of a "sportive" body, and certainly not accidentally also representing his client base beyond the old continent—who accompanied him back to France, to then present his designs in Paris.[24] Given this previous work, it was little wonder that Grund and her colleagues perceived the shift in tone and silhouette as particularly poignant. From the tennis court and the beach to the salon and the soiree, "waists are up and skirts are down" meant from "girls" to "women"—and gowns.

An onscreen vignette: L'Herbier, Helm, Louiseboulanger

One of the earliest yet most enduring manifestations of this newly emerging look—which would eventually be termed "the line of the 1930s" (a description that at least captures the fashion trends of that decade's first half)—can still be seen onscreen, as well as on the pages of one of period's leading fashion magazines, the French revue *Femina*. The film in question is Marcel L'Herbier's 1928 *L'Argent*, a loose adaptation of Émile Zola's 1891 novel of the same title, and widely regarded as a stylistically and technologically innovative and formally complex masterpiece of the ending silent era. One of the film's outstanding cast members is German actress Brigitte Helm, who in L'Herbier's film acts the part of the sultry, manipulative, and business-savvy Baroness Sandorf. The entire wardrobe for *L'Argent* was overseen and largely created by Jacques Manuel, initially an art department assistant on L'Herbier's 1926 *Le Vertige*, who would go on to work in this function on the director's films for the coming decade.[25] On the outfits for Helm's character, however, Manuel collaborated with the couturier Louise Boulanger, and among the fruits of this collaboration are two gowns that anticipate and fixate tendencies of the emerging silhouette in a remarkable manner.[26] This anticipatory quality exists in spite of a number of general mitigating factors, reflected by Manuel himself at a later point in his essay "Esquisse d'une historie du costume de cinéma," by which the presentation of an outfit that at a given point is considered to be in fashion doesn't necessarily figure as such onscreen. Manuel considers aspects such as the difference between the face-to-face perception of a garment vs. its visual approximation through the lens in close-ups, the framing through the format of the screen, as well as differences in perspective, all of which could—to a certain extent—be considered as parallel arguments to the Benjaminian trope regarding the non-congruency between the world as it presents itself to human vision, and as it presents itself to the filmic or photographic camera (whose products become, in turn, visible to the human eye)—anticipations, if you will, of how fashionable vestments will be warped once they enter the optical unconscious.[27] Manuel also mentions the crucial temporal marker that stamps fashion, making for the fact that "from the time a film is made until its first public showing a minimum of sixth months elapses, often much longer where big productions are concerned," leading to the result that "because fashion is in its essence ephemeral and current, the film may seem out of fashion by the time it makes it to the cinema."[28] Resorting to the concept of *photogénie*, a term initially coined by silent filmmakers Louis Delluc and Jean Epstein to account for the fundamental aesthetic transformation of certain profilmic elements in the moment of entering the filmic dimension, Manuel defines this act as a filmic stylization of fashion[29]—a stylization which, in the case of his collaborations with Louise Boulanger on the costumes for Brigitte Helm, was remarkably successful.

The first standout look is a dress made from what in the literature is described as gold lamé; on black and white film this translates into a metallic silver surface, whose color echoes the film's (and Zola's novel's) French title

2.4a

The Contingent Primacy of Sex(es) 69

2.4b

2.4c

Figure 2.4.a–e Brigitte Helm in Marcel L'Herbier's "L'Argent," costume by Louiseboulanger with Jacques Manuel (1928), film stills. Cinégraphic / Société des Cinéromans / Universumfilm.

L'Argent, meaning both money and silver (Fig. 2.4a–e).[30] The dress's tightly fitted bodice accentuates the slightly undulating, elastic, yet forceful movements of Helm, its reflective surface visually sculpting the shapes of her hips and waist in motion, as she strides across a salon and, in particular, when, her back toward the camera, she climbs a set of stairs. In its shimmering and reflective effects, the garment also produces a strange visual cinematic echo of Helm's appearance in her previous film, which burned itself into the canon of Western film history and visual imagination at large—namely one part of her role as Maria and the android in Fritz Lang's *Metropolis*, which had been released a year earlier. The Louiseboulanger gown here looks like a sort of liquefied partial reiteration of her shiny robot armor (down to her tightly fitted skull cap that recalls her helmet). Its effect is particularly strong when, stretched out on a chaise longue and lying on her back, Helm's torso is captured in close up, wringing and wiggling as she engages in a dialogue with her aggressive counterpart, Saccard, played by French actor Alcover. When reclining from under Saccard's assault, the dress has the effect of particularly accentuating her previously invisible hip bones, giving prominence to her lower abdomen in a manner that exemplifies the corresponding tendencies in fashion at the moment. When upright, Helm's nude shoulders—the gown is held by two halters—and her elongated neck merge with the curve initiated from chest down to the forward-thrust hips in a pattern that echoes the more eccentric, abrupt, and tic-ridden, yet characteristically hunched movements of the robot, disguised as a woman, in *Metropolis*. This pose can also be seen as presenting a slightly exaggerated and camera-compatible version of what fashion historian Caroline Evans has identified as the characteristic slouching and drooping stance adopted by models in fashion shows of the period.[31]

These sculpting and kinetically profiling effects of the reflective and tightly tailored bodice are supplemented by tides of visual movements generated by the dress's enormous train. Visible as Helm traverses the set, but most prominently and astonishingly presented on her aforementioned stair climb, captured in a static long shot, the train here unspools into a seemingly unending silvery flow; the higher the baroness steps, the longer the waterfall of shining lamé garment spouts forth behind her.

This image, as well as the enormous volants attached to the sleeves of another garment, whose voluminously layered tulle skirt fans out from

2.5a

2.5b

Figure 2.5.a–c Brigitte Helm in Marcel L'Herbier's "L'Argent," costume by Louiseboulanger with Jacques Manuel (1928), film stills. Cinégraphic / Société des Cinéromans / Universumfilm.

underneath a tightly tailored jacket, giving Helm onscreen, as she elegantly rests on a sofa, the air of a bundle of pristine white seaweed, afford us with a palpable impression of what Franz Hessel captured only slightly later when he praised the affluence, the flood of too much, and the sliding trains and gowns which the new look of the beginning 1930s was going to embody (Fig. 2.5 a–c).

Offscreen, on the pages of *Femina*, this look was anticipated by the latter outfit that Helm wore in *L'Argent* and which she modeled here, perched atop a plinth, the at once massive and light volants and layers of tulle cascading like the feathers of an exotic bird (Fig. 2.6). With no mention of any participation by Jacques Manuel, simply listed as a regular Louiseboulanger gown, this page at once magnifies and exaggerates, yet quintessentially condenses what fashion would bring in the coming years. Particularly palpable through its mediation in L'Herbier's film, where the garments were shown in motion, filmically modified yet true to the impression a viewer would have at a fashion show, Louiseboulanger here formulated essential qualities which, outside the cinema, most discovered in the work of a different designer: Patou.

Figure 2.6 Brigitte Helm in a Louiseboulanger negligée; *Femina* (January 1929). Kunstbibliothek der Staatlichen Museen zu Berlin.

Should Benjamin have attended fashion shows?
Helen Grund, the expert

It is a hardly acknowledged, if not entirely ignored fact that in his Parisian exile during the 1930s, Walter Benjamin must have visited fashion shows.[32] We can deduce as much from a letter that Benjamin sent on July 29, 1935 to his close friend Gretel Karplus. In it he writes: "If all goes well I will be able to treat myself again with one or two fashion shows" (Wenn alles gut geht, werde [ich] also wieder diese oder jene Modenschau mir vergönnen können).[33] We neither know the work of which couturiers Benjamin had seen at that point, nor if his planned further attendance at the Paris *défilés* actually took place. However, we do know without a doubt whose mediation and recommendation Benjamin was intending to rely on for gaining access to the Paris presentations: he writes to Karplus that he recently, "after a break of several years, had taken up contact again with Helen Hessel" (nach einer Unterbrechung von Jahren den Umgang mit Helen Hessel . . . wieder aufnehmen können). She had also, Benjamin continues, "written a small pamphlet about the Paris fashion business, indeed first rate in its presentation of its social conditions" (ein Schriftchen über den pariser Modebetrieb geschrieben, (. . .) in der Darstellung seiner gesellschaftlichen Bedingtheit durchaus erstrangig) which he had now acquired.[34]

The "Helen" in question, whom Benjamin here refers to by the last name of her husband Franz Hessel (his close interlocutor, collaborator on one of the earliest sketches on the subject of the *Arcades*, and the author of the above quoted piece, "Company for a Fashion Show") is of course none other than Helen Grund, who signed her published texts with her maiden name.[35] And, due to her expertise, no other person in his milieu would have been better suited to establish contacts (and provide him with information about) the métier and products of fashion. Her texts had also earned her a reputation among Benjamin's interlocutors. Gretel Karplus, who at that point managed the leather manufacturing business founded by her parents that specialized in gloves, and who thus to an extent also worked "in the industry," accordingly responded to Benjamin's letter on August 28, 1935:

> I would love to talk to Helen Grund, and not just about the fashion creations of the grand *maisons*, but about the laws according to which fashions

establish themselves as they trickle down into the provinces and the middle class. I encounter this problem in my job on a nearly daily basis, but I'm not merely interested in it for the sake of business. This process has always puzzled me and I would almost say that the closer I get the more difficult it is for me to find a solution. The concept of taste becomes ever more questionable.

Mit Helen Grund würde ich mich für mein Leben gern einmal unterhalten, und zwar nicht nur über die Modeschöpfungen der großen Häuser, sondern über die Gesetze, nach denen sich die Mode nach unten hin in der Provinz und beim Mittelstand schließlich durchsetzt. Jetzt stoße ich in meinem Beruf beinah täglich auf das Problem, aber ich interessiere mich nicht nur dafür aus Geschäftstüchtigkeit, sondern schon früher war mir dieser Ablauf ein Rätsel, und ich möchte beinah sagen, je näher ich dran bin, desto schwieriger erscheint mir die Lösung, desto fragwürdiger erscheint mir der Begriff des Geschmacks.[36]

Also, Karplus's partner, Theodor Adorno, points out Grund's firsthand knowledge when he suggests to Benjamin, in response to the exposé for the *Arcades Project* which Benjamin had sent him, to consult her in relation to "the passage on fashion, which I find very significant": "Frau Hessel, whose reports in the FZ [Frankfurter Zeitung] we follow with great interest, certainly is an expert here" (zur Stelle über Mode, die mir sehr bedeutend scheint: sicherlich weiß Frau Hessel, deren Berichte in der FZ [Frankfurter Zeitung] wir stets mit großem Interesse verfolgen, damit Bescheid).[37]

And Benjamin indeed *did* rely on Grund's expertise, partly excerpting the mentioned "little pamphlet about the Paris fashion business" in the *Arcades Project*. While the reference certainly has a slightly patronizing ring to it, the hue of condescension is balanced by the actual recognition and respect which Benjamin also expressed when he called Grund's text, as far as it delivers a "presentation of the social conditions" of fashion, "first rate." Said text is Helen Grund's lecture "Vom Wesen der Mode" (On the Essence of Fashion), which she gave in 1934 (and possibly in a slightly altered form again in 1936) at the Munich Meisterschule für Mode (Fashion School). The institution printed and published the text as a slender booklet with a print run of 1000 copies. Benjamin's characterization of Grund's approach as providing an analysis of the "social conditions" of fashion makes her work sound considerably more "sociological" than it actually is. For instance, while Grund, at least in one of the lecture versions, in all likelihood did treat the question of taste (see chapter 3), she seems quite simply not interested in what Gretel Karplus, in her letter to Benjamin, referred to as the social implementation of fashion phenomena from top to bottom, from the center to the periphery. "On the Essence of Fashion" entirely disregards what nowadays is called (and refuted) as the "trickle-down" model of fashion, which was prominently espoused by Thorstein Veblen, or, with regards to matters of class, also by Simmel.[38] In the *Arcades Project*, Benjamin quotes from this text on several occasions, and without a doubt "On the Essence of Fashion" must be regarded as the most important strictly contemporary analysis of the systematic aspects of fashion, as well as the concrete realities of current Paris fashion production to figure in the fashion convolute.

The only contemporaneous fashion thinker

Benjamin's other fashion materials largely pre-date the moment of his working on the *Arcades Project*, with a vast number of them, unsurprisingly, dating to the nineteenth century. It is not always easy to ascertain the potential status which texts—such as the already quoted von Jhering reflections about fashion and media, or the eminently fashion-phobic observations of philosopher and philologist Friedrich Theodor Vischer, whom Benjamin occasionally excerpts on theoretical and systematic matters—would have had within the logic of the *Arcades Project*. Were these intended to provide him with elements for a meta-framework on his topic, or would they have figured *as articulations of the nineteenth century*—which they were—as elements to be treated and worked through, just like the poetry of Baudelaire, or the architecture of the *Arcades*? Even Simmel's *Philosophy of Fashion*—which Benjamin clearly excerpts with an eye to constructing a theoretical framework, and whom scholarly reception has come to treat as a more or less contemporary thinker to Benjamin, and whose diagnostics of the modern metropolis are treated as synchronous with Benjamin's study of the same subject—strictly speaking isn't "of" the *Arcades Project*'s moment. *Philosophy of Fashion* was written in 1905, circa thirty years prior to Benjamin's work on the *Arcades*—a period in which, arguably, the conditions of fashion production and consumption, in particular during the 1920s, had changed considerably.

Surrealist writers and publications occupy threshold positions with regard to chronology, in that a number of them, such as the journal *Minotaure* to which Benjamin refers in the fashion convolute, are strictly contemporary, while others, such as Apollinaire's 1916 novel *Le poète assassiné* which Benjamin treats as a proto-Surrealist text, pre-date his working period. The question of the "when" of these texts' writings is not as acute as the question of when certain styles and fashion aesthetics are articulated, disappear, and reappear—the import of which for Benjamin's work will be weighed in chapter 4; although this question should matter to readers of the *Arcades Project*, as long as they take its intention—to work through the disappeared formations of the nineteenth century—seriously, in that it raises the issue of what, among the fragments and notes gathered here, would have counted as "subject matter" and what as discursive framing; what as primary and what as meta; what as "source" and what as "comment"; and when and where these distinctions would have been difficult or impossible to maintain.

Helen Grund's accounts, by contrast, constitute something like a real-time feed for Benjamin. Not only are her general observations regarding the fashion system—its aesthetics, economic aspects, practices and practitioners, etc—the result of nearly a decade of participant observation;[39] her knowledge is also immediately tied to a feedback loop vis à vis the current fashion production in the Paris of Benjamin's working on the *Arcades Project*.

The contingent primacy of sex

One core preoccupation of the notes and fragments gathered in the fashion convolute is sex, and, as we shall see, Grund's work is one of the main sources for this particular slant, which is also present in other voices. There is, for example, a passage extracted from writer Eduard Fuchs, in which the "origins of the frequent changes in fashion" (Ursache des häufigen Modewechsels)—i.e., one of the fundamental challenges when thinking about fashion: why does it change?—is in part explained through its connection to sexuality and eroticism: "the function of erotic stimulation in fashion ... operates most effectively when the erotic attractions of the man or the woman appear in ever new settings" (AP 77) (die erotisch stimulierenden Zwecke der Mode, die dadurch sich am besten erfüllen, wenn die erotischen Reize des Trägers oder der Trägerin immer wieder auf andere Weise auffallen [PW 128]). If fashion is hence defined as a generator for renewed erotic encounters between people, so to speak, Benjamin also casts fashion as a sexual blocking agent in other configurations, when he states that "[e]ach generation experiences the fashions of the one immediately preceding it as the most radical antiaphrodisiac imaginable" (AP 79) (Jede Generation erlebt die Moden der gerade verflossenen als das gründlichste Antiaphrodisiacum, das sich denken läßt [PW 130]). If the permanently reconfigured presentation of the body through the change of fashionable styles helps to keep attraction going, its inverse effect is not just indifference, but attraction's kill-off. While the transformation of styles perpetually renews the turn-on, the looks of preceding generations equate turn-offs. Fashion is thus described as a chronolibidinal engine, a pharmakon that perpetually sparks new sexual interest while smothering other potential attractions ("Don't date backwards"). Benjamin, finally and also rather famously, conceived of fashion not just as some sort of maieutic force for the erotic encounter between people, as an enabler for interhuman sex, but also as that instance which enables a coupling between person and thing, between human subject and material object through sexual desire, which is the scenario of fetishism: "Every fashion couples the living body to the anorganic world ... The fetishism that succumbs to the sex appeal of the inorganic is its vital nerve" (AP 79) (Jede Mode ... verkuppelt den lebendigen Leib der anorganischen Welt.... Der Fetischismus, der dem sex-appeal des Anorganischen unterliegt, ist ihr Lebensnerv [PW 130]).

Now there is a note in the fashion convolute in which Benjamin gives us one of the sources for what could perhaps be called his theory of fashion as an assistance for sex. In this note he cites Grund's "On the Essence of Fashion." Benjamin introduces the quotation by referring to what he characterizes as Grund's "biological theory of fashion that takes its cue from ... the abridged Brehm" (AP 73) (biologische Theorie der Mode im Anschluss an [the] Kleinen Brehm [PW 123]) (the *Brehm* was the German standard encyclopedia of the animal world). The passage in question begins with Grund talking about the stripes that mark the zebra's fur. She assumes—a view disproven nowadays—that this visually prominent pattern, although it dominates the animal's appearance, does not correspond to any evolutionarily beneficial function (i.e., Grund does not explain the zebra's striped pattern as camouflage, for example):

> What do these stripes signify? A protective function can be ruled out ... The stripes have been ... preserved despite their unsuitableness or harmfulness, and therefore they must have a particular significance. Isn't it likely that we are dealing here with outward stimuli for internal tendencies, such as would be especially active during the mating season? ... Ever since humanity passed from nakedness to clothing, 'senseless and nonsensical' fashion has played the role of wise nature ... And insofar as fashion in its mutations ... prescribes a constant revision of all elements of the figure, ... it ordains for the woman a continual preoccupation with her beauty.
>
> AP 73, TM

> *Was bedeutet dieses Streifung? Schützend wirkt sie sicher nicht. ... Ihre Streifen werden ... erhalten, trotz ihrer 'Zweckwidrigkeit' und—daher müssen sie ... eine besondere Bedeutung haben. Sollten wir es hier nicht mit äußeren auslösenden Reizen für innere Bestrebungen zu tun haben, die in der Paarungszeit besonders lebendig werden? ... Die 'sinnwidrige' Mode übernimmt, seit die Menschheit von der Nacktheit zur Kleidung übergegangen ist, die Rolle der weisen Natur ... Indem nämlich die Mode in ihrem Wandel ... eine dauernde Revision aller Teile der Gestalt anordnet ... zwingt sie die Frau zu einer andauernden Bemühung um die Schönheit.*
>
> PW 123

What Grund thus effectively proposes—and Benjamin integrates her proposal into his work—is an evolutionary genealogy of fashion; a genealogy that traces fashion's function as a sexual facilitator back to those transformations and differences in the appearance, morphologies, and anatomies of individual bodies—or the body ornaments—which Charles Darwin in his *The Descent of Man, and Selection in Relation to Sex* had already connected to the forces of sexual attraction and sexual selection that he saw at work in the evolutionary process. In fact, as recent scholarship in the field of evolutionary aesthetics has pointed out, Darwin himself compared the variations in the "looks" of individual exemplars of a given species—for example, the slightly varying lengths or patterns of a peacock's or an argus pheasant's tail feathers—to "caprices of fashion."[40] And he explained these otherwise "non-functional" or even positively harmful traits by arguing that these differences in appearances gave the respective individuals an advantage over others, because they made them "stand out," attract attention, and increase their chances of finding potential mating partners. The analogy is exactly the one that Grund operates with, namely a comparison between the various looks that differentiate the individual members of a species, and the ongoing differentiation of styles of dress in fashion.

In his 1872 article "Development in Dress," George H. Darwin—Charles's son—had already extended the argument into the field of literal fashions, arguing, for instance, that fashion, in its foregrounding of non-utilitarian aspects of dress, could be understood in

> analogy to the 'sexual selection,' on which so much stress has recently been laid in the 'Descent of Man'... Some parts of... dress have been fostered and exaggerated by the selection of fashion, and are then retained and crystallized, as it were, ... notwithstanding that their use is entirely gone (e.g., the embroidered pocket-flaps in a court-uniform, now sewn fast to the coat).... [Such] cases have their analogue in the peacock's tail, as explained by sexual selection.[41]

It should be noted that Grund—and both Darwins—hence do not equate sexual attractiveness (in fashion) with the fulfillment of a hypothetical body-norm or a stable ideal of beauty. Rather, it is the capacity for *permanent rearrangement*, the ability to recompose one's appearance (i.e., the difference and variation in comparison to a panorama of earlier looks) which sparks sexual attraction (in Charles Darwin's terms, "variety" and "novelty"). In this sense, Grund's theory takes full account of the fundamentally temporalized nature of fashion and what Simmel called the fact that "change does not change." Grund wires this impermanence in permanence to attraction and hence casts the temporal tides of "in" and "out" as streams that pulse through a power station that charges sex.

These passages are not only indicative of the central importance which Benjamin and Grund ascribed to sexuality in the genesis of fashion—i.e., they are not only indicative of how Benjamin and Grund thought about *fashion*. They in turn also reveal a peculiar understanding of sexuality, especially where Benjamin leaves the level of sexual encounters between individuals and talks about fashion in relation to the libidinal set-up of entire collectives, as is the case with his theories about the "generational" effects of fashion (new fashions instigate attraction and so forth, not just in relation to one particular individual that might need to enhance his or her attractiveness, but as a pervasive stimulation of sexual activity through the general presence of fashion in a collective). If thought through to its logical consequence, there can only be one reason as to why one would assume that fashion would need to function as a *systemic* sexual stimulant, and this reason would consist in a view, or a theory, of insufficient or waning libido—on a systemic level. That is, in Benjamin's view, fashion needs to compensate for the depletion of sexual energy in culture (or the human species?) at large. Which is to say that underneath this sexualized understanding of fashion on the broadest scale lies an entropic scenario in which sexual activity as a whole is at a permanent risk of dying off. Broken down into its most basic components, this theory could be summarized as: without fashion, sex *tout court* might die. Or, to put it less dramatically: there is fashion because there isn't enough sex. With a concept coined by psychoanalyst Ernest Jones, we could speak of *aphanisis* as an overall backdrop to these fashion theories: a generalized fear not of underperforming or of failing to perform in sex; nor is the assumption here that an individual's ([self-] perceived) lack of attractiveness would drive him or her (in most cases actually "her"; more on this below) into the arms of fashion to make up for said fault. Rather, such approaches assume—or fear—that *desire* might wane, not in relation to a particular object, but *in toto*.[42]

If the above mention of Grund's "wiring" of the problem of sex to the question of fashion gave the impression of referring to an intellectual (although not necessarily deliberate) operation, that impression was fully intended. For in the last resort, it is clear that to explain the existence of fashion by pointing to sexuality is, if prevalent, far from necessary. Or, to put it differently: to respond to the question "Why fashion?" by answering "Because fashion fixes shortcomings in the field of sexuality" misses the many occasions on which the processing of fashionable difference does not align with the axes of sexuality (and that these are not derivative from an originary sexual scenario). Among the authors Benjamin quotes (and with whom Grund was certainly familiar), we could point again to Simmel, who, as we saw above, explains the thriving of fashion formally by pointing to its coincidence with requirements of the social form. If we were to locate individual desires or "drives" in Simmel's model, these would, again, not be sexual, but relate to the needs of belonging and distinction; and even if we were to base our argument on such hypothetical drives, we would still need to account for and appreciate Simmel's theoretical sophistication when he points out that fashion's functionality and its success do *not* rest on supplementing solutions for these drives *individually*; rather, through the temporalized, ongoing negotiation of such difference, fashion successfully produces "solutions" that respond to both of these, technically speaking, contradictory needs, hence "handling" not only difference but contradiction, without needing to "resolve" it. We could also turn to more contemporary phenomena and observe how, for instance, fashion appropriates and transforms underground styles, or how it begins to twist the aesthetics of genuine subcultures. In each case, there is a moment of difference involved, but this difference isn't prima facie "sexual."

(Schiaparelli's) Genital millinery

Another aspect to be noted here consists in the "gendering" of sexual attraction that occurs in Grund's text. In her—in this respect staunchly conservative— view, the female as opposed to the male body is the site upon which fashion permanently reconfigures forms and re-generates attractiveness. In the *Arcades Project* there is another reference to Grund, this time in the form of a semi-paraphrase, in which Benjamin applies her theory about the fundamental interconnectedness between fashion and sexuality to the concrete case of millinery. In the fashion convolute, Benjamin writes:

> There is hardly another article of clothing that can give expression to such divergent erotic tendencies, and that has as much latitude to dress them up as a woman's hat. . . . the shades of erotic meaning in a woman's hat are virtually incalculable. It is not so much the various possibilities of symbolic reference to sexual organs that is chiefly of interest here. More surprising is what a hat can say about the rest of the outfits. H[elen] Grund has made the ingenious suggestion that the bonnet, which is contemporaneous with the crinoline, actually provides men with directions for handling the latter. The wide brim of the bonnet is turned up—thereby demonstrating

how the crinoline must be turned up in order to make sexual access to the woman easier for man.

AP 80, TM

Es gibt schwerlich ein Kleidungsstück, das so divergierenden erotischen Tendenzen Ausdruck geben kann und soviel Freiheit sie zu verkleiden hat wie der weibliche Hut. ... unabsehbar sind die Abschattierungen der erotischen Bedeutung am Frauenhut. Es sind nicht sowohl die verschiedenen Möglichkeiten, symbolisch die Geschlechtsorgane zu umspielen ... Überraschender kann der Aufschluß sein, der etwa vom Kleid aus dem Hute werden kann. H[elen] Grund hat die geistvolle Vermutung geäußert, die Schute, die gleichzeitig mit der Krinoline ist, stelle eigentlich eine Gebrauchsanweisung der letzteren für den Mann dar. Die breiten Ränder der Schute sind aufgeklappt—derart andeutend, wie die Krinoline aufgeklappt werden muß, um dem Mann die geschlechtliche Annäherung an die Frau leicht zu machen.

PW 131

This passage is of interest not only because Grund, qua Benjamin's paraphrase, here provides us with one of the most peculiar interpretations of one, or actually two items of clothing. Interpreting the bonnet as a sartorial instruction manual that will enable a male audience to more swiftly unpeel potential female sex partners from their obstructing crinolines gives us a whole new angle on the mantra of "form follows function" (fashion's function being here, once again, to enable sex). While just briefly pointing out that with the crinoline and the bonnet Grund and Benjamin are here talking about two nineteenth-century items of dress, these sentences also contain an encrypted reference to the fashion of their own moment (i.e., the early 1930s), or at least to a set of critical writing dedicated to the fashion of that moment.

At first the claim that a series of women's hats "playfully and symbolically alludes to genitalia" seems bizarre, yet in its oddness the formulation unmistakably refers to an identifiable source, namely a series of hat designs by the couturier Elsa Schiaparelli. Photographed by Man Ray, and one of them modeled by the designer herself, these images accompanied an article by the Surrealist poet Tristan Tzara titled "D'un certain Automatisme du Goût" (On a Certain Automatism of Taste), which was published in the Surrealist journal *Minotaure* in 1933.[43]

The Contingent Primacy of Sex(es) 85

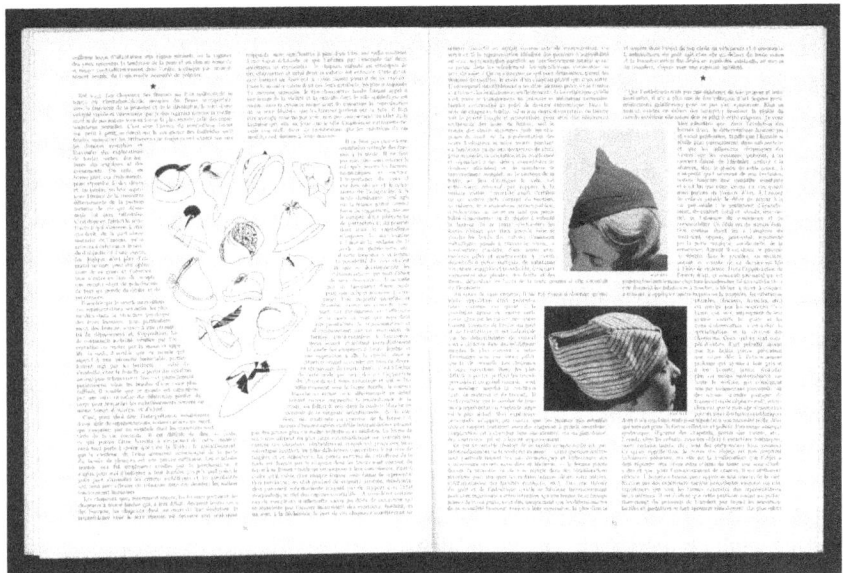

Figure 2.7 Minotaure No. 3/4 (1933), pagespread. Kunstbibliothek der Staatlichen Museen zu Berlin. Man Ray photographs: © Man Ray Trust / VG Bild-Kunst, Bonn 2019.

The three Man Ray photos—one of them famously showing what at first looks like a man's hat (the design is based on a fedora and appropriately titled "Savile Row")—all taken from a steep upper angle, visually plunging down onto the heads of the wearers, were supplemented by a set of illustrations, again displaying a host of examples of contemporary millinery, fashion magazine, the Savile Row model occupying the position second from right in the illustration's upper row. (Fig. 2.7).

If the fedora introduces the topic of the sexes in a small maneuver of cross dressing – a standard fashion trope, at least as long as the vector of redistribution flows from "masculine" to "feminine" position, the two other specimen of millinery photographed present the topic more obliquely, yet also strangely concretely. One, a diagonally positioned patched and patterned monochrome cap, elongates the shape of the model's head into a pointy protrusion, hence evoking the image of a singular large nipple. The other – this one modeled by Schiaparelli herself and, in the parlance of her maison referred to as the crazy cox comb, also builds from the wearer's head; yet – the result of a method of folding the item's textile, the structure created here resembles more a slightly geometric mound on an oval base.⁴⁴ If seen in profile, this hat might mount to a considerable crown. Its motivic tendency, which Man Ray's photo doesn't make entirely clear, is reinforced when glancing to the left-hand page in Minotaure, with its assortment of illustrations. These reduce the material width and thickness of the millinery object to graphic clarity, highlighting both the intended volumetric dimensions, as well as in higher detail the repeated technique of creating folds across the head's dome which resemble slits. The resulting image lets nothing to be desired in terms of clarity: with only a few odd examples out whose biomorphic prodding of folds looks slightly labial, we are seeing here a grouping of headpieces that somehow incorporate distinctly phallic imagery. The head of the hat's wearer thus ideally propping up – or popping into – what very much resembles the head of a penis, with either the urethera or the foreskin slightly opening; or, in some cases, the foreskin perhaps being already pulled back. The visual-vestimentary equation being one between the skull's bony stability and a solidly tumescent penis. Glancing back to the right and Man Ray's shot of the designer in her own creation, it is now clear that Schiaparelli's modeling move was indeed an audacious one, giving herself a dickhead. The "automatism of taste" mentioned in the title of Tzara's piece refers to an alleged function (posited by Tzara himself) which explains the manifestations of fashion—the wares and styles of the author's present in particular, but also generally—as results of an overwhelming, unconscious, and collective expression of libidinal force.⁴⁵ To be more precise, as an exemplary specimen of the gender-biased position described above, Tzara explains the manifestations of fashion as articulations of a libidinal force that pulses primarily through *women*, whose aggregated consumer choices irrevocably provoke designers and manufacturers to produce garments whose erotic charge and message become ever more pronounced. What is called fashion (appelée la mode) is thus defined as "the miraculous world of representations of sexuality, which is seated deeply in the psychological structure of human beings, in particular women. It stands under a strange law of surpassing and opposition, a law of ongoing mobility, verified through the acceptance or rejection of the masses" (le monde merveilleux des representations sexuelles les plus reculées dans la structure psychique des êtres humains, plus particulièrement des femmes, soumis à une étrange loi de dépassement et d'opposition, loi de continuelle mobilité, vérifiée par l'acceptaction ou rejetée par la masse).⁴⁶

For Tzara, the fashion panorama of summer 1933 (like any year in principle, but that year in particular) thus encodes "a whole world of desires and perversions" (tout un monde de désirs et de perversions), and in a strange, temporally compressed and literalized, not entirely unfaithful travesty of Darwin's argument, by which the shapes of body ornaments can be regarded as the results of accretions of a multitude of choices exercised by mating partners of the opposite sex, Tzara here explains the concrete forms of fashion as the products of the push and pull of the forces of erotic desire.[47] And if Darwin organized his evolutionary fashion theory around both shapes of bodies and organs and the function of the intercourse, so does Tzara, with the modification of expanding the concept of the fashionable and erotic body to the realm of clothes, which, as mediated through the posited activity of the libido, here become a sexualized morphology. More precisely, fashionable dress here re-engenders the "real morphological state of organs correlating" (état morphologique réel des organs corrélatifs) with sex—i.e., sexual organs—and the styles of fashion are deciphered as "idealized representations of possibilities of accessing the sexual organ" (la représentation idéalisée des pouvoirs d'accessibilité au sexe).[48] Or, to render Tzara's peculiar graphically "functionalist" interpretation in all clarity:

> It seems that this world, which responds to an inescapable, partly instinctively driven urge for embellishment that occurs in the female sex from relatively low zoological levels (...) is characterized by the emphasis of several parts of the body for which these embellishments serve at once as advertisement and signal.
>
> *Il semble que ce monde qui répond à une nécessité inéluctable partiellement régis par les instincts—celui de s'embellir, chez la femelle, à partir des échelons zoologiques relativement bas (...) est caractérisé par une mise en valeur des différentes parties du corps pour lesquelles les embellissements servent en même temps d'enseigne et d'appel.*[49]

The parallels to the ideas of Grund and Benjamin are evident, and they are so striking that it is perhaps permitted to speculate about a relation of direct influence, or at least the participation of all three protagonists in a common conversation about the matters of fashion at that moment. Benjamin's share is the more unfortunate here, when he varies Tzara's concoction of evolutionism, perversion, and fashion in convolute B by speculating about an evolutionary stage at which man had already transitioned to upright gait, while woman still remained his "four footed companion"; this is a position, Benjamin opines, more favorable to the development of the pregnant belly—a function later catered for by all sorts of supportive belts and garters—marking frontal sexual intercourse as "perversion" on an evolutionary scale, departing from the "original" act from behind (AP 81, PW 132).

A potential relation of Grund's ideas to "D'un certain Automatisme du Goût" relies on Benjamin's already mentioned report of her speculating about the bonnet's function as a user's guide, so to speak, for how to "access" a woman's body for sex by removing a crinoline. One clear connection here exists in the specific garment, or rather accessory, that both Grund and Tzara chose as relays between fashion and sexual instruction: hats. Tzara focuses on the "women's hats" (chapeaux de femmes) of the year 1933 as "sexual representations," which Schiaparelli's designs in the context of *Minotaure* exemplify:

> The hats worn by women very recently, hats that display a cracked form, which in the beginning were intended as imitations of men's hats, hats whose resemblance to the female sex, in the course of their evolution, has become not only striking but on a number of counts significant have—in these two exemplars—finally come to confirm my view in the most illuminating manner.
>
> *Les chapeaux que, récemment encore, les femmes portaient, les chapeaux à forme fendue qui, à leur début, devaient imiter ceux des hommes, les chapeaux dont, au cours de leur évolution, la ressemblance avec le sexe féminin est devenue non seulement frappante, mais significative à plus d'un titre, ont enfin confirmé d'une façon éclatante ce que j'avance par l'exemple des deux spécimens ici reproduit.*[50]

Tzara expands this vision into a full-blown projection by seeing "reproductions of the female sex which women wear on their hats" (la reproduction de ce sexe féminin que les femmes portent sur la tête), whose shapes in turn derive from "a maximum number of representative forms of a sexual function" (un maximum de formes représentatives à fonctionnment sexuel).[51] These he locates in a morphological shift that leads from the mentioned parallel between hat and phallus to a reading of the hat's crack—previously presumably seen as the opening of the urethra—as a vaginal opening. A reading which, as we saw, is to an extent indeed based in Schiaparelli's aesthetic.[52] The female hat thus not only becomes a representation and morphological displacement of the prime female genital organ in the medium of clothes—vagina heads, essentially—but also alleged instructions and solicitations for intercourse.

The point here is that Tzara's commentary on Schiaparelli's headgear, which reads its protrusions, bulges, slits, and mound-like openings as a collapsing of the morphological inventory of genitalia onto the form of the hat, accentuates in an admittedly pointed manner what correspondingly became evident to many observers of his period. The Surrealist view, while exaggerated communicated with the actual overall development of fashion at the time; namely that fashion increasingly turned into an arena in which not only sexual encounters were facilitated, but in which the very morphology of these (sexuated) bodies was remodeled—in the shape of garments.

This process began with a development that *Vogue* in 1930 summarized in the dictum "strict is a thing of the past," which referred to the abolishment of the androgynous and geometrical silhouettes of the 1920s and the adoption of a more curved outline in women's fashion, and which, of course, Grund had observed.[53] This was a movement away from the androgynous, more gender-equalizing looks that had dominated the 1920s, toward the emergence of a quasi-anatomically "sexed," post-pubescent body type *in dress*. Apart from the described narrowing of the waist and the corresponding emphasis on hips and chest (i.e., apart from the tendency to produce the proverbial hourglass silhouette which could rely on the popularity of the shaping capacity of spanks underwear bodices), this trend also encompassed a forceful modeling of the female behind—"l'ampleur en arrière" (plenty of "back" or bountiful bottom), as fashion critic Martine Rénier put it in a review of Schiaparelli's designs which appeared in *Femina*. The development perhaps reached its most pronounced articulations in Schiaparelli's designs for Hollywood star and producer Mae West's 1937 film *Every Day's a Holiday*, in which West struts across the screen as singer and petty criminal Peaches O'Day, dressed snugly in the most figure-hugging, shaping gowns (Fig. 2.8a–d).

That silhouette was also immortalized in the design which the couturier selected for the bottle of her perfume, "Shocking," a female torso modeled into a dramatically curvaceous shape, with ample bosom and behind, its glass

2.8a

2.8b

Figure 2.8.a–d Mae West in A. Edward Sutherland's "Every Day's a Holiday," costume by Schiaparelli (1937), film stills. Paramount Pictures.

carvings insinuating the bodice and possibly garters that would have accompanied an encounter in the boudoir. A shape which, lore has it, Schiaparelli lifted from the form of a tailor's dummy, manufactured in Hollywood to the scale of West's impressive torso, hips, and behind, which had been sent to Paris so the designer could work on the costumes for *Every Day's a Holiday* (Fig. 2.9).[54] In an advertisement from 1937, Schiaparelli also situated the scent firmly within the realm of an iconography of the genital. Here the flacon, placed under a glass casing – a luxurious mode of packing with which the perfume was indeed sold – is doubled by the image of West's familiar roundings, here incorporated as a tailor's dummy. The figure's lower section – its non-existent legs – is cloaked in classically draped, shiny, heavy cloth – a maneuver which makes the prop's torso appear nude. Popping out from just behind it is a set of white calla lilies, their retouched fleshy petals echoing the dummy's drape and the folds of a massive curtain further back. The flowers' conical openings, their labial texture, and the protruding stems once again putting in place a solid set of allusions to human genitalia of various sexes. Executed as a photomontage, the entire advertisement further depicts this scene in front of a view of the Place Vendôme in Paris. This was indeed the address of Schiaparelli"s legendarily decorated perfume boutique which opened that very year, and where the designer had a painted bamboo mock up of a human-scaled bird-cage installed through which customers entered the premises. In the context of the ad this site is chosen clearly for one of its major attractions. By the far right edge of the image, the Place Vendôme's column – originally erected to commemorate Napoleon's victory at Austerlitz – is just that: seen to to be standing straight up. As the column joins the genital inventory of the foreground, the overall composition seems to insinuate that in Paris behind every curtain there's a boudoir and that the city, at least in Schiaparelli's vision, always makes room for an erection.

To critics, it was clear that this reconfiguration of women's fashion along an exaggeratedly curvaceous outline and the pronounced, voluminous protrusions of breasts, hips, and bottom did *not* equate a "grounding" in the anatomical givens of the female body. For instance, in another amusing twist of her "evolutionary" argument, Grund considered that, whereas the fashions of the late 1920s, with their short skirts, had favored women with attractive legs, now it was the "turn" of those who had "good waists."[55] The changes of fashion thus

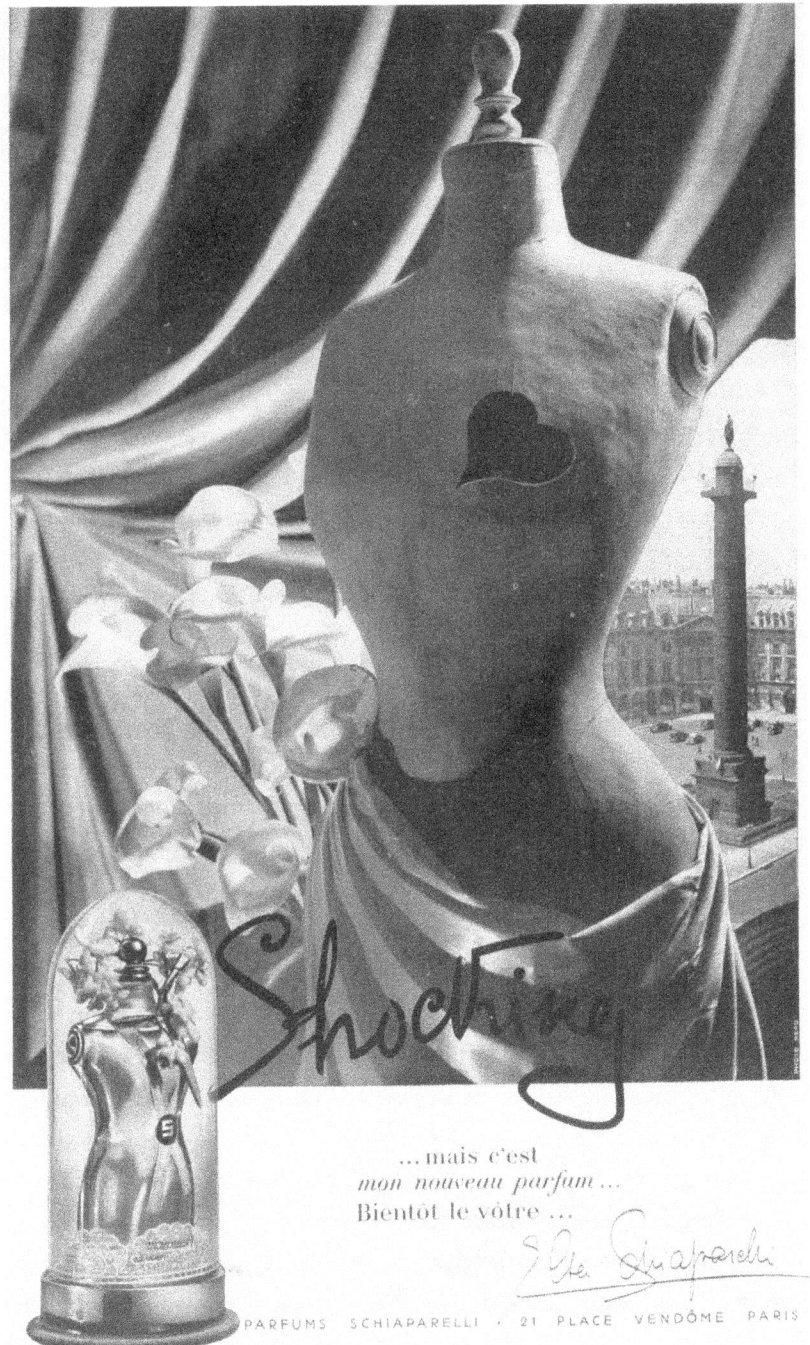

Figure 2.9 Advertisement for Schiaparelli perfume "Shocking" (1937). Kunstbibliothek der Staatlichen Museen zu Berlin.

serve to distribute a bizarre form of "justice" for different body types across generations of style. What *is* significant, however, is that with the model of 1930s fashion, the interpretation of fashionable difference as sexual is, again, remodeled as sex between "the" two sexes (whereas the androgynies of the late 1920s allowed for a much wider spectrum of this meta-interpretation of fashion difference as relating to sex).

It is not quite clear what conditions motivate or even "cause" such a sexualized understanding of fashion. And it would of course be patently wrong to deny the close intertwinement of fashion on the one hand and sexual erotics on the other. Given that clothing is one of the prime material strata in which fashion plays out, and given clothing's literally intimate relation to the human body, it would be astonishing if fashion weren't also a playing field for sexuality. But mutual implication doesn't mean unilateral foundation of one element by the other.

What we can undeniably assess, however, is that the gender distribution that undergirded the fashion scenario of 1933 was, again, contingent, rather than necessary. Not only does a look at our very own contemporary fashion panorama suggest that, while in terms of economic impact womenswear (still) outweighs menswear, it is clear that already on the level of social groupings and their styles, youth cultures, etc we are witnessing a nearly equal distribution of fashion capital among genders. Historical research of course also points us to periods in which the distribution of greater and lesser degrees of adornment was exactly inverse to the constellation described by Grund, Benjamin, and Tzara. Before, to quote Fluegel's canonical diagnostic term, "the great male renunciation" which coincided with the social ascent of the bourgeoisie, it was the male wardrobe of the aristocracy that was subjected to the highest degree of ornamentation.[56] (Given these examples, we should also bear in mind that a maximum of adornment shouldn't be confused with the highest propensity for fashionability: reduction and understatement are fashion strategies just as valid [and arguably just as intense] as rich ornamentation, and entire social groups may choose to forsake "bling" in favor of, for instance, foregrounding the discrete materialities of weave and textile, and participate to the exact same degree in fashion as their bejeweled counterparts.) We can, finally, point to examples that fell within the range of Benjamin's interest, in which the relationship of fashion and gender was conceived differently. None other than Georg Simmel in *Philosophy of Fashion* argued that woman's "propensity" for fashion was a result of the comparative "weakness" of her "social position" (PoF 196, PdM 22). The point here is not so much whether the argument in itself (and in particular its inherent view of fashion as an *ersatz* for other activities) is convincing. What matters is that Simmel recognized that a position which others (Benjamin among them) saw as inherently bound to the execution of fashion—and a prime recipient for validation through fashion, namely "woman"—was circumstantial and contingent, rather than inherent.

Fashion, whores, Surrealists (The pitfalls of allegory and the forgetting of labor)

It is hardly surprising that within this sexualized fashion panorama, including the increasing modeling of what was (in line with "traditional" views) understood to be a more "womanly" body (in a staff-authored piece reviewing the latest developments at Chanel, *Vogue UK* called it "the new femininity," highlighting the difference to the designer's customary "sponsor[ing] of the straight . . . dress and the boyish silhouette"), we also discover a distribution of gender positions that is problematic.[57] The general problem lies in the exclusive and unilateral identification of the body of "woman" as the locus of fashion, and as the site of sexual desirability along an axis of gender dimorphism. While reminiscent of the old adage against woman's sexual objectification through the means of fashion, what we are looking at here actually functions slightly differently. The problem is, firstly, the grounding of fashion in sexuality and, secondly, the exclusive nomination of the "feminine" body as its carrier. According to the logics of desire that is not so much invoked as instituted as the default position, the characteristically unseen (i.e., unmarked) position beyond fashion and sexualization is of course "man" (i.e., "straight man").[58] Benjamin participates in these maneuvers, for instance, when he writes, slightly comically from our vantage point, about the late nineteenth-century trend of bicycling costumes—an early form of sportswear—that in "these halls the figure of the woman assumed its most seductive form: as cyclist" (AP 62, TM) (In diesen Hallen nahm das Weib seine verführerische Gestalt an: als Radlerin [PW 110]).

A further example, which also demonstrates the closeness of his thinking to Surrealism here, is his grouping of the sight of a woman (actually a wax mannequin) fixing her garter—a staple of erotic and pornographic imagery, which he finds depicted in Breton's novel *Nadja*, under the rubric of fashion (cf. AP 125, PW 185). The point here is, again, that such an association, while not being implausible at all (in fact, there are many instances in which fashion production has recourse to the rhetoric and inventory of lingerie), marks one *instantiation* of fashion, as opposed to fashion's fundamental generative engine.

Less anecdotal, namely structural, and thus more consequential is Benjamin's pronouncing of fashion as the "dialectical trading place of woman and ware" (AP 62, TM) (dialektischen Umschlageplatz von Weib und Ware [PW 111]). The German term *dialektischer Umschlageplatz* is a Benjaminian neologism and not easy to translate: without the adjective "dialectical," an *Umschlageplatz*—more commonly spelled *Umschlagplatz* without the antiquated *e*—can be a marketplace; the term denominates the site of economic transactions, in the sense of a buying and selling of goods. The combination of the adjective "dialectical" with the substantive *Umschlag*, however, denotes the basic dialectical figure by which a given state, quality, or position reverses into a different, perhaps even opposite state, quality, or position. Joined by Benjamin in the form of a portmanteau expression, the idea of the *dialektischer Umschlageplatz* is that of a site on which economic and dialectical exchanges take place. The tone clearly gestures toward the *Schauplatz*, the site of action, as which Benjamin identified the stage of the Baroque mourning play, on which he famously situated the machinations of allegory. This invocation here indicates that Benjamin indeed vises an allegorical scenario, an allegorical view of fashion as the site of commodity exchange, but also the exchange of woman *and* commodity.

Two further passages from this fragment in convolute B support this reading. One is the, again allegorical, description of fashion as "parody of the motley corpse, provocation of death through the woman" (Parodie der bunten Leiche, Provokation des Todes durch das Weib) holding "colloquy with decay" (Zwiesprache mit der Verwesung [AP 62/63, PW 111]). Beyond the drastic vocabulary of material withering, Benjamin inscribes fashion here into a familiar conceptual configuration. The semantics of death belongs, firstly, to his theory of allegory, where its mortificatory qualities are associates of the imagery of frequently physically dismembered corpses on the stage of the mourning play (and later in the poetry of Baudelaire). The vocabulary of death, secondly, forms part of a theory of commodification, understood as a process by which labor, initially imagined as "alive" (cf. the Marxian notion of 'living labor'), mortifies into "dead labor," ready for the exchange process (the *Umschlag*, the circulation of commodities) to ensue. Fashion, as the site for these processes, is thus defined as the frame in which the mortification of woman into allegory and woman into commodity take place. The logic is complemented by the end of the fragment, where Benjamin invokes the figure of the whore, which he casts as a real-life allegory of commodification—the woman whose body *is* a commodity.[59]

The configuration thus positions fashion as an instance or agency in which, following the model of the prostitute, the female body figures as commodity, in which *Weib* flips into *Ware*; to be more precise, fashion here becomes the allegory for this mortificatory dialectical reversal, while in turn casting the prostitute as an allegory for fashion's deadening machinations. While the parallelization of allegory and commodity, and the figuration of one through the other, are undeniably among Benjamin's most influential and consequential arguments, their specific instantiation in relation to the field of fashion is problematic, and in particular where the figure of the prostitute is concerned.

Comparing Benjamin's discussions of the flaneur and the whore as figures who "loiter" in the *Arcades*, Susan Buck-Morss has pointed out how unequally Benjamin valorizes their seeming "lack of productivity": whereas the male flaneur is merely cast as a loiterer (and, we could add, as someone who is seen as refusing the pressure to produce by conspicuously "wasting" his time), the prostitute, who loiters, figures depreciatively as "whore."[60] Whereas the flaneur figures as an example of a modern *subject*, according to which Benjamin can model transformations of perception, the prostitute is "the allegory for the transformation of *objects*, the world of things."[61] Pointing to Marx's diagnosis that all wage laborers under capitalism are sellers and commodities at once, Buck-Morss deduces that, accordingly, prostitution is only a specific expression of the general prostitution of the worker.[62] The prostitute, she continues, figures as commodity, and she points to Benjamin's view that "[p]rostitution can lay claim to being considered 'work' the moment work becomes prostitution. In fact, the *lorette* was the first to carry out a radical renunciation of the costume of the lover. She already arranges to be paid for her time; from there it is only a short distance to those who demand wages" (AP 348) (Die Prostitution kann in dem Augenblick Anspruch erheben, als "Arbeit" zu gelten, in dem die Arbeit Prostitution wird. In der Tat ist die Lorette die erste, die auf die Verkleidung als Liebhaberin radikal Verzicht leistet. Sie lässt sich schon ihre Zeit bezahlen; von da ist es kein sehr weiter Weg mehr zu denen, die auf "Arbeitslohn" Anspruch machen [PW 439]).

The problem with the proviso of Benjamin's diagnosis seems to be that the prostitute's services, in the service of producing a theory of commodification, are always already obfuscated precisely to the extent that they are merely addressed as commodities, or as their allegorical figuration (as fashionable woman).[63] One may or may not find what a prostitute does palatable, but she *does* things. She works. (And should we add that not all prostitutes are female?) Her elevation to the status of an allegory of the state of all labor under capitalism as commodified, on the condition of her position becoming "emblematic," comes at the cost of disregarding her actual work, in its particularity and existence. And because Benjamin so intimately ties the structure of allegory to the structure of the commodity, there is little chance of him describing an allegory of *labor* (as opposed to an allegory of the commodity). In this view, "woman," as reduced to commodity and salesperson, does not "work." "Living labor" always already disappears into the deadness of the allegorical commodity. In this framework, we could say, a woman's body is the place where labor goes to die.

Beyond the logic of the placeholder. Schiaparelli's (and Dora Benjamin's) fashion work

Undeniably these issues are much more far-reaching than the question of fashion, but they are immediately connected to the problem of figuring fashion as an allegory of commodification. By the same consequence, in Benjamin's view, nobody "works" in fashion. Fashion, always already a commodity, is a labor-free zone, at least as far as its intellectual realization in Benjamin's writing is concerned. This view doesn't lack a certain irony, given the size of the fashion industry, which was considerable. It should be noted that already in Benjamin's time this was also a field in which a comparatively high percentage of workers, as well as entrepreneurs were women. Where the present analysis turns to the practice and aesthetics of fashion, it privileges what could be called "authored" positions, turning to the work of couturiers such as Louise Boulanger, Schiaparelli or later Vionnet. We could add the names of colleagues such as Coco Chanel, Augusta Bernard, or Jeanne Lanvin. Or writers and editors like Helen Grund or Martine Rénier. Beyond these there are – still known by name – photographers like Lee Miller, and models such as Toto Koopman; and no less impactful the masses of unnamed workers who created and sold dresses for the Parisian maisons. Particularly well known is the case of Lanvin who started out as a small milliner to eventually count over a thousand employees working for her company. To merely allegorize fashion as an instantiation of commodification in the face of this rather powerful female workforce seems quite a feat of repression. Or, given its all too quick absconding of the factor of women's work we could even be tempted to call this mode of thinking partly complicit in the very circumstances which the critique of capitalism wanted to tackle: the forgetting of labor.

All this hits even closer to home – Benjamin's home, that is – if we consider the fact that for a good while his then-wife Dora was the bread-earner of the family, receiving a salary for her work in the publishing business—as of 1927, for a magazine called *Die praktische Berlinerin: Das Blatt der Bazar-Schnittmuster* (The Capable Berlin Woman: The Magazine of Bazar Cutting Patterns).[64] This bimonthly publication, published by the Bazar Actien Gesellschaft, featured descriptions and illustrations of outfits – dresses, skirts, jackets etc – into which the editors had condensed the overall trends of current fashions. These were numbered, so readers could order or, in the case of later issues, were directly provided with cutting patterns for executing these generic looks, the magazine also informing its readers/customers approximately how much cloth would be required when they went about to tailor these looks at home. In addition to addressing its audience not just as *praktische*, but also as resolutely active women who were perfectly capable of making their own clothes, *Die praktische Berlinerin* also featured photojournalism and articles – of a distinctly emancipatory bent. The second January issue of the year 1927 – the year in which Benjamin's wife took up her position, for instance, opens with a photopage of "Frauen die ihren Mann stellen" (women who man up). Here the reader sees Germany's first female police detective, a female engineer and a female exterminator, from New Jersey and New York respectively, or a group of London's first female housepainter apprentices. The issue continues with an articel about "The Creative Woman" (Die schöpferische Frau), here meaning the German sculptor Käthe Kollwitz, and also features a report about daycare institutions for the children of salaried women.[65] On the masthead Benjamin's soon to be former wife tellingly appears under her maiden name, Dora Sophie Kellner, and it is clear that her post came with a good deal of responsibilty. She was the publication's "Schriftleitung", i.e. the editor in charge of all textual content. Dora Kellner clearly was a working woman, and it is clearly the case that the sphere of her and her colleagues' work was not sealed off from that of her husband. As of the beginning of the year 1927, when the magazine's ownership had changed from the Ullstein publishing house to the Bazar Actien Gesellschaft, and when Dora Kellner's name appears on its pages, the publication also had a new graphic designer who modernized its previously rather timidly illustrated covers by integrating elements of photomontage and bold moments of color blocking. That designer was no other than Sasha Stone, who would, only a year later, also design the cover for the first edition of Benjamin's collection of short prose titled One Way Street, which appeared with Rowohlt Verlag. – This entire panorama in which salaried labor and the everyday production and materialization of fashion play out – a panorama which paid the Benjamins' bills – somehow seems to evaporate once the heights of the equivocation of allegory, commodity and fashionable woman are reached.

A similar problem marks the manner in which Benjamin and Tzara conceive of the interrelation between fashion and Surrealism. In convolute B, Benjamin famously declares, "Fashion is the predecessor—no, the eternal placeholder—of Surrealism" (AP 64) (Die Mode ist die Vorgängerin, nein, die ewige Platzhalterin des Surrealismus [PW 113]). The contents of this relation are quite convincing: for instance, the movement of Surrealism, with its professed investment in the world of outmoded objects, influenced Benjamin's own interests in the *Arcades* as environments that had gone out of style (Aragon's novel *Le Paysan de Paris* being of particular importance here); and through this dedication to the *démodé*, Surrealism could also be seen as providing Benjamin with another model for his theorization of fashion's rearticulations of the outmoded; a theorization which, as Hal Foster reminds us, was intended to discover a radical potential in the démodé.[66] However, just as in the case of fashionable woman as allegory for the commodity, this logic of the "placeholder"—a symbolic representation—while enabling systematic and conceptual comparisons, also obfuscates the dimension of real work and production. For what is obviously missing in this equation, which establishes a general equivalence between fashion and Surrealism on an abstract level, are the concrete contributions of Surrealist practitioners to fashion, rather than general ruminations on the nature of fashion as per the logics of Surrealism. A photographer such as Man Ray, who was affiliated with the movement, produced works for fashion magazines such as *Harper's* or *Vogue*, employing techniques and aesthetic tropes like solarization, otherwise deployed in his Surrealist artworks. This is not to suggest that the photographic aesthetic of Man Ray's fashion work is identical with that of his pictures produced for avant-garde publications such as *Minotaure*, or for exhibitions in gallery spaces. In order to place a picture in a commercial fashion magazine of the period (and in order to be paid for it), the photographer would, within certain parameters, have had to accept that the image indeed displayed the depicted garment with a sufficient degree of clarity and recognizability. This compositional prerogative excludes a number of the more radical, estranging formal strategies, like multiple superimpositions, the use of distortions, or cropping decisions that deliberately violated the integrity of the captured human figures. However, compositionally more neutral features such as the employment of unexpected props (in one picture for *Vogue*, Man Ray shoots a model in a Vionnet directoire gown reclining in wheelbarrow from a bird's eye angle) or solarization can be easily reconciled with the requirements of *Harper's* or *Vogue*, not to mention the extant connections between a Surrealist sensibility and the general aesthetic imaginary of the period, like the interest in statues, dolls, and mannequins.

The environment of the avant-garde publication, however, was far less inclined to acknowledge the fashion producer's share. In fact, the name of the couturier Schiaparelli is entirely missing from *Minotaure*. In "D'un certain Automatisme du Goût," Tzara merely mentions "the creators of these items" (les créatrices de ces modèles), simply bypassing the authorship of the woman who had designed the very hats he was commenting on; a person who not only went on to collaborate with Dalí, but who also participated with individual items in Surrealist exhibitions and, once a number of the protagonists of the avant-garde had escaped the Fascist rule over Europe for the United States, was also instrumental in staging one of them. In New York Schiaparelli had a shared responsibility in organizing the 1942 'First Papers of Surrealism' show. More or less aligned with a Surrealist aesthetic, Schiaparelli's work, rather than exemplifying a structural correlation between Surrealism and fashion in total, was one arguably very important, particular, and *real* contribution to fashion. Tzara surely must have known (at least of) her, yet he refuses to attach her name to the millinery creations he discusses. The result is a foregrounding of his symbolic reading at the cost of an acknowledgment of the labor and actual logics of fashion and its producers—in this case, which does not lack its exemplary qualities, the work of (a) woman, a body of work which will occupy us more fully in the following chapter, along with that of her contemporary Madeleine Vionnet.

Morphology of the silhouette (Benjamin vs. Focillon)

The slightly hysterical and dramatizing deciphering of the manifestations of millinery as part of a displaced morphology of sexual organs could, finally, be seen as another case in which a logic of the placeholder is implemented, rather than deploying an analysis that would be situated on the more fundamental, if not to say actual level of fashion.[67] Benjamin did excerpt passages from a contemporary treatise in which, although the topic of fashion occupies a merely marginal position, central impulses for a better grounded combination of *mode* and morphology could be found. In the fashion convolute, Benjamin includes a fragment from Henri Focillon's 1934 meditation *La Vie des Formes* (The Life of Forms in Art):

> Fashion … invents an artificial humanity…. Such a humanity, … obeys much less the rule of rational propriety than the poetry or ornament, and what fashion calls line or style is perhaps but a subtle compromise between a certain physiological canon (which is, moreover, highly variable, as are the successive canons of Greek art) and a pure fantasy of shapes [*figures*].[68]

> *La mode invente … une humanité artificielle … Cette humanité … a pour règle … la poétique de l'ornement, et ce qu'elle appelle ligne … n'est peut-être qu'un subtil compromis entre un certain canon physiologique … et la fantaisie des figures.*

PW 131

What we find in Focillon is a theory of form, i.e., a morphology, that is also much better suited to Benjamin's understanding of fashion as mediating questions of time and temporalization (see chapter 1). Its articulation in our present context depends on a certain proviso—namely, first, to underline that Focillon's morphology differs markedly from what could be called a post-Goethean strand of morphological thought that is implicit to Benjamin's thinking, and to his fashion theory as well, which is connected to the concept of the dialectical image. This implication will be briefly unfolded in chapter 4. A second categorical difference between Focillon's thought, as well as a number of subsequent more or less prominent morphological models which have partly declared allegiance to his ideas, is that Benjamin's forays into morphological terrain seem to do without the category of environment or milieu, at least if understood as a spatial category, as a surrounding territory or zone, which is central also to Focillon's ideas about fashion, who writes, "Fashion thus invents an artificial humanity that is not the passive decoration of a formal environment, but that very environment itself"[69] (La mode invente ainsi une humanité artificielle qui n'est pas le décor passif du milieu formel, mais ce milieu même [PW 131]) These ideas still reverberate until today where they surface in the rediscovery of the work of philosophers such as Gilbert Simondon, who, as historians of science inform us, had a keen interest in Focillon.[70]

With a view to our present concerns, Focillon's account does not get tied up in the denominating game by which specific forms of fashion (hats) are taken as extensions, developments, and substitutes for organs, body parts, and as supports for their respective functions. What Focillon refuses, in other words, is a theory of fashion as a "substitute" body. Rather, what he focuses on is the general transmutability of form, marking his morphology as another case in which form cannot be thought of as being separate from transformation. At other instances in *The Life of Forms*, not quoted by Benjamin, Focillon explicitly connects fashion to this principle of alteration in its purest form, listing fashion as one of "those imponderables ... that modify whatever they touch."[71] In this framework, morphology is inseparable from metamorphosis, and together these qualities account for the temporalized form that is fashion.[72] Bracketing the vitalist background of the art historian's theory of a *life* of forms (a stance that would seem difficult to reconcile with the position of Benjamin, who reserved harsh criticism for the related, similarly vitalist approach of Bergson in his Baudelaire essay), we can still identify a point at which Focillon allows us to grasp an elementary configuration which contributed to the overall fashion situation from which Benjamin's and Grund's mentioned approaches and comments emerged. Focillon describes the invention of a new humanity—new shapes—by way of what in fashion is called *ligne*, which we can here translate as "a" line in fashion, meaning partially a given silhouette. That Focillon is thinking of something that we would call silhouette is indicated by the particular logic and constraints that he maps out for these inventive transformations. They occur in a zone in which the fantasy of shapes (figures) is matched with and checked by the "physiological canon," i.e., the morphological realities and boundaries of the human body. The fashionable "line" or silhouette is thus defined as a becoming of form in the zone between invention and the delimitations of anatomy. Neither complete reimagination nor symbolic substitution, fashion here is deployed as a transformation between potential forms and their anchoring in real (i.e., non-symbolic) bodies. If we were to search for an example of such a transformation, we wouldn't have to look far. As a matter of fact, we might pinpoint it at one particular historical moment—others would be possible, too, but this one would have had an impact on Benjamin's and Grund's understanding of fashion. It could be the difference between 1929 and 1930: waists went up, skirts went down, and the observers of fashion were wondering, "What are we going to do about it?"

3

In/Elegant Materialisms

Grund's additional notes on the essence of fashion (an unpublished fragment from the Walter Benjamin-Archiv)

If we want to assess Helen Grund's intellectual contribution in "On the Essence of Fashion" (Vom Wesen der Mode) more systematically, we had best turn to the author's own words: she describes her general intention as wanting to elaborate on "principle[s] and intellectual characteristic[s] of the concept of fashion" (Prinzipielle[s] und Ideelle[s] des Modebegriffs). Or, as Grund also puts it, she aims to think through the "buried and surviving laws" (verschütteten und überlebenden Gesetze) of fashion to counter the assumption of its mere capriciousness (Modelaunen),[1] while at the same time sketching a "picture of the creation of fashion in Paris" (Bild[s] des Pariser Modeschaffens).[2]

As we shall see, several of Grund's central concepts have counterparts in Benjamin's work, and across a number of pronounced differences these two bodies of fashion thought could be described as exemplars of a contrast between two guiding aesthetic ideals: Grund's work posits *elegance* as this guiding value, whereas Benjamin's writing implicitly revolves around a program of what could be called an "obdurate" fashion form, the closest associates of which in fashion are perhaps instances of hard edge chic. While neither author in these specific texts makes reference to concrete examples of Parisian couture, their respective arguments can still be clearly connected to contemporaneous positions in fashion aesthetics, sometimes directly, sometimes indirectly, where they have corresponding elements in the design practices of Elsa Schiaparelli and Madeleine Vionnet, as well as tying into general currents of the fashion panorama, as they became evident, for instance, in the presentation of Parisian couture in the context of the so-called *Pavillon de l'Elégance* for the 1937 Paris World Fair. We shall also see that in the context of Benjamin's writing, his ideas lead us to a particular intersection of other intellectual strands in his work, familiar and less so, such as his theorization of "material" and "matter."

This dialogue between Grund and Benjamin, which is one of the central concerns of the present chapter, relies on an intellectual exchange whose textual basis was never fully formulated, and not merely due to the *Arcades Project*'s fragmentary status. The exchange also relies on a piece of writing by Grund, which—to the best knowledge of the present book's author—has until today remained unpublished: an eight-page typescript that was in Benjamin's possession and that is kept today at the Walter Benjamin-Archiv at the Berlin Akademie der Künste. The document addresses a readership, or more likely an audience, to whom these paragraphs were directly delivered by Grund, which the grammatical form of the original German clearly marks as female (Sehr geehrte Damen . . .). This allows us to surmise that the fragment might have originally been presented as part of Grund's lecture to the students of the Munich Fashion School, whose student body will have consisted of young women. Certain segments of the text's content, namely remarks on a number of German fashion brands, whom Grund generally compares rather unfavorably to their French counterparts, further support the assumption that these pages must be notes for her presentation in Munich, whose part goal was (as was also the case for Grund's published criticism) to inform and educate the interested German public about the Parisian fashion scene.

The reasons as to why Grund didn't include these passages in the printed version of her lecture are subject to speculation. She might have also formulated them on the occasion of a subsequent visit to the Munich Fashion School, which—as literary scholar and curator Julia Bertschik has researched—occurred in 1936 when she spoke about "Die Beziehung der Frau zu ihrer eigenen Erscheinung" (Woman's Relation to her Own Appearance), when the print booklet of "On the Essence of Fashion" had already appeared.[3] If they had been part of Grund's initial lecture, they might have been retracted from publication either on the author's or her publisher's request, or in a joint initiative, for being too sensitive: Grund's critique of the German designers whom she mentions is trenchant and she makes no effort to sugarcoat her assessment of their output as provincial at best. In 1935, only two years into National Socialist rule, when her text went to print, one might have refrained from putting to the page, and hence to permanence, what already in the spoken form could be considered a risk, namely to talk unfavorably of the Reich, and favorably of its trans-rhenian neighbors, where Grund had made her home. Had this indeed been the assessment, it would have proved accurate: after her 1936 visit to Munich, Grund became the target of National Socialist officials who—as Germanist Mila Ganeva has found out—initiated a vicious attack against her (as well as against the directors of the Modeschule and the *Frankfurter Zeitung*) in the SS publication *Das Schwarze Korps*. They took particular insult at the fact that Grund—a denizen of Paris, married to a Jew, and writing for a medium which National Socialist propaganda had singled out as being the "most Jewish newspaper of all"—lectured "German" women about "German women's culture" (deutsche Frauenkultur).[4] As a result, Grund's employment at the *Frankfurter Zeitung* was terminated.[5] Her unpublished notes, however, made their way into Benjamin's hands; in all likelihood he received them from the author herself.

What concerns us in the following is not Grund's assessments of the failings of German fashion production. In addition to these, her typescript contains a number of general reflections, which complement the argument that she unfolds in "On the Essence of Fashion," and which stand in marked contrast to Benjamin's fashion aesthetics. Held side by side, both works become legible as theories of the elegant and the obdurate fashion form, and, beyond, as complementary contributions to a theorization of the question of matter and material.

A theory of elegance: The animation of garments according to Helen Grund

As if responding directly to Gretel Karplus's already quoted remark (see chapter 2) that within the fashion system the notion of taste is a questionable category, in "On the Essence of Fashion" Grund provides a functional definition of this concept: "Taste is indeed a mere regulator in fashion" (Der Geschmack ist nämlich tatsächlich nur ein Regulator der Mode).[6] And, connecting her reasoning to the tradition of philosophical aesthetics, Grund relates the question of the judgment of taste to the issue of the beautiful, which, she says, fashion regularly touches upon and traverses, but which within its systemic parameters is manifest at best as a transcendental value, rather than a de facto aesthetic goal to be realized:

> As we are carried onward by time it is as if we are circling around and thus gain ever different views of beauty. This compulsion to change goes so far that we frequently give up what has been achieved and exchange the intuitively beautiful for the counterintuitively beautiful (we could also call it the ugly), so that we follow its trace also along detours.
>
> *Es ist, als ob, indem die Zeit uns weiterträgt, wir die Schönheit umkreisen und somit jeweilig eine andere Sicht auf sie haben. Diese Nötigung zum Wechsel geht so weit, daß wir nicht selten das Gewonnene wieder aufgeben und das sinngemäß Schöne mit dem sinnwidrig Schönen (wir können es auch das Häßliche nennen) vertauschen, daß wir also auch auf Umwegen die Fährte verfolgen.*[7]

Grund here determines the stylistic and systemic course of fashion development as a play of transformations over time, a to-and-fro between "intuitively" and "counterintuitively" beautiful styles, of fashion phenomena appealing and "ugly." She situates the category of taste (or, rather, the fulfillment and execution of a certain subcategory of taste, namely the beautiful) not on the level of individual phenomena. Rather, taste comes into effect as a regulatory instance in relation to the entirety of systemic activity—i.e., the change of fashion(s) as such, not individual styles. This position surely entails a certain terminological blurriness. For isn't the "intuitively beautiful" closer to the transcendental value of *the beautiful*—which fashion chases after and which is safeguarded by the regulator of taste—than to the "counterintuitively beautiful," i.e., the ugly? (This is a question which could be countered by observing that the everyday fashion judgment, i.e., the positive evaluation of a look, only in a few subordinate cases actually amounts to stating that an outfit is *beautiful*. Much more frequently, and much more accurately, one states that something *looks good*.)

While Grund treats taste as the mere systemic regulator of fashion, she does not assume that beyond this meta-control lies a field of *anything goes*. As a critic, she takes a decisive stance, which isn't entirely clearly positioned in relation to fashion's systemic logic. For in addition to her assumption that good looks in fashion take on many forms as styles oscillate, Grund unmistakably privileges certain aesthetic values which in her view contribute to successful fashion. These values clearly emerge from her familiarity with the Parisian panorama, which she sketches for her German readership. In "On the Essence of Fashion" Grund mentions the most important value in passing when she defines the guiding ideal of the French, and in particular Parisian style, by stating that for Parisian women "wanting to be 'elegant,' rather than 'pretty,' i.e., 'impeccably put together'" is central (weniger daran lieg[e], für 'hübsch' als für 'elegant', das heißt 'untadelig zurechtgemacht' zu gelten).[8]

In her unpublished typescript at the Walter Benjamin-Archiv, Grund unfolds her casual observation regarding the centrality of elegance in a more substantial manner. In that text, she sets out by defining the goal of any fashion pedagogy as follows: "How can we assist the production of 'elegance,' rather than a mere 'dress'?" (Wie kann man dazu helfen, dass die 'Eleganz' hervorgebracht wird und nicht nur das 'Kleid'?)[9] At the same time she observes that "motifs, pretty textiles, great lines, pleasant colors – remain powerless if they don't disappear under the impression of elegance that is produced by the wearer of dresses" (Motive, hübsche Stoffe, gute Linien, angenehme Farben – sie vermögen nichts, wenn man sie nicht über dem Eindruck der Eleganz, den die Trägerin der Kleider hervorbringt, völlig vergessen kann).[10] In all cases elegance is thus defined in relation to dress. Elegance refers to a certain quality of styling, the impression of flawlessness ("impeccably put together"); elegance also refers to a quality of the garment itself, where it describes a certain more, a surplus in relation to the mere textile and its materiality, which resides in design. Or, more precisely, Grund defines the elegance of a dress negatively in that, in its absence, the materiality and "objectness" of that garment are making themselves felt. Elegance is thus defined as a "more" than the respective garment in and on which it appears (not "just" the dress), and at the same time this more implies a state in which the garment, as matter, disappears (the impression of elegance makes the viewer forget about the material aspects of the vestment).[11] A dress is thus defined as the material medium in which the quality of elegance unfolds, and the unfolding of which leads to the obfuscation of this materiality in the perception of the fashion audience.

Or, as Grund puts it differently, "The lure of a dress does not result from its objectness (i.e., from its qualities as an object), but from the effect of its elegance. A dress 'in itself,' even the most beautiful, even the most modern, lacks essence until it is animated through attitude and lively movement" (Die Verlockung der Kleider entsteht nicht aus ihrer Gegenständlichkeit, sondern aus der Wirkung ihrer Eleganz. Ein Kleid 'an sich' auch das schönste, auch das modernste ist wesenlos, ehe es von der Haltung und lebendiger Bewegung beseelt wird).[12] As if belatedly responding to the basic question of her lecture regarding the *essence* of fashion, Grund here names at least the essence of fashionably successful outfits. These are garments which have the potential and propensity to be "animated" through a certain attitude, bodily posture, and lively movement. This definition carries several implications: firstly that Grund's concept of elegance—just like her concept of taste—and her criteria for what counts as "looking good" in fashion are not identical with the beautiful (or the pretty), let alone the modern. Grund's fashion judgment doesn't target what is merely "in." Being "modern," in the sense of contemporary, isn't sufficient; her discerning eye, schooled and disciplined in Paris, demands elegance. Secondly, elegance is defined here as a momentum of animation of material that would otherwise appear inert, or "dead."

Theory of modeling

Grund develops her ideas regarding the elegant "unmarking" of (textile) materiality further in a small theory of modeling, which is based on an analysis of the performance of the Parisian mannequins:[13]

> A model (the name implies as much) is the more perfect the less she is a 'presentation lady'. Just like an actress she has to represent a being that would be insufferable in real life. She has to exaggerate her agility. She has to convey the impression as if she consisted of views of her front, back and both sides at once. When an actress, through clumsiness or a poor choice of tempo, makes us realize that she 'acts,' the audience will not be affected any more [teilt sich keine Erregung mit]. When a model makes us realize that something is 'presented' to us, we notice dresses, coats, in short 'things,' but the mediation of elegance is lost.
>
> *Das Mannequin (das liegt schon im Namen) ist umso vollkommener, je weniger es eine 'Vorführdame' ist. Es hat nämlich, der Schauspielerin verwandt, ein Wesen darzustellen, das uns im gewöhnlichen Leben unerträglich wäre. Es hat seine Beweglichkeit zu übertreiben. Es muss den Eindruck erwecken als bestünde es gleichzeitig aus einer Rücken-, Front- und zwei Seitenansichten. Lässt uns eine Schauspielerin durch eine Ungeschicklichkeit oder ein schlechtgewähltes Tempo darauf kommen, dass sie 'spielt,' so teilt sich dem*

> *Zuschauer keine Erregung mehr mit. Lässt das Mannequin uns spüren, dass uns etwas 'vorgeführt' wird, so bemerken wir Kleider, Mäntel, kurz 'Dinge,' aber die Vermittlung der Eleganz geht verloren.*[14]

Also on the level of modeling, elegance is thus defined as a function of animation, and it is determined as a quality that results from agility and suppleness. This "movement process" (bewegte ... Vorgang) is essential for Grund's concept of elegance, and it is once again combined with a rejection of prettiness, as well as with the demand for a strictly non-private formalization:

> A model is neither supposed to be 'intellectual,' nor 'sentimental,' neither moral, nor immoral. Her private life must not cross the audience's mind. She doesn't even need to be particularly pretty if she only has the pluck to be confidently elegant.
>
> *Mannequins haben weder 'intellektuell,' noch empfindsam noch moralisch, noch unmoralisch zu wirken. Man darf an ein Privatleben überhaupt nicht denken. Sie brauchen nicht einmal besonders hübsch zu sein, wenn sie nur den Schneid haben selbstverständlich elegant zu sein.*[15]

And, even more concretely, Grund is concerned with the models' actual movement, and its qualities. Models need to be "taught not to 'show' the dresses, but rather to move freely and lightly, and to present themselves in an exaggeratedly swift rhythm of steps and turns as fleeting images of confident elegance" (beizubringen, dass sie nicht Kleider vorzuführen haben, sondern sich frei und leicht und in einem übertreibend hurtigen Rhythmus des Schreitens und Wendens als flüchtige Bilder der sicheren Eleganz zu zeigen haben.)[16] Grund's assessment is clearly in line with the period's fashion public opinion that particularly appreciated the gliding walk of Parisian models.

In Grund's conceptualization of elegance as a quality of movement (which could be connected to predecessors at least as far back as Balzac, who included a *Théorie de la Démarche*, a theory of the step or the gait, in his "Traité de la vie élégante," we encounter a case in which the production of theory is profoundly informed by the historical, medial, and economic fashion system, and we find in it an aspect that tends to be overlooked in a number of accounts of fashion, partly due to a privileging of a certain medial (and perhaps even media-ideological) bent in thinking through fashion, which has, however, in recent years been questioned.

The question to begin with is simple enough: how do we know of the fashions that we are not immediately privy to, for instance, the fashions of the past, or of distant places? For a long time the most basic answer would have pointed to two types of media (apart from the archiving of individual garments in institutions, such as museums): written accounts (i.e., criticism and narrative) and visual fixation first in drawings, sketches, and illustrations, and later in photography. Combined with the overall awareness of fashion's changing character, this combination has contributed to a certain polarity in which, in particular, the visual fixation in the technological medium of photography, including its entire ballast of aesthetic-ideological "arrests," serves to highlight the other pole which, by contrast, acquires characteristics of a fleeting, ephemeral event which is, by definition, difficult if not impossible to capture. As we shall see, that dichotomy—whose individual factual components are perfectly accurate, but whose polar counter-stabilization is perhaps not as necessary as it is usually considered—informs, for instance, the fashion poetics of Charles Baudelaire, which of course is canonical material for Benjamin's reflections on the subject.

A recent shift in scholarship, which has not only begun investigating the first periods of studio film (i.e., ca. the period between 1910 and 1930) in relation to fashion history, but is also focusing on the role of fashion shows, has begun correcting this perspective. Fashion historian and theorist Caroline Evans emphasizes the coemergence of film as an art form and entertainment industry, and the earliest fashion shows.[17] This amounts to the insight that, for the fashion aesthetics of Grund's and Benjamin's moment, movement was not just an exterior condition in the sense of a progression from one season to another, from one collection to another, or with the turning of magazine page by magazine page in order to see the next shot. Rather, movement counted as an inherent aesthetic quality; it was part of the immanent ontology of vestments and their appreciation.[18] Grund's argument clearly develops from a position that takes these realities into account; hardly a surprising fact, given that through her work as a fashion correspondent she was both familiar with and dependent on the Parisian *défilés*, where models in outfits ambulated in front of an audience of clients, buyers, and journalists. As in other cases, Grund also included this aspect, understood not least as an aspect of the overall fashion economy, in her writing.[19]

The immanence of elegance

Elegance as a guiding and concrete value of fashion is not only realized by whisking the dress away from a mode of mere, clumsy presentation. Grund thinks this process of "animating" materiality as comparable to the strictly formal, hyperagile movement patterns of good models. The mentioned "images of confident elegance" are moving images, and as effects of animation processes that rely on actual movement (or processes that resemble movement) these images are transient; and in their animating agility and transient movement they form the counterpart to the perceivable materiality of the textiles, which they must tackle. However, they deploy their effects *within* the medium of the textile, or *in* the model's walk. As such they are immanent, not transcendent. They animate textile and matter, but they don't supersede them.

In Grund's circumvention or bracketing of any potential understanding of textile as a "beautiful" medium, we not only encounter the reason for why elegance is a concept that is proper to the system of fashion, whereas beauty is not. (Moments of beauty, in the rigorous sense of the term, may be desirable correlates to the work that is done in fashion, and as Grund underlines, beauty may serve as its transcendental regulator, but as such transcendent values they lie beyond its germane machinations.) We also here come across a configuration that indicates why fashion must be regarded as (one) end of even the last remnants of an idealist project.

It seems clear that the concept of elegance, and in particular Grund's development of it, is, further, related to the more established notions of grace and gracefulness.[20] Just like grace, elegance is intricately connected to the phenomena of habit, attitude, posture, and, first of all, movement. However, in contrast to these notions, and their venerable history dating back to classical antiquity, elegance again lacks the at least latent connection to an instance situated beyond the plane of its own execution, from which it would receive its ultimate legitimization. Graceful movement, as with the realization of the quality of grace, is—already etymology suggests as much—in the last instance a gift. One either possesses grace or one doesn't, because one has been gifted with it. In this lies the at least subliminally transcendent character of grace which, for all its inherent fascination, ultimately points to an instance beyond itself from which it has been bequeathed upon the individual who comports themselves "with grace." Not so elegance. The historic root of the word—eligere—points the way, indicating a way of choosing. The first usages of the term that anticipate the way in which we still employ it date back to the 17th century, when the expression 'elegant diction' refered to a choice way of speaking. Elegance thus derives from the context of rhetorics, from courtly communication, and it refers to a skill, a technique—for the technique of choosing one's words with discernment.[21] The logic of elegance is actually the inverse of the logic of grace, which relies on distinction because one has been chosen (to receive the gift of grace). To put it more concretely: elegance promises no claim to transcendent revelation, because it is an exemplar of a worldly quality and/or practice; it is an aesthetic skill and a social technique. As such it communicates its worldliness. Elegance is mundane in the best possible sense of the term. Inherent to the world, to culture, and its forms, it is immanent.

Taking it to the industry

Grund's analysis of fashionable elegance has, finally, a surprising counterpart in her reflections on a number of commercial and production-related aspects of the fashion industry. In these she departs from a number of commercial failures, which the houses of Chanel and Lanvin allegedly suffered when they entered the field of textile manufacturing: "It has never been to their benefit when Parisian fashion creators surrender to the temptation of taking over the fabrication of textiles themselves. Chanel and Lanvin have lost a lot of money in such endeavors" (Es hat noch keinem pariser Modeschöpfer gut getan, wenn er sich verlocken ließ, die Stofffabrikation selbst zu übernehmen. Chanel und Lanvin haben viel Geld dabei verloren.)[22] Grund argues that the functional differentiation of the fabrication of textiles and the design and production of dresses benefits both parties' performances: "To produce textiles 'in the spirit of fashion', encompassing the full risk of such explorations, motivates peak performances among the manufacturers" (Die Stoffe im 'Geiste' der Mode zu fabrizieren, mit all dem Risiko, das solch ein Voraustasten in sich schließt – das regt die Stofffabrikanten zu Höchstleistungen an), and: "To receive textiles as 'raw material,' which to engage with, sparks the imaginations of the fashion tailor" (Die Stoffe als "Rohmaterial" geliefert zu bekommen, mit dem man sich auseinanderzusetzen hat, das beflügelt die Phantasie der Modeschneider).[23] One final point leads back to Grund's theory of elegance: "In general such an engagement [Auseinandersetzung] with the material is necessary in order to supersede [überwinden] its materiality (Im Allgemeinen ist eine Auseinandersetzung mit Material nötig, um seine 'Stofflichkeit' zu überwinden).[24] In Grund's story—which, incidentally, has a correlate not just in the realm of the grand fashion houses but also on the pages of the period's press, where titles such as *Vogue*, *Harper's*, or *Femina* regularly included illustrations of and short reports about new textiles—the Parisian woman celebrates her fashionable victories because she masters (beherrscht) the raw material (das Rohmaterial) through composition (indem sie es komponiert), thereby executing the elegant working through and animation of materiality which Grund demands.[25] This the expert also recognizes on the level of the fashion industry, where the textile suppliers produce cloth, which the couturiers in the production of their own creations "work through" once again.

Grund situates her development of the aesthetic value of fashionable elegance only in the broadest terms. While she provides systematic arguments, she doesn't furnish references to positions in the history of aesthetics, or criticism. And while she clearly identifies Paris, and with it France, as the cultural center for the production of elegance (offsetting these further in her text against a number of German fashion brands), she is at her most specific in her discussion of the commercial failures of the houses of Lanvin and Chanel in the field of textile production. It is thus perhaps interesting to note that her advocacy for the fashion value of elegance, and her functional definition of it as an immanent animation of materiality, corresponds with a number of positions in the historical poetics of fashion that were contemporaneous with the writing of her text.

For within the course of the development of Paris fashion in which the more androgynous looks of the 1920s were gradually replaced by gender-dimorphous silhouettes—a development which Grund had called for her German readers (see chapter 2)—we also see the emergence of certain positions that correspond surprisingly closely with her analysis of the formal conditions for elegance. At this point we can observe, firstly, in conjunction with the term's origin from a concept of socio-aesthetic (the rhetoric of elegant diction), that within the overall rejection of the aesthetics of the second half of the 1920s, with their affinities for the more casual codes of sportswear (e.g.,

Patou designing for Lenglen, the idolatry of the tennis champion, the importance of the resort and beachwear of Deauville and the Côte d'Azur), there is now a re-institution of the more socially "elevated" registers of eveningwear, which make themselves felt in the emphasis on the classical dress, and even gowns (on the economic preconditions of these tendencies, see chapter 4). While there is no reason that, for instance, a flapper dress couldn't be elegant, and while one could in all validity claim that the 1920s, in the work of Coco Chanel, gave fashion an epitome of elegance in the form of the little black dress the overall tone of 1930s fashion presentation communicates the principle of exclusiveness and selection—which is *nolens volens* integral to the genesis of the concept of elegance—more openly than before. We shall look at a concrete example—the couture of Madeleine Vionnet—later on.

Thing and dress (Schiaparelli, Apollinaire)

For Grund's reader Walter Benjamin, the term "elegance," by contrast, was of marginal relevance at best. As much is evident from Benjamin's notes in the *Arcades Project*. In the fashion convolute, the term "elegance" figures only once, as marginalia of Parisian fashion history. In the dress of the female cyclist—an early form of sportswear that Benjamin took an interest in—the "sporting expression still struggles with the inherited ideal of elegance" (AP 62, TM) (der sportliche Ausdruck [kämpft] noch mit dem überkommenen Idealbild der Eleganz [PW 110]). And where Grund in her reports and analyses of the creations from the salons of Parisian couturiers increasingly focuses on the gowns and robes of Patou, Lanvin, or Lelong, one note from the *Arcades Project* gives a poetically mediated yet sufficiently concrete idea of a dress that sparked Benjamin's attention. The difference between his and Grund's prerogatives are of such a fundamental nature that they deserve to be called a genuine contrast. The text in question is a passage from Apollinaire's 1916 novel *Le poète assassiné*, in which the author unfolds a proto-Surrealist account of fashion:

> This year ... fashion is bizarre and common, simple and full of fantasy. Any material from nature's domain can now be introduced into the composition of women's clothes. I saw a charming dress made of corks.... A major

couturier is thinking about launching tailor-made outfits made out of old bookbindings done in calf.... One often sees delicious young girls dressed like pilgrims of Saint James of Compostella; their outfits ... are studded with coquilles Saint-Jacques. Porcelain, sandstone and faience have suddenly entered the vestimentary arts.... Fashion ... no longer looks down on anything. It ennobles everything. It does for materials [les matières] what the Romantics did for words.

AP 70, TM

Cette année ... la mode est bizarre et familière, elle est simple et pleine de fantaisie. Toutes les matières des différents règnes de la nature peuvent maintenant entrer dans la composition d'un costume de femme. J'ai vu une robe charmante, faite de bouchons de liège.... Un grand couturier médite de lancer les costumes tailleur en dos de vieux livres, reliés en veau.... On voit souvent de délicieuses jeunes filles habillés en pèlerines de Saint-Jacques de Compostelle; leur costume ... est constellé de coquille Saint-Jacques. La porcelaine, le grès et la faïence ont brusquement apparu dans l'art vestimentaire.... La mode ... ne méprise plus rien, elle ennoblit tout. Elle fait pour les matières ce que les romantiques firent pour les mots.

PW 119[26]

This example contradicts Grund's principle of elegance in several ways, and not just through the exorbitant proliferations of imaginary vestments which—in line with Benjamin's predilection for the fantastical worlds of Grandville—eschew any preference for supple yet formally restrained examples of light movement. We could also hardly think of a fashion model that would contradict the animation and dissolution of materiality more emblematically than the dresses in Apollinaire's novel which are literally tailored from things: bookbindings, pilgrim scallops, porcelain—none of these materials would be suitable for the elegant movement of textiles which Grund discusses. By contrast, these fashions carry their thingliness on the sleeve, so to speak.

It is worth noting that, in spite of the fantastical element of the poet's writing, a number of elements here are far from relegated to the realm of pure fiction. Rather, what Benjamin recognized in Apollinaire's literary description has correlates in the fashion production of his period. And it is, unsurprisingly, again in the work of couturier Elsa Schiaparelli, with her Surrealist sensibilities and collaborations, that we find, if not literal equivalents to the poet's vision of dresses as assemblages of pre-existent objects, then at least models for an approach to a conceptualization of outfits that posits them on a shared tangent with thingly entities.

Already Schiaparelli's self-presentation signals as much—for instance when, in 1931, she showed up in the social circles of Saint Moritz wearing a silver lacquered wig created for her by the hairdresser Antoine, an appearance documented by society and fashion photographer d'Ora.[27] The logics of this accessory is captured and extended by another photo in which Schiaparelli sports the wig, her chin resting on a headless female white plaster torso, positioned in such a manner that it hides the designer's upper body (Fig. 3.1).

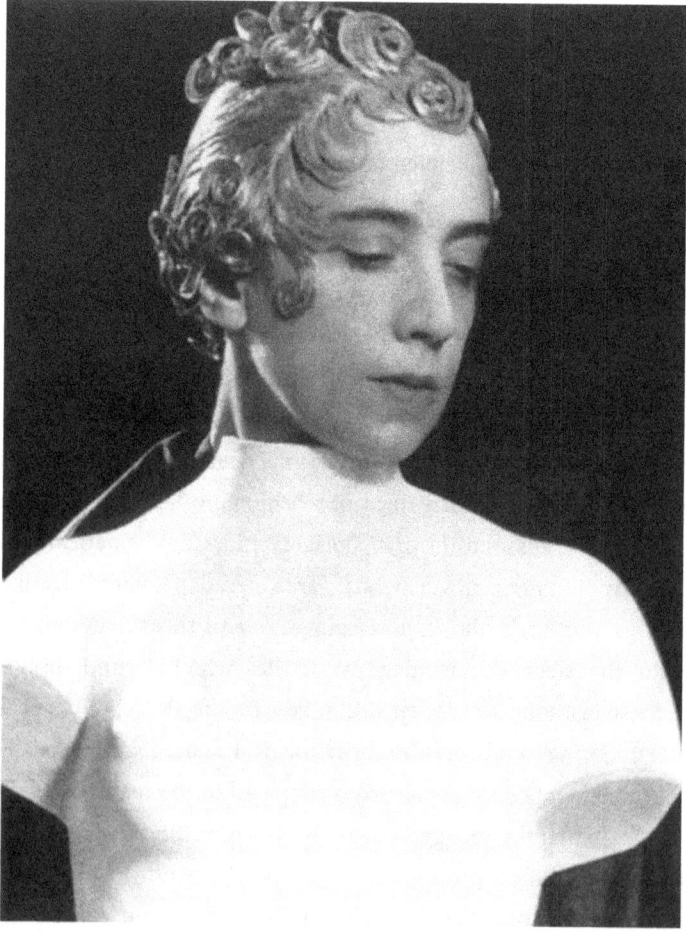

Figure 3.1 Man Ray: Elsa Schiaparelli, head on plaster torso, coiffure by Antoine (1933). © Man Ray Trust / VG Bild-Kunst, Bonn 2019.

In/Elegant Materialisms 119

Figure 3.2 Horst P. Horst: Mrs. Reginald Fellows with coiffure by Antoine and white Mandarin collared Schiaparelli coat. *Vogue* (1935). © Condé Nast/Getty Images.

This picture was taken by Man Ray, who used it, along with a host of other motifs, to illustrate his essay "L'Age de la Lumière" in the 1933 double issue no. 3/4 of *Minotaure*, in which Tzara also published "On a Certain Automatism of Taste," and with it Man Ray's photographs of Schiaparelli's designs. The point is driven home visually: those sections of hair that attach closely to the shape of Schiaparelli's skull, slicked back, display a metal sheen; the other sections, growing across her upper ears, running back along the crest of her head, and framing her forehead are draped into a small torrent of curls, all of which are fixed into a repellant appearance. One strain of hair curls its way across the height of her eyes and brows and onto her right cheekbone, where it twists into a spiral. Sprayed into a compact and slightly reflective surface, Schiaparelli's skull looks as if it is encased in mother of pearl, the material matrix for the formation of pearls, which—in their irregular shape—served as inspiration for the metaphorical naming of the style, whose intricate convulsions and decorative garlands also inform the shiny twists and turns that stretch into the designer's face: *rocaille*, rococo. This was an aesthetic which Antoine, the maker of the wig, had invented and which he successfully capitalized throughout the decade and beyond (Fig. 3.2).

The cap/helmet clearly functions as an equivalent to the white plaster torso, a visual bracket for the gray-tone rendering of the flesh colors of Schiaparelli's face. An animate body sandwiched between a mimetic rendering of its physique and its extensions, each hardened into lifeless doubles and appendages.[28] Schiaparelli's "helmet" wig makes the case with particular force: an (in)organic, already dead, yet usually supple outgrowth of the body—hair—that normally would yield and react to movements, drafts of air, turns of the head, etc, is here arranged into shapes whose visual rhetoric signals drastic animations (eddies, vortices), but which in this arrangement are literally stuck.[29]

This logic of a material juxtaposition of spatially contingent objects ("things"), which Man Ray's photograph stages, also extends to the details of Schiaparelli's own designs, where one of its arenas is the field of accessories and applications—for instance, in the form of buttons interpreted less as semi-functional, semi-decorative items attached to the garment, but rather in acts of displacement and imitation cast as objects with an independent presence (think of the bullet casings that "embellished" and fastened a coat in the early 1930s, or the miniature grand pianos closing a suit jacket in the 1939 'Music' collection).[30] Or, also relying on witty mimeses, this tendency is amplified in pieces of millinery such as the iconic shoe hats (1937), which not only partake in another morphological reworking of the silhouette (see chapter 2), but which in their displacement and upscaling of footwear to the measures of a human head position items of apparel firmly in the realm of "things"—i.e., concrete material objects (Fig. 3.3, 3.4).

Schiaparelli's most pronounced designs in this direction, however, are possibly her drawer suits from 1936. Working from a sketch by Dalí that shows

Figure 3.3 Maison Schiaparelli, design sketch (collection winter 1937). Paris, Musée des Arts décroatifs – collection UFAC. Copyright MAD, Paris / Jean Tholance.

a humanoid figure in a nightgown-like garment rhythmically structured by a pattern of drawers extending into the interior of the depicted figure's body, the knobs partly doubling as nipples and navel, Schiaparelli's suit jackets, and a corresponding coat, position applications—a set of breast pockets and frontally placed waist pockets—on the front of the torso (Fig. 3.5). Executed as rectangular patches in the same dark velvet out of which the suit jackets were constructed, to which circular black plastic knobs had been attached, these applications (constructionally displaced epaulettes, so to speak) generated the impression of a superimposition of the wearer's torso and a bureau drawer, of vestment and furniture.[31]

Staged by Cecil Beaton in a sparse, painted studio landscape, three variations of this model appeared, harshly lit, more silhouette than sculpture, in the 1936

Figure 3.4 Schiaparelli Shoe Hat (collection winter 1937). © Ullstein Bild/Getty Images.

Figure 3.5 Maison Schiaparelli, design sketch (collection winter 1936). Paris, Musée des Arts décroatifs—collection UFAC. Copyright MAD, Paris / Christophe Delliäre.

September issue of *Vogue* (Fig. 3.6a-b). One model holds up, as if reading from its pages, another magazine, or rather a journal—the eighth issue of *Minotaure*, which had just been published, with another Dalí drawing on its cover: a female minotaur whose breasts had been replaced by another opened drawer.

Figure 3.6 a, b Cecil Beaton: Models in Schiaparelli Drawer Suits. *Vogue* (1936). © Condé Nast/Getty Images.

The strange steadying and morphing of vestment and fashion into the object world of furniture occurs most graphically concrete in the drawer suits, but the trope can be observed in other Schiaparelli garments as well: in her winter 1938/39 Zodiac collection, the designer studded the jacket of a dinner suit with tiny rectangular mirrors set into gold-embroidered baroque "frames" (executed in sequins and metallic thread) to transpose the effect of the mirror-paneled Salon de la Guerre and Salon de la Paix in the Versailles Galerie des Glaces.[32] The visual explosion of ornament certainly pushed the concept of exuberance to a new level, but the basic concept is also present, for instance, in Schiaparelli's 1937 summer collection, in which evening jackets were trimmed with white leather, executed in graphically reduced but clearly recognizable rococo appliqués, generating once again a strange effect of vestimentary *ameublement*.[33]

It was again Cecil Beaton who picked up on the idea—shortly after he had shot the drawer suits in 1936—and reinforced it elegantly yet markedly when, for another *Vogue* commission, he photographed Wallis Simpson, the soon-to-be Duchess of Windsor and wife of the no-longer king of England Edward VIII (soon to be Duke of Windsor), in the aforementioned costume jacket

Figure 3.7 Cecil Beaton: Wallis Simpson in a black Schiaparelli evening jacket with white trimming and a Schiaparelli dress. *Vogue* (1937). © Condé Nast/Getty Images.

which, along with a number of other Schiaparelli designs, formed part of Simpson's wardrobe (Fig. 3.7).[34] In this picture, Simpson combines the jacket with a slim dark dress, also designed by Schiaparelli, giving her the characteristic column-like silhouette of the period. She stands next to a wooden chest of drawers that is embellished with intensely labored, intricately twisted, vegetal metalwork around the keyholes, handles, and side edges. The characteristically spiked and flaming shapes echo those of a dark bouquet of flowers and branches placed on the piece of furniture's marble top. Behind the bouquet, on the wall, we spot a clock that inverses the color attribution of light tones which characterize the rococo ornamentation in this picture (here it is the dark wood case that branches out into the characteristically dynamic shapes, set off against the white of the clock's face). The entire picture skillfully highlights the opposing tendencies of the inventory of rococo forms which we already saw varied in Schiaparelli's portrait by Man Ray, donning her Antoine wig—a dialectic of dynamism and freezing, the vegetal and the hardened—which here extends to the design of the dress jacket. It further sets a tone in which Simpson's immaculate white skin acquires a strange touch of porcelain deadness, while the fashionable *pièce de resistance* that anchors and occasions the entire construction—her dress jacket—visually joins the realm of objects which furnish a room, rather than dressing a person.

The concept, or trope, wasn't exclusive to Schiaparelli: a manuscript note on nineteenth-century fashions, grouped with the *Arcades* materials (yet not included in convolute B), in all likelihood partly informed by Grandville's graphic object metamorphoses, underlines the connection between Benjamin's identification of Apollinaire's literary deployment of vestments-as-things as a significant contribution to the subject of fashion, and the styles of his own moment that worked in proximity to Surrealism, e.g., Schiaparelli. In that note, Benjamin simply jots down in the shortest manner "architectural forms on clothes, or dresses" (AP 900, TM) (Architekturformen auf Kleidern [PW 1221]) and then mentions an unidentified design from "1850/1860," among others, in which the jacket appeared as a "double door" (AP 900) (zweiflügelige Tür [PW 1207])—a design logic and form-generating principle that is strikingly close to Schiaparelli's shifting of dress into dressers, of vestments into pieces of furniture, constructing a similar appearance to the architectural in the vestimentary.

In Apollinaire's text—Benjamin's primary source—the constructional logic is, obviously, different. It is in contrast to the narrator's commentary, which asserts that the observed fashions ennoble and enchant everyday objects and materials in a manner reminiscent of "the Romantics'" treatment of words. Rather, Apollinaire's text here returns to models from literary aestheticism and *decadence* (for instance, Huysmans or Wilde), in which the enumeration of precious materials (metals, jewels, textiles, etc) created literary evocations of sumptuous scenarios, a richly textured, "expensive," and abundant imaginary. Another background—evoked through the prominent mention of the pilgrim's scallop—might be the inventorial mode of the depiction of Saint's attributes (the original French *coquille de Saint Jacques* serving as a prompt), or of course the attributes of allegories. Apollinaire integrates this technique of "listing"—a naming itemization of a fictional inventory—and, in a maneuver that anticipates fully fledged Surrealist techniques, produces incongruences between the items comprised in this act of listing and the overall framing which they "fill"—the description of a fashion panorama.[35]

In a slightly displaced form, the passage in question also displays a central characteristic which Peter Bürger has identified in Surrealist narrative. Whereas, like a number of their contemporary avant-garde projects, the Surrealists in their films, texts, and artworks do employ strategies of discontinuity—as realized on the plane of motifs and semantics, e.g., indicating varying ontologies, "levels of reality," combinations of "dream" and "waking," etc—Bürger observes that such disjunctions are largely kept at bay from the level of form.[36] In contrast, for instance, to Dadaist works, linguistic or visual material itself is never fragmented; montage/collage components as such do not become material; words aren't broken apart into letters and sounds; disjunctive statements are never combined with the intention of drawing attention to the "disjunct" state of the artistic product, be it filmic, visual, or literary. Rather these structures appear in terms of syntax, paragraph structure, or with regard to cinematic editing, etc perfectly "intact." The combination of these two features—semantic disjunction and formal/structural intactness—to a large extent creates the characteristic "surreal" experience of decoding the text: a deciphering movement that facilitates a "flow" through the unpredictable semantic discrepancies and across "reality shifts" which figures as a literary and artistic equivalent of "trancelike" states, of moving through a stream of dreams.

Bürger's observation can be productively extended to the version of fashion that is deployed here; a version that Benjamin took an interest in, and a version that, finally, to an extent even characterizes Schiaparelli's work. For what remains perfectly intact in Apollinaire and Schiaparelli are the concepts of fashion and the garment themselves. Just as a Surrealist narrative doesn't lose track of syntax in order to veer into "altered" semantic trajectories, there is no disruption here of dress and vestment. Rather, the vestimentary is the medium in and through which encounters of strange materials and objects occur. In the realm of fashion aesthetics, these encounters do not challenge the cohesion of dress and fashion. In this sense they are formally and systematically conservative—a conservatism that can be understood literally, in the sense of preserving the existing articulations of fashion, and which may very well have contributed to the rather seamless transition of Surrealism's protagonists and the movement's aesthetic idiom into the fashion industry. However, they do contribute to the definition of one peculiar take, or view, on fashion; they unlock one specific aspect of fashion, and this is the "thickening" of dresses into arrays of things, assemblages of stuff. And "stuff" doesn't move. "Stuff" is not elegant.

The extraneous temporality of the fashion phenomenon

A second important divergence between Benjamin and Grund makes itself felt when both think of the temporality of fashion, and in particular its transient character. Grund talked about the models who in their movements created images of ephemeral elegance on the runways of the Parisian *maisons*. Benjamin also turns to the transitory appearance of a dress and its wearer, and his medium is again literature. In his essay "Über einig Motive bei Baudelaire" (On Some Motifs in Baudelaire), Benjamin analyzes Baudelaire's sonnet "À une passante", a poem that evokes a fashionable encounter on a roaring, deafening street in which a tall, slim woman in mourning—in majestic grief—passes the subject from whose perspective the poem is enunciated:

> La rue assourdissante autour de moi hurlait.
> Longue, mince, en grand deuil, douleur majestueuse,
> Une femme passa, d'une main fastueuse
> Soulevant, balançant le feston et l'ourlet;

Agile et noble, avec sa jambe de statue.
Moi, je buvais, crispé comme un extravagant,
Dans son œil, ciel livide où germe l'ouragan,
La douceur qui fascine et le plaisir qui tue.

Un éclair... puis la nuit! – Fugitive beauté
Dont le regard m'a fait soudainement renaître,
Ne te verrai-je plus que dans l'éternité?[37]...

Benjamin here focuses on the irrevocable character of the moment: "The delight of the urban dweller is love – not at first sight, but at last sight. It is an eternal farewell, which coincides in the poem with the moment of enchantment"[38] (Die Entzückung des Großstädters ist eine Liebe nicht sowohl auf den ersten als auf den letzten Blick. Es ist ein Abschied für ewig, der im Gedicht mit dem Augenblick der Berückung zusammenfällt).[39] As the passer-by lifts and swings festoon and hem of her dress with her 'splendid hand' (une main fastueuse), and as she displays her 'statuesque leg' (sa jambe de statue), a particular affect occurs; an affect that, in Baudelaire's description, leads to a spasmic contraction:

> Thus the sonnet deploys the figure of shock, indeed of catastrophe. But the nature of his emotion has been affected as well. What makes the body contract in a spasm – *crispé comme un extravagant*, goes the poem – is not the rapture of someone whose every fibre is suffused with eros.[40]

> *So stellt das Sonett die Figur des Chocks, ja die Figur einer Katastrophe. Sie hat aber mit dem so Ergriffenen das Wesen seines Gefühls mitbetroffen. Was den Körper im Krampf zusammenzieht* – crispé comme un extravagant, *heißt es – das ist nicht die Beselignung dessen, von dem der Eros in allen Kammern seines Wesens Besitz ergreift.*[41]

In the *Arcades Project*, Benjamin further focuses on the "detailing of feminine beauties" (Detaillierung der weiblichen Schönheiten) which in Baudelaire's poetry feeds into a model of the "parceling out of feminine beauty" (Zerstückelung der weiblichen Schönheit), a "dissection" (Sektion) in which body parts are compared to "inorganic formations" (anorganischen Gebilden). It is a process of "dismemberment." In the "Passante" sonnet, such tropes could be recognized in the isolated naming of a single leg (sa jambe), which is presented not only without its counterpart—a missing limb—but also compared to the inanimate body of a statue: fragmented, fixed, hardened. This mode of representation extends to the mention of the passerby's imposing, "majestic" hand. It is, again, rendered in the singular, as if the ambidextrous human figure had been cut in half.[42]

Grund's concept of the transient image of elegance and Benjamin's account of the transitory nature of the Baudelairean *rencontre* with the *passante* have different contextual framings and respond to different conditions of fashion (infrastructures). Grund's theory is quite literally sketched next to the runway; the transient image comes together under the closely focused conditions of the salons of the fashion houses with their emphasis on presentation and sales. Her observations are made in a socio-economic interior space. Benjamin's account, with its orientation toward the Baudelairean scenario, has its setting in the exterior of the street. Its site is the boulevard of the urban masses, where transience does not *inhere* to a gradually deployed play of movement. Rather, transience here—at least in Benjamin's post-Baudelairean scenario— determines the appearance and disappearance of the fashionable apparition *in total*. Again, Grund's concept of the transitoriness of elegance shows itself to be immanent to the fashion phenomenon; by contrast, Benjamin's conceptual version of the transitory frames the fashion phenomenon as such. In his analysis of the Baudelairean sonnet, this corresponds to a collection of stases and cutouts: the shock-like cramp of the viewer/the lyrical "I"; the passerby's "statue's leg"; her hand; the seam of her dress.

The tendency of Benjamin's thought also shows itself where he omits semantics and imagery from Baudelaire's poem. Benjamin's silence on the *agilité*, the agility and skillfulness, which in Baudelaire's description sets the passerby's handling of her mourning garb apart, is telling (d'une main fastueuse / Soulevant, balançant le feston et l'ourlet; / Agile). In this infidelity to Baudelaire's wording, we not only see the difference to Grund's theory; we also recognize a parallel to Benjamin's tendency of collapsing women's work into an always already assumed state of commodification in his equation of the female body (of the prostitute) with the commodity (see chapter 2), which is here realized in his omission of the skillfulness of her hand, and of her lifting and balancing of the dress as she navigates the Parisian crowds. (Baudelaire's poem renders these in the grammatical form of the gerund, which, while casting verbs as participles, still transports the qualities of actions.) In the contrast to Baudelaire's sonnet, if the pun is permitted, rather than recognizing that the passerby *works* her dress, Benjamin is content merely to itemize her.

The problematic character of Benjamin's approach here results from its specific connection with the manner in which fashion and gender are correlated (see above). We find similar—yet unproblematic—structural motifs on a number of other occasions in Benjamin's fashion thought. As compared to Grund's theory, they overall tend to cast the category of the transitory as the condition of appearance of the fashion phenomenon, while refraining from situating (the impression of) transience and the ephemeral as a quality that would inhere to the materiality of the fashion phenomenon. On the contrary, as given emblematically in Apollinaire's description of dresses made of things, and as exemplified in Benjamin's reading of Baudelaire, the constituents of Benjamin's fashion imaginary are characterized by a thingly concreteness, even permanence, that almost contradicts the only momentary appearance (and disappearance) of the Baudelairean passerby. For transience and the ephemeral would seem to be conventionally more closely associated with a reduced substantiality, and a related effect is of course the goal of the work toward elegance which Grund demands, namely the immanent dissolution of (the perception of) materiality in the process of its animation.

We could thus provisionally speak of two different rudimentary dialectics which confront each other in the encounter of Grund's and Benjamin's fashion thought. While Grund demands the compositional and animating "working" of the material with the goal of its "vanishing," the Benjaminian dialectic aims at articulating material in its persistence in a paradoxical manner: while marking its appearance as momentary, and transient, materiality itself becomes monumentalized, physically persistent, obstinately thingly. In contrast to the process of animating working through, material is cast here only in cutouts, brief, suspended, while materially insistent. Material is thought of—and this is hardly a surprise given Benjamin's status as a prime theorist of ruination and destruction—as fragment.

This stance also informs the theory of the dialectical image and its implications for fashion theory (see chapter 1). For "fashion's tiger's leap into the past" also presents a model in which the transitory forms a framing condition, while again—and perhaps even more markedly than in the case of the theory of fashion's treatment of material—refraining from localizing the transitory within the appearing phenomenon as its immanent, qualitative characteristic.

When Benjamin writes that "the true image of the past flits by" (OCH 390) (Das wahre Bild der Vergangenheit huscht vorbei [BG 32]), he refers to a model of the transitory, in relation to the overall, systemic changes of fashion, which does not apply to the individual fashion phenomenon—as Grund had done in her description of the supple movements of elegance. This divergence is partly a result of the limits to which Benjamin takes the fashion model, as we saw in chapter 1. Historical *apocatastasis*, the rearticulation of the entirety of history with the tendency toward an end of history *tout court*, may be a liminal function (see chapter 1), but the limit against which it infinitely progresses also marks the end of time. Or, to put it differently, and within the bounds of Benjamin's more fully formed ideas, the figure of the "time kernel," which inheres to the dialectical image, stipulates that at the core of these trans-historical constellations lies time (see chapter 1). If, as Simmel held, the basic law of fashion is that *change doesn't change*, the Benjaminian model ultimately, although implicitly, emphasizes that *time is not transitory*. Time also cannot be temporalized.

This is to say that the entry of time into Benjamin's fashion theory is strictly systematic, not poetic, in the sense of an immanent poetics of individual fashion phenomena. This privation of the transitory and the transformative from the individual dress, in which it could unfold into manifold variations and plays of appearance has its counterpart in the temporality of the (fashion) image which "flits by." But in Benjamin's thought this rushing through perception, this fleeting appearance and disappearance characterizes the image, not the dress.

In this context figures also Benjamin's remark that the "'eternal is in any case far more the ruffle on a dress than some idea' dialectical image" (AP 69) ('daß das Ewige jedenfalls eher eine Rüsche am Kleid ist, als eine Idee' Dialektisches Bild [PW 118]), whose logic is of course partly driven by the rhetorical provocation of a *contradictio*. First of all, Benjamin here posits the provocative hallmark of fashionable playfulness and superficiality—the ruffle—against the venerable philosophical concept of the idea, and transfers the latter's state—exempt from time, as Platonic doctrine had stipulated—to one of the most frivolous and most profoundly discredited vestimentary applications. And a type of textile ornamentation which, it should be noted, enjoyed a particular hausse at the very moment in which Benjamin was putting down these thoughts. Volants, ruffs and in particular flounces had been important elements in the reconfiguration of womenswear at the beginning of the 1930s, when they were part and parcel of the visual dissolution of the more severe geometrical layout of the garçonne silhouette into an overall more frilly appearance.

However, beyond this maneuver of a strategically vamped-up thought, in which *froufrou* poses as idea (or in which the idea poses in a ruffled dress), in short, in which historical epistemology poses in drag, there is a close connection to actual fashion theory here. As much is indicated in a further note from the fashion convolute which, again, refers to Surrealism. Benjamin here focuses on the particular ecstasy of the everyday which characterizes André Breton's poetic program, and which in Breton's *Nadja* chances upon the novel's protagonist at the Paris Musée Grevin: "No immortalizing so unsettling as that of the ephemera and the fashionable forms preserved for us in the wax museum" (AP 69) (Keine Art von Verewigung so erschütternd wie die des Ephemeren und der modischen Formen, wie die Wachsfigurenkabinette uns aufsparen [PW 117]). The connector here is obviously the category of "immortalization" (Verewigung; literally "eternalization"), in which ephemeral (i.e., transitory) fashionable forms are cast into permanence at the museum, on the wax mannequin.[43]

In this regard, the ruffle, which—at least in Benjamin's intellectual operation—is *eternalized*, does not merely mark a vestimentary and ornamental *investment* in the realms of epistemology and the philosophy of history; it also acquires its significance in fashion theory as an item that has been set to permanence. Its material obstinacy, fixed on the wax mannequins at the Musée Grevin—counter-examples of the elegantly strutting models at the fashion shows—replaces the figure of the ephemeral, at least as far as its impression on the viewers is concerned. All lightness has left it. Fashionable form becomes heavy.

The supple and the rigid: Two tendencies in 1930s Paris Couture—Vionnet and the Pavillon de l'Élégance

The juxtaposition between Grund's fashion theory with its demand for elegance, and Benjamin's approach that foregrounds inert fashion forms, is conjectural. Emerging as it does from a corpus of mostly unpublished fragments, the conceptual contrasts and polarities that tie its positions to each other aren't consciously and fully developed by their respective authors, nor do they take shape through a sustained exchange between them. Without pretending to systematically chart a discursive field, we can refer to them as *structural* positions whose logic, if not entirely symmetrical, is one of opposition. As such, they exist within a field that extends beyond criticism and philosophy, and it is possible to find correlates among the vestimentary fashion practices of the historical moment at which they were formulated, namely the field of Parisian couture of the 1930s. While plausible, the identification of such correlates can—at least in the present case—not rely on direct references in the writings of Benjamin and Grund. As we already saw above, it is indeed possible to recognize a certain congruence between elements of his fashion theory that amounts to a poetics of "obdurate" form and a Surrealist programmatic in couture (Schiaparelli), in which dress is cast as a medium where thingly components assemble into vestments.

Grund's fashion criticism, of course—qua the nature of its genre—relies on references to individual positions in fashion production that are to be reviewed. However, in the Walter Benjamin-Archiv typescript, Grund does not point to any specific exemplars for what she considers "elegant" dress, hence treating the term in its generality really as the overall conceptual hallmark for successful fashion design, whose maximum specificity is provided by its provenance: Paris. Or, Grund is asymmetrically specific in naming—in effect calling out—those empirical cases in which she observes failures in the implementation of the principle of elegance (the mentioned German designers, and by economic proxy case the alleged fiscal debacles that were the result of Lanvin's and Chanel's short-lived forays into textile production). There exists, however, a certain streak, a tendency, in 1930s Paris couture that exemplarily embodies a number of the characteristics that Grund includes in her concept of elegance, and that in our context can serve as the counterpart to the association of Benjamin's aesthetic with the Surrealists and Schiaparelli.

If the prime characteristic of Grund's concept of elegance is the immanent animation of matter and the production of a pleasurable play of movement in and through which matter is "made light," its most prominent articulations within the fashion panorama of her and Benjamin's shared historical moment are certainly those looks which, again, gained prominence from the beginning of the 1930s, when the waistlines had moved up and the hems down. In magazines like *Vogue* and *Harper's Bazaar*, these attenuated garments were frequently shot on models adjoint to no less attenuated columns (or props thereof) (Fig. 3.9). The stylistic code in which these items registered was that of (neo-)classicism—arguably a register particularly fitted to the general photographic aesthetic of core protagonists such as George von

Figure 3.8 George Hoyningen-Huene: Model Toto Koopman in an Augustabernard evening dress. *Vogue* Paris (1934). © Hoyningen-Huene Estate Archives / Horst Estate.

Hoyningen-Huene or Horst, who perfected the transformation of studio photography into the production of clearly structured visual spaces with occasionally dramatic but always "clean" relations between light and darkness.

In these pictures—crystalline expanses whose clarity matches the parallel development of depth-of-field technologies in cinema—designs by Lanvin, Lelong, Alix, or Vionnet, frequently executed in white—one of the dominant colors of the decade—echo the stylistic inventory of antiquity, either directly or in references to empire dresses whose cuts, of course, in turn refer to (Roman) antiquity. As evening gowns from which the drama of the grand skirt is subtracted (a fashion feature that gains prominence in other parts of the fashion panorama), and frequently shaped as sleeveless sheath dresses, these designs enabled a particularly supple deployment of movement in the garment (both in the wearer and in the reacting textile). While not susceptible to the impulses of any light waft of air (no feathers or veils here), and nearly always executed in opaque cloth, these designs combined a certain rigor (as was characteristic for the neo-classical inventory) with malleability and a flowing quality, which made, from a formal standpoint, for nearly ideal realizations of a number of aspects that Grund had identified as contributing to the phenomenon of elegance (which through its distinguished character also encompasses a certain nuance of restraint).

The couturier who arguably articulated these features at the height of technical intelligence was Madeleine Vionnet (Fig. 3.9). One of her central techniques consisted in exploiting the fabric's bias to maximum effect. In the technical vocabulary of tailoring, the term "bias" refers to a woven textile's diagonal orientation—i.e., a vector that marks a 45-degree angle to the orthogonal threads of warp and weft. Initially—that is, still during the 1920s—the designer "hung" her fabrics on the bias, meaning to employ them in the tailored garment at a "biased" orientation; to later on fully embrace the procedure of cutting textiles on bias. To a growing degree, these bias techniques make a garment behave less rigidly. In either case, the "stacking" of a warp/weft pattern that is oriented in parallel to an assumed bottom seam, or the floor (as if replicating the structure of a wall), is made more malleable, while retaining the garment's stability. When "hung" on bias, threads "flow" diagonally upwards and downwards; when cut on bias, that quality is quasi sewn into the garment's infrastructure. In either case the effect is one of a different "flow" of the garment and, importantly, an increased

Figure 3.9 George Hoyningen-Huene: Model Marion Morehouse in a Vionnet dress. *Vogue* (1933). © Condé Nast/Getty Images.

elasticity. Vionnet perfected these effects into a style that looked "poured" onto the body. Her dresses frequently also lacked fasteners or zippers, needing to be put on by being pulled over the head. The garment thus gave room into space, as it adapted to the shapes of the wearer's body by stretching, while also "moving" freely.[44] The garment retained visual conciseness and precision of cut, but lacked the stiffness of an unyielding infrastructure that wouldn't transmit movement. Vionnet's particularly "sculptural" approach was also furthered by her abandoning of sketching as a design tool in favor of muslin drapes, as well as by her predilection for working with crêpe, a textile that offered both "grip" and elasticity, because it flowed optimally in the bias.[45]

Already in 1931, Martine Rénier, the editor-in-chief of *Femina*, stenographically summed up the stylistic tendencies which the exploitation of the textile's newly acquired flexibility and agility enabled, incidentally giving a concise characterization of the central characteristics of Vionnet's work: "Toujours: La taille haute, les mouvements en bias, ... l'influence de l'antique (Throughout: high waist, movement on bias, ... the influence of antiquity.)"[46] In terms of a relation to antique styles, this meant less a specific *reference* than a—no less specific and intentional—active harnessing of the properties of ancient costume for the purpose of furnishing a current aesthetic, as witnessed in Vionnet's shift from the 1920s to the 1930s. During the earlier decade, Vionnet tended to model her designs on the rectilinear *peplon*, a tunic-style garment that in its layout corresponded with the silhouette of the *garçonne* or *Neue Frau*. Moving into the 1930s, Vionnet turned to the model of the ionic *khiton*, which, with its loose handling of flowing pleats, lent itself to the demands of textile movements that dominated as of the turn of the decade (see chapter 2).[47]

The flowing quality, combined with a visual sharpness of shape, give the idea of swaths of textile pouring along and at the same time adherent to the wearer's body: a near antithesis to the visual and material obtuseness and obstinacy of the articulation of the dress as "things" that can be observed in Schiaparelli, in whose work this aesthetic not only became manifest through object-mimeses and assemblages in the vestimentary medium, but also, for instance, in the employment of so-called tree bark crêpe, a crunched fabric that gave the impression of the surface of an untreated wooden "stem" to its wearer.[48]

That these two positions are indeed two opposing poles within the stylistic options of the overall fashion aesthetic of their historical moment is suggested, for instance, in the realization and visual documentation of the *Pavillon de l'Élégance* that was set up for the 1937 Paris World Fair. It was organized by an exhibition committee which was chaired by the designer Jeanne Lanvin, housed in an extensive container structure covered in corrugated sheets, and situated on the Quai d'Orsay. Its interior was decorated with a massive set of partly architectural, partly quasi-geomorphic plaster elements set in brownish and ochre tones that evoked the impressions of a grotto (contemporaneously referred to as "Calypso's Grotto") or of a city turned to stone (Fig. 3.10).[49]

In/Elegant Materialisms 139

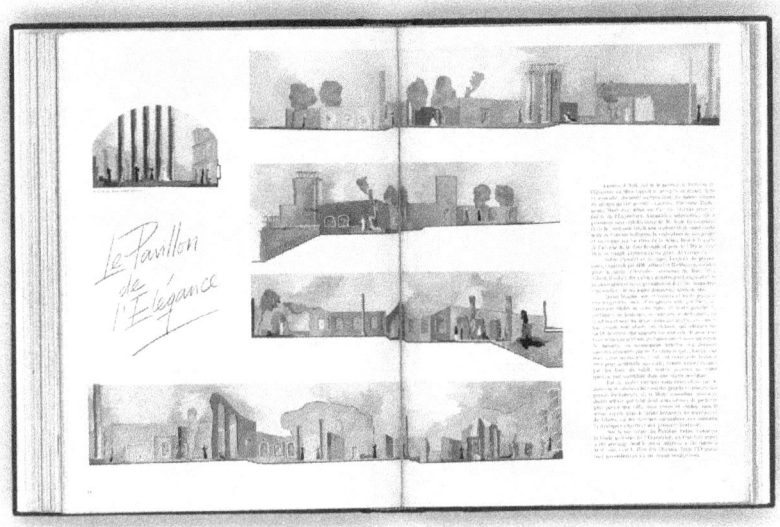

Figure 3.10 *Vogue Paris* (June 1937)—page spread. © Condé Nast.

In this scenario, 29 members of the Paris Chambre Syndicale de la Couture were invited to present a number of select creations. These were displayed on imposing, roughly textured plaster mannequins produced by the manufacturer Siégel, according to the ideas of the sculptor Robert Couturier, who had them colored in a slight rosy hue (Fig. 3.11a, 3.11b).[50] Numbering 200 and measuring over two meters in height each, they not only shunned any conventions of frail and fragile femininity, effectively requiring that all participating designers fabricate larger than life-size versions of the dresses they intended to exhibit;[51] they also tapped into an erotics and aesthetics of what we could colloquially refer to as the "imposing woman" or the female giant, which had artistic and literary precedents in nineteenth-century French culture. At the dawn of aesthetic modernism it was evoked and celebrated, for instance, in Baudelaire's sonnet "La géante," whose enunciating subject dreams of having lived a life "close to a young female giant, like a voluptuous cat at the feet of a queen" (auprès d'une jeune géante, / Comme aux pieds d'une reine un chat volupteux); or in Manet's full-body portrait of Baudelaire's lover Jeanne Duval, reported by some of the poet's contemporaries to have in reality been exceptionally tall: the 1862 *Dame à*

l'éventail depicts her as a figure of imposing proportions, reclining on a chaise longue, her voluminous dress taking up a vast amount of visual space, her massive hand holding on to an armrest.[52]

The unsettling tone of Couturier's mannequins would be developed further in a show that was also held in Paris, about half a year later, at the beginning of 1938. Refering explicitly to the earlier installment of the world fair, the Exposition Internationale du Surréalisme famously featured works on actual shop window mannequins—on one of them garments by Schiaparelli, draped by Dalí—which the movement's various protagonists and affiliates had deployed as an engagement with the spectacular logic of

Figure 3.11a, b Pavillon de l'Élégance booklet (1938). Bibliothèque Nationale de France.

commodity display while also maximizing the disquieting effects of the humanoid life-size doll—the arch-denizen of the uncanny valley. In the Pavillon de l'Élégance the uncanny stance was reinforced by the declamatory gestures which Couture chose for the execution of the mannequins.[53] They combine a capacity for curved shapes with a disquieting degree of formal underdifferentiation. Both "organic" and rigid, they give the impression of humans turned to stone, as if the Parisian high chamber of couturiers had decided to show the seasonal creations of its members on an inventory of casts from body molds in the lava fields of Herculaneum and Pompeii;[54] fashion presented on shapes that had lain dormant for millennia.

As such, Couturier's mannequins sit well with the Surrealist conception of fashion as an assemblagist and, in turn, intentionally "crudely" "mattering" medium: each dress that is presented on them stands out as an "item" in its objectness, not least because the mannequin on which it sits dramatizes its awkward warping of the proximity-yet-distance between human and object to begin with (rather than fusing the wearer's body and the dress in a single impression as Grund demanded in her theory of elegance: appreciate the garment and forget it in the same cognitive-aesthetic movement). They perform their effect even on those outfits which, by design, should escape heaviness into flights of elegance: intricately draped, stretched, and pleated garments by Vionnet and Alix.

Or, to be more precise, the mannequins perform these effects particularly well in the visual documentation of the *Pavillon de l'Élégance*, the vast majority of which was produced the young German artist Wolfgang Schulze, who, adopting for the first time in his career the pseudonym Wols, was the *Pavillon*'s official photographer and whose press pictures were sold as postcards on-site, as well as serving as the prime source for the exhibition's coverage in the pages of international magazines from *Vogue* and *Femina* to *Harper's Bazaar*. (In August 1937 Vogue Paris illustrated their editorial column "Point de vue de Vogue," with a large number of Wols's pictures.)[55] These pictures combine a crypto-Surrealist sensibility for bequeathing a sense of "psychic" personality to the mannequins with an embracing of dramatic light–dark contrast and the deployment of a rhetoric of shadows that does not stay behind the tradition of chiaroscuro dramatizations which connect German expressionist cinema of the Weimar years and Hollywood noir. In this harsh light, complemented by dramatic perspectives in which the mannequins seem to interact with each other, with their shadows, or with the camera—as if a battalion of grotesque Claymation figures had been set loose in a fashion boutique—even the most delicate draping of an Alix gown or a Vionnet sheath dress gives the impression of having been stuck to the odd humanoid shapes on which they are presented with a wet gypsum paste, and hardened into a crusty shell rather than a smoothly flowing textile (Fig. 3.12).

Figure 3.12 Wols: Mannequin at the Pavillon de l'Élégance (1937). Kunstbibliothek der Staatlichen Museen zu Berlin. @ VG Bild-Kunst, Bonn 2019.

The double tendency that becomes visible in such examples—a tendency whose two poles, in their own ways, correspond to the theoretical premises of Benjamin's and Grund's works—is perhaps best illustrated in yet another set of visual material of the period, which is only in part directly related to the fashion context.

One set of images situated at the heart of the fashion system, on the pages of *Vogue* in November 1931, is a series of pictures of the model Sonia taken by the photographer George von Hoyningen-Huene (Fig. 3.13a, 3.13b). In them Sonia wears a crêpe romaine pajama suit with matching scarf, all designed by Vionnet. Extended into a several motifs, realized as page spreads in the various editions of *Vogue*, her movement—and the movement of the garment—is light, captured in a strictly formalizing profile and reduced to a clear contrast of light/white and dark/black, which here—unlike in the case of Wols's images—is neatly separated into figure and ground. Sonia, against the generality of a black field devoid of features, seems to engage in a series of easy gaits; her elegant garment is animated into a play of drapes, curling lines, and fanning shawls. Produced in the photographer's studio by placing the model's body against a diagonally inclined black plank, her left foot carefully and discretely prodded against a nail so as to prevent her from sliding, both her body postures and the wafting drapes are all carefully arranged by the photographer who thus produced a *Bas-Relief*—this is the series' title—for his fashion present (Fig. 3.14).[56] We could position this work against other types of photographic bas-reliefs, made about the same time, not for a fashion context, but by Surrealist artists, such as Raoul Ubac. In his series *Penthésilées*, Ubac transforms a group of female figures, some nude, some veiled, through a combination of procedures such as photomontage and multiple solarisations into unsettling pictures in which the exactness of the lens-based image of the human body fuses with the appeal of ashen stone. The human bodies are sunk into the gray materiality of the picture plane, giving the impression of a bas-relief, but a deadly one, which has half swallowed the formerly distinct and freely moving figures.[57] This juxtaposition of Hoyningen-Huene's and Ubac's works—we could think of a number of the latter's other pictures executed by employing the so-called paraglyph technique which visually turn the visual motif into petrified scenarios; fossils of culture, as it were—pinpoints a central double tendency theorized by Grund and Benjamin with regard to fashion form: one animates matter, the other dis-animates it; one teases lightness and movement out of the garment, the other makes the vestment appear heavy and imposing, weighty.

In/Elegant Materialisms 145

Figure 3.13a George Hoyningen-Huene: Model Sonia in Vionnet pale crepe romain pajamas. *Vogue* (1931). © Hoyningen-Huene Estate Archives / Horst Estate.

Figure 3.13b George Hoyningen-Huene: Model Sonia in Vionnet pale crepe romain pajamas. *Vogue* (1931). © Condé Nast/Getty Images.

Figure 3.14 V*ogue Paris* (November 1931)—page spread. © Condé Nast.

Both have a correlate in the field of visual-medial fiction in Jean Cocteau's film *Le sang d'un poète*, which opened the decade, and in which Lee Miller serves as a flesh-and-blood counterpart to a classicizing white statue—presumably plaster. She is, over the course of the film's meandering, Surrealist maneuvers and plays of substitution, superimposed with her figural peer, producing sliding montages, visual dissolves, as well as (through the frankly theatrical use of make-up) being positioned between states of animation and collapse into the inanimate (Fig. 3.15a-d).

In their joint reference to the formal repertoire of (Greek) antiquity, all of these also point to the latent script that informs these different theoretical and artistic approaches to fashion. It is Ovid's *Metamorphoses* from which two plots are here culled and set against each other: Pygmalion's Galatea, and the story of Niobe, or, if we look to Schiaparelli's couture shapeshifts (such as the tree bark crêpe dress, or other garments whose ornaments and patterns took the forms of leaves and plants), the story of the sylph Daphne, turned into a bush of reeds.[58] One is the story of a marble statue coming to life; the others are stories of moving bodies turning into motionless mineral and vegetal forms. Beyond and bereft of their plots and characters, and twisting their eminent elaborations of questions of

3.15a

3.15b

Figure 3.15a–d Lee Miller in Jean Cocteau's "Le Sang d'un Poète," (1930), prod. Charles de Noialles, filmstills.

figuration (i.e., the protocols of passages from one state into another), they now help model the transformations of material and matter played out in all of these fashion programs, as well as their discursive elaborations.[59]

Versions of inertia: Persistence of the fashion form

The two poles within the fashion poetics and practice of 1930s Paris charted here do not exist as self-declared "positions," and, in spite of the possibility of being to an extent associated with individual couturiers and œuvres—Schiaparelli and Vionnet—they do not represent the outcome of explicitly formulated artistic "programs." The same holds for their respective associations with the theories of Grund and Benjamin (which, like each of the couturiers' œuvres, in themselves of course are deliberately developed). Rather, it seems most plausible to think of them as stylistic options and tendencies that emerge from processes and interactions that play out within the layers and relations—design choices, criticism, theorizing, economic, technological, in relation to the properties of textiles, options for mediation, etc—that make up the fashion context of their moment.

The common vantage point under which they are considered here, and which in their contrasting perspectives indeed functions like a hinge for them, could be seen as the "treatment" of matter, or as an elaboration of the problem of material. One core feature of Grund's concept of elegance is the immanent animation of matter, and Vionnet's works indeed provide examples for formally concise yet flowing, sharply tailored yet undulating garments in which materiality becomes "light." Benjamin's explorations of Apollinaire's and Baudelaire's literary fashion poetics both amounted to an "aggravation" of matter, a subtraction of inherent potentials for its animation—a "deadening," if one will; a making steady, yet also devoid of motion (which, in turn, may appear in a flash only)—the production of inertia. The corresponding programs in Surrealist fashion displays and couture are the articulations of the dress as a "thing," emphases of its obdurate objectness which either riffs off the freakish body of the mannequin or which, through couture strategies, is mimetically transformed into the appearance of other things, and in this gaining prominence is placed as a thing among things.

We are now in the position to make another observation regarding Benjamin's theory of the "obdurate," "weighty" fashion form: its condition as form, and the corresponding aspect of materiality it conveys, rely, again, on an intervention in the temporal dimension that corresponds with an operation of fragmentation. In contrast to Grund's theory of elegance, Benjamin's development of the monumental and monumentally fragmented fashion form relies on the idea of the withdrawal of temporalization from the immanence of the fashion phenomenon and its deployment as that phenomenon's contextualization. This fragmentation, this interruption, however, does not attack the integrity of the material in which it is conveyed and couched: there is no "chopping up" of language or of the fashion form here, which—as described earlier in the cases of Apollinaire and Schiaparelli—is conserved in its integrity. The emphasis lies on the withdrawal of the capacity of temporalizing the material and its various segments, of "fixating" it, and this results in the impression of "inertia."

This implies, further, that the theory of the inert form that we are considering here differs categorically from other epistemic *dispositifs* in which weight and its lifting, the heavy and the light, were thought. One approach that comes to mind is Simmel's, as formulated, for instance, in his "Aesthetics of Gravity" (Aesthetik der Schwere). In that short text, taking his central cues from Rodin's sculpture, Simmel develops an idea of the aesthetic object in which, as he explains, two opposing forces—gravity and will—generate form as a result of their conflict.[60] In comparison, the Benjaminian "aggravation" of form, its drift toward petrification, does not rely on a comparable vectorialist approach. Benjamin does not think of textile—or the body—as a site upon which opposing forces engage with one another, and in such a contest produce a certain quality of that form. Rather, the quality of "gravity" emerges once material has been momentously been removed from the working of time, just as the gravity and gravitas of Baudelaire's *passante* with her majestic hand have been thrown into stasis, not as the result of the interplay of kinetic forces. In this, his approach is again congruent with a Surrealist (fashion) aesthetic.

Even at the risk of stating the obvious, it is perhaps helpful to point out that, in contrast to Simmel's champion Rodin, no Surrealist sculpture, from Max Ernst to Man Ray, or even Giacometti in his brief moment of affiliation with the movement, thrives on a comparable rhetoric of imbuing and permeating material, preferably marble, with the (illusion of) forces. This is particularly evident, for instance, in the mannequins—essentially thrift store and flea market assemblages—that formed part of the First International Surrealist Exposition in Paris in 1938. Here it was precisely the assemblage-character that, while articulating the material presence of the component objects, never fuses into a material continuum in and through which such 'forces of form' could be deployed. It is also the case for the designs of Schiaparelli, in which the effect of "thingly" concretion is achieved through object-mimeses, the transformation of the supple into the fixed, or the material juxtaposition of textile and object; not through a formal elaboration of force and counter-force—i.e., not through engaging with a rhetoric of gravity.

The non-givenness of material

There are at least two interrelated instances in which Benjamin employs the term "material" in a manner that could help us outline the particular operations of his and Grund's fashion theories in this domain more clearly; and their suitability is partly due to the fact that Benjamin, in both cases, concerns himself with a phenomenon that is situated in close proximity to his and Grund's elaborations on the question of fashion, namely movement. There is, first, the description in the artwork essay of the filmic take (i.e., a moving image) as the material from which the editor composes the film in the process of montage: "The sequence of positional views [Stellungnahmen], which the editor composes from the material supplied (to) him constitutes the completely edited film" (Die Folge von Stellungnahmen, die der Cutter aus dem ihm abgelieferten Material komponiert, bildet den fertig montierten Film).[61] There is, second, the passage in the later version of Benjamin's two essays on Brecht's epic theater (which Benjamin, along with Brecht, describes as fundamentally "gestural" [gestisch]): "The gesture is its material and its task is the purposive utilization of this material" (Die Geste ist sein Material, und die zweckmäßige Verwertung dieses Materials seine Aufgabe).[62] (In an alternative version, Benjamin refers to Brechtian gesture as "raw material" [Rohmaterial]).[63]

These two examples display, firstly, certain particular traits compared to what one would or could, as per common sense, understand by "material." For one, rather than operating with a concept of material as a *given*, as a set point of departure, both quotes present it as the result of prior processes: the filmic take is, obviously, the result of a camera recording, and also gestures Benjamin understood as having been *produced*, albeit unconventionally: for him they are the result of an interruption of actions and movement. Pointing to the primacy of caesuras in Brecht's theater practice ("the interrupting of action stands in the foreground in epic theater" [für das epische Theater steht die Unterbrechung im Vordergunde]), Benjamin characterizes gestures through "strict, framelike closure" and declares, "the more frequently we interrupt someone engaged in an action, the more gestures we obtain" (Gesten erhalten wir um so mehr, je häufiger wir einen Handelnden unterbrechen).[64]

Keeping this in mind is helpful in our present context as it reminds us that—at least on Benjamin's side of in/elegant materialism—we shouldn't assume a ready availability of "material" which the obdurate fashion form would simply "expose." There is no prior matter "onto" which form would be cast. Benjamin's is not a hylomorphic position. To put it differently, neither Benjamin's Baudelairean understanding of the fashion form, nor the Surrealist fashion poetics of, for instance, Schiaparelli, would be in the position to articulate the "obdurate" character of a fashionable dress by merely employing (or pointing to) a type of textile manufactured from a heavy, less supple, densely woven thread, which would put more grams on a scale per meter as compared to a "lighter" type of cloth.

This is, of course, not to deny the relevance of such positive qualities for an analysis of work from the perspective of construction. Regarding the fashions of the 1930s, the flowing qualities of gowns by Vionnet or Alix rely centrally on a number of technological innovations in the production of textiles, such as new silks and synthetics; new featherweight silk gauzes, muslins, and chiffons, all based on refinements of the jacquard loom; new finishing techniques and the employment of lamé, which allowed for a metallic finish while preserving a relatively light weight; as well as the incorporation of new fibers such as rayon and high-twist threads, which allowed for suppleness and elasticity.[65] But a dress by Vionnet, while making ample use of these achievements, does not "expose" these qualities. Rather, the classicizing interface, the undulating, elegantly plunging form is emphasized, not the innovative threads or the revolutionary method of constructing on bias. Consider, on a related note, the way in which the material of Vionnet's work engages with the force of gravity. Rather than visualizing or exposing its pull in the textile medium, the principle of working on the bias harnesses gravity's impact in order to stretch and "liquify" the garment, as it were, enhancing its flowing quality and generating the impression of lightness. Techno-aesthetically shrewd, this procedure does not aim to articulate the matter of textile in its actual weight, but rather to transform it into a medium in which movement, not at least the movement of its wearer, becomes visible. Vionnet's is a similar intention to Schiaparelli's, Grund's, or Benjamin's. There is never a recourse to matter through the category of material here as positive.

A further point at which Benjamin's conception differs from other materialist frameworks that operate with the notion of a positive recourse to material (with which he was indeed familiar) is exemplified in the field of architecture. In the *Arcades Project* we find at least one convolute that, qua its thematic dedication, would seem ideally suited for such elaborations on the question of "material"; namely convolute F on "Iron Construction." (There is, of course, also the early fragment "The Ring of Saturn, or Something on Iron Construction" [Der Saturnring oder Etwas vom Eisenbau]). This is not only due to the fact that the fragments and notes collected in the convolute revolve around one, if not *the* most central material for the development of modernist architecture, namely iron (or its derivate, steel). This convolute is also, arguably, closest to a perspective developed in a text that must be regarded as Benjamin's most important source for questions of architecture and, given the *Arcades Project*'s centering around an *architectural* figure, namely the *passage*, one of the central points of departure for Benjamin's whole undertaking: Sigfried Giedion's 1927 *Building in France*.

In his study and manifesto, Giedion famously deduced a formal language for modernist architecture through a recourse to the physical and constructional qualities of steel (and glass) as *material(s)*. While Benjamin clearly acknowledges the logics of these arguments, he no less clearly does not make them his own. On the contrary, the overall logic of Benjamin's argument focuses on the asynchronies—anticipations, misuses, etc—of manifestations of iron and glass which he recognizes in the architectures of the nineteenth century. This is an essential complication as well as the indispensable prerequisite for his critique of the Giedionian idea of a deduction of forms through an immediate recourse to material and its properties, and of Giedion's concomitant program of merely dispensing with any such asynchronies, failures, phantasmagoric overdrives, etc that did not deliver such straightforward recursion. Again in line with Surrealists, and ultimately Freud, the category of "material" in Benjamin's project would seem to refer much rather to the (unconsciously) articulated, already formed productions of drives, wishes, etc that need to be *worked through*, rather than material that needs to "worked" in the production of form.

One crucial difference would lie in Benjamin's equation of the infrastructural element of iron construction, not, as Giedion does, with repressed psychological content to be "uncovered" and "retrieved," but rather to the *bodily process*—a stratum that, in Freud's model, interferes in psychological production, but that is not susceptible to hermeneutic, interpretative, etc approaches. Closer to a media-archaeological Kittlerian notion of the "technical real," "material" here would form a framing and enabling condition, rather than the object of a potential uncovering, referencing, etc.[66]

These examples demonstrate that to assume a positive recourse to the stratum of the material—including the concomitant assumption of its mere "given-ness"—would be equivalent to assuming that Benjamin's interest in the realm of things could form the basis of a hypothetical materialism. The dedication to the world of *Dinge*, in particular those of his childhood, which we find primarily in Benjamin's literary works, is of course undeniable, but it is *physiognomic*—an approach whose compatibility with the framework of (historical) materialism, as Benjamin's first editors have pointed out, is questionable.[67] We may add that such a physiognomic approach would be equally difficult to reconcile with Benjamin's professed anthropological materialism, which—contra Adorno's reproach—with its basis in a media-technologically articulated history of perception (Wahrnehmung) clearly did have a material and historical dimension.[68] It has, further, been convincingly argued that categories such as the fetish and phantasmagoria—quasi-objects—would have had their place in this framework.[69] But "things," in the sense of concrete objects, would not have been its points of departure.[70] Rather, its primary points of departure would have laid, as mentioned, in the realm of media-technology and perception.

The argument doesn't merely concern Benjamin's share. It also touches on fashion practice—for instance, Schiaparelli's. As laid out above, the articulation of the "objectness" of dress as one of the characteristics of the obdurate fashion form is the result of a number of formal strategies: mimeses, disruptions, arrangements, and assemblages, etc; or, in the case of Baudelaire's fashion poetics, of a subtraction of temporality from the immanence of the fashion phenomenon—neither of which amounts to "pointing" or "referring" to the dress-as-a-thing, or to "exposing" its materiality. As a matter of fact, the counter-example which we have been investigating—the elegant designs of Vionnet—serves to prove the point as well: the effect of its elegance does not rely on *canceling* the factor of its materiality from its appearance. If that were the case, Vionnet's craft—or Grund's theory—would call for a cutting down, a making transparent of cloth—both operations that would yield quite different effects, obviously. Rather, what Grund in her writing calls "forgetting the dress," and what we have referred to as an "unmarking," amounts to a "making light" of matter, not its immaterialization or subtraction.[71]

The idea that the base for such operations within the realm of fashion could be the dress as a material entity would also fail to take into account the fact, pointed out by Caroline Evans, that even in the 1920s the prime economic entity, in the sense of a commodity, wasn't necessarily manufactured dresses. Rather, while French fashion houses, of course, did produce garments, their business could rely just as much on selling patterns and the rights to execute them (i.e., intellectual and aesthetic property)—for instance, to manufacturers in the United States who would retail these items on the North American market under the label of the French houses.[72] In other words, licensing is part and parcel of the commercial aspects of fashion, and so is the production and marketing of knowledge. Rather than merely and straightforwardly manufacturing garments, fashion, in its industrial and commercial form, revolves around designs in the full sense of the term. This coincides with the insight that the material base of fashion is not the dress-object, but rather a look, rules for its execution, instructions for its production, and skills, including its complex *materializations*.

None other than Madeleine Vionnet, the master of individualized construction and the harnessing of the techno-material properties of textiles for the purposes of elegant couture, realized this and sought to control the resulting runaway processes of copying. She lobbied successfully to institute intellectual and artistic property rights for designers, depositing her designs with the Office National de la Propriété Industrielle; she also fought lawsuits against unauthorized replicas, successfully arguing that a revolutionary law from 1793 which protected "créations artistiques" should also apply to "modèles de robes, costumes et manteaux" (in addition to a law from 1909 that protected couture creations), as well as founding the Association de Protection Artistique des Industries Saisonnières in 1921, which existed until its dissolution through the German occupiers. She also devised a label that was sewn into her designs, which included both replicas of her signature and her fingerprint, in order to indelibly mark a vestment's origin in her house, and went on a publicity offensive, taking out ads in fashion publications that were intended to educate potential customers that the original products of her *maison* could not be purchased through subsidiaries ("Madame Vionnet ne vend ni aux commissaires, ni aux couturières").[73] She, finally, instituted photographic documentations of her creations against mirrored corners in which the full three-dimensional extension of the dress and its make would be prismatically broken down and folded onto a single picture plane, the so-called copyright shot (Fig. 3.16a-b).[74]

Photography was instrumental in documenting the entirety and the make of a given outfit, and was thus harnessed for the purpose of fixating a position of verifiability within the described economy of licensing. More the equivalent of a technical drawing submitted along with a patent, the copyright shot charted the engineering of a dress, precisely because the dress, as a material entity, was only one particular instantiation of the fashion commodity, the pattern to be copied, including its dynamics for potentially economically uncontrolled–read illicit, pirated—reproduction.

Materialism à la mode

If none of these frameworks provide us with the possibility of elucidating the approach to material and materialism latent in Benjamin's and Grund's fashion theories, a more promising road perhaps leads through a reinvestigation of the two quotes from the artwork essay and Benjamin's analysis of Brecht's work.

What, then, do Benjamin's cast of the filmic take and the *gestus* on the epic theater have in common? One hint lies in Benjamin's addressing the camera shot as a *Stellungnahme*, a taking position. It is clear that Benjamin not merely implies advocating a certain viewpoint here, taking a stance, or making a declaration, all of which are meanings comprised in the original German

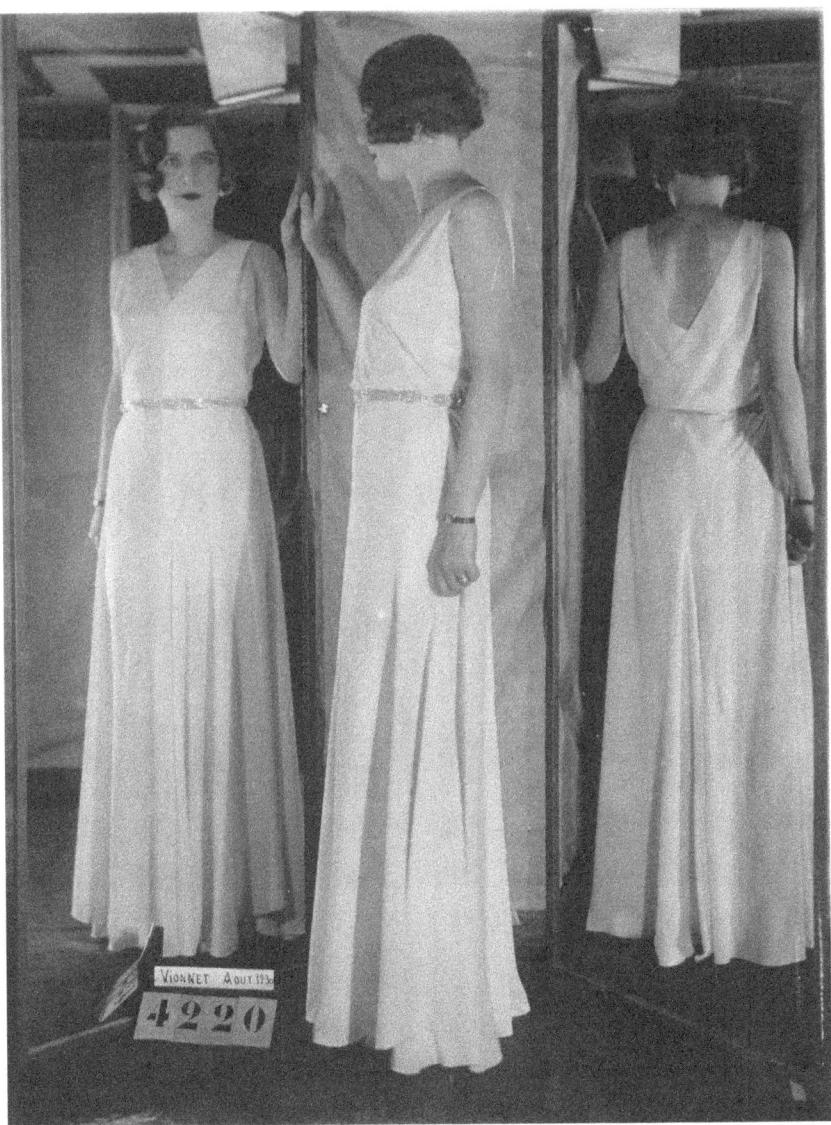

Figure 3.16a Maison Vionnet, copyright shot (collection winter 1930, model 4220). Paris, Musée des Arts décroatifs—collection UFAC. Copyright MAD.

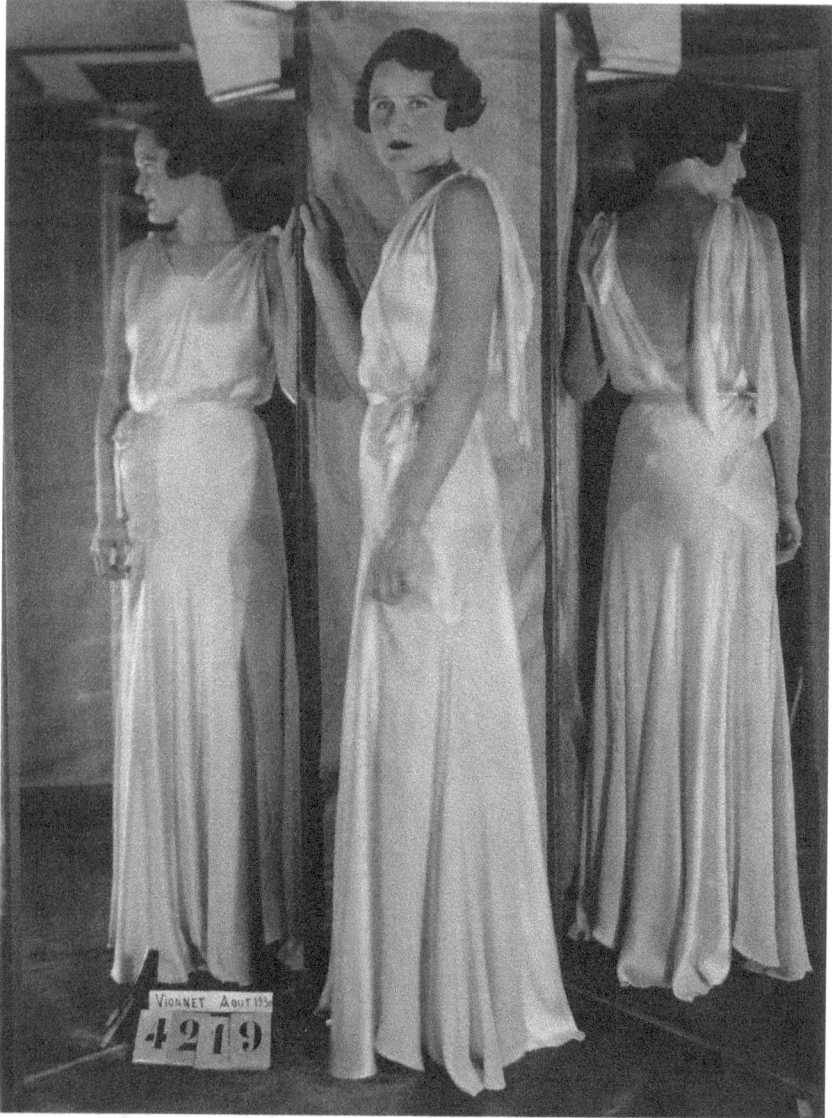

Figure 3.16b Maison Vionnet, copyright shot (collection winter 1930, model 4219). Paris, Musée des Arts décroatifs—collection UFAC. Copyright MAD.

expression. Rather, Benjamin here also varies the word *Einstellung* (*Stellungnahme/Ein-Stellung*), the *terminus technicus* for the filmic shot, which also signifies "attitude" or "stance": the shot is the stance—to formulate the idea that what the camera shows is coeval to the articulation of a stance *toward* what it shows. Such a positional theorem is, of course, also central to the Brechtian concept of the *gestus*, to which Benjamin refers as *gestural*. In Brecht's theater theory (and its concomitant practice), the idea of *gestus* is closely related to *habitus*, indicating a stance, position, and attitude that describes the way in which an actor on stage performs a certain action or movement, implying both its fundamental iterability and ability for modification according to a different (in turn iterable or, famously, "quotable") *gestus* in which said action or movement is executed. The execution as filtered through varying *gestus* would enable varying perspectivations onto the performed actions and movements.[75]

In what way, then, could the concept of the filmic take as *Stellungnahme* and Brecht's (self-declared "materialist") concept of gesture help us model the materialist dimension of Benjamin's—and Grund's—fashion theories? The answer lies in the capacity, comprised in both theorems, of adopting a stance, view, *gestus*, and of casting an *Einstellung* onto something. Or, more precisely, of providing modes of articulation in which matter as material would be cast in such an *Einstellung*, *gestus*, or mode.[76] While obviously by far not the only characteristics in these two fields (film, Brechtian theater), shot and gesture are each examples of a specific kind of form—a form that filters that which is formed in a particular way, that presents it in a certain mode. This may be an apt way to consider the way in which Benjamin and Grund theorize the articulation of matter in their writings; both assume that specific formal interventions will make certain traits of matter appear in and through the fashion form: elegance reveals matter's lightness; the obdurate brings out matter's "rigidity." Or, to slightly restate this, elegance means to cast matter as light; the obdurate casts matter as obstinate and resistant. The place of "material" and of "materialism" in these two fashion theories would, then, coincide with the intersection of form and matter, and they would mark out the possibility of such a revelatory component in which, through this or that specific form, certain traits and qualities are brought to light.

On this basis we are now in the position of making a few further observations regarding the materialist element of Benjamin's and Grund's fashion theories. Rather than operating with the assumption that matter can be seen as having an essence—an essence that could be understood as calling for being articulated in a set and determinate repertoire of forms, which could in turn be understood as "expressing" the essence of matter (and dignifying it through elevating it to the level of cognition)—we find a model in which certain formal operations, in their articulation of matter as material, bring to light certain *aspects* of matter.[77] Matter, by consequence, would then appear as having certain *potentials* rather than bundles of essence. Matter has the potential for lightness *and* heaviness, for seeming animated or inert, rather than "being" any of these to begin with.

In particular in view of the specific set of features that we find in Benjamin's and Grund's theories the pairing of lightness and heaviness, of animation and "mortification," we can extend this situating operation both with regard to our own contemporary panorama of critical theory and to the current dispositions of so-called "new materialism," which rejects the idea of matter as inert, or dead.[78] Held against this setting, one specificity of the Benjaminian/Grundian approach becomes clear: whereas this recent perspective tends to reverse the valuation of matter along the axis between what is considered animate and what is inanimate, opting against the alleged dominance in "modern" thinking of approaches that conceptualize matter as "dead," Benjamin's and Grund's fashion theories do not fall on either side of the debate, hence also not engaging in a similar operation of reversal. Rather, the animate and the inanimate, just like the light and the inert, are potentials that both inhere matter, which can be coaxed out through the appropriate fashion/formal operations. Matter here is *neither* dead *nor* alive, neither animated nor inert—and not because it couldn't be materialized as such through the corresponding interventions. Rather, in Benjamin's and Grund's model, the predication "matter is …" in the strong meaning of an ontological assertion, doesn't make sense.[79]

In Benjamin's and Grund's fashion theories, form via the category of material articulates a quality, rather than an essence of matter, and matter is not conceived as an ontologically set entity, but rather as an agglomeration of potentials to be articulated through form. And, with an eye to a point made earlier, we could speak of the mode of being that fashion assigns to matter as formed material. To make this point is not to claim the intellectual heritage of Grund and Benjamin for the sake of legitimizing the neo-ontologies into which actor-network theory has now turned. It is even less to assume an intellectual genealogy, which clearly does not exist here.[80] Rather, this is a reverse operation, in which what is currently being widely discussed is referred back to a regularly overlooked and excluded context in which related questions have stood at the center of attention for quite some time indeed. As already indicated in chapter 1, the derivation of the term *mode* (i.e., fashion) from *modernité* is misleading and tends to obfuscate the relation between *la mode* on the one hand, and those *modes*, grammatical and logical, by which various types or manifestations of being were referred to on the other. This is to assert that with Benjamin's and Grund's writings, or with the practices of Schiaparelli and Vionnet, we do have examples for thinking of the modality of matter through the rather unexpected detour of fashion, and that, while materialism is currently distinctly *en vogue*, (re)turning to the materialism à la mode framed by fashion and its theories seems a leap worth taking.

4

The Tiger's Leap and the Expression of History

The charm of the previous century

On one occasion in the *Arcades Project*, Benjamin opens a direct window into his own fashion present and its past. Among the systematic reflections in convolute N ("Epistemology and Critique of Progress") we find the following observation, part of which was already quoted (in chapter 1):

> The stream gradient of every fashion current ... originates from what is forgotten. This downstream flow is ordinarily so strong that only the group can give itself up to it; the individual – the precursor – is liable to collapse in the face of such violence, as happened with Proust. In other words: what Proust, as an individual, directly experienced in the phenomenon of remembrance, we have to experience indirectly (with regard to the nineteenth century) in studying 'current,' 'fashion,' 'tendency' – a punishment, if you will, for the sluggishness which kept us from taking it up ourselves.
>
> AP 393, TM

> *Jede Strömung der Mode ... hat ihr Gefälle vom Vergessen her. Es ist so stark, daß gewöhnlich nur der Verband sich ihm überlassen kann, der einzelne – der Vorläufer – droht unter ihrer Gewalt zusammenzubrechen, wie es Proust geschehen ist. Mit anderen{n} Worten: was Proust am Phänomen des Eingedenkens als Individuum erlebte, das haben wir – wenn man so will als Strafe für die Trägheit, die uns hinderte, es auf uns zu nehmen – zu 'Strömung,' 'Mode,' 'Richtung' (aufs neunzehnte Jahrhundert) zu erfahren.*
>
> PW 496/97

What occurs only in brackets here—the connection between questions of fashion's systemic implementation as a chronotechnics and the specific temporal location of the moment at which these reflections are formed; or to be more exact, the location between the moment of articulation of these reflections and a different specific point in history—is even more pronounced in a different passage in which Benjamin observes that "contemporary fashion" (die gegenwärtige Mode) is fixated on the "charm ... of the previous century" (AP 458) (Reiz ... des vergangenen Jahrhunderts [PW 572]).

For both observations, Helen Grund's work provided cues that are quoted in the *Arcades Project*: in *On the Essence of Fashion* she talks about the general connection between the past and the present in fashion: couturiers "are inspired by the ... ferment ... which the busy present day can offer. But since no present moment is ever fully cut off from the past, the latter will also offer attractions to the creator" (AP 72) (their inspiration "entzündet sich an den ...

Figure 4.1 Edouard Manet: Berthe Morisot With a Bouquet of Violets (1872), oil on canvas. Wikimedia.

Anregungen, ... die eine bewegte Aktualität bietet. Da nun aber keine Gegenwart sich völlig von der Vergangenheit loslöst, bietet ihm auch die Vergangenheit Anregung" [PW 122]). She also provides a concrete example from her, and Benjamin's, fashion present that establishes exactly the connection between the 1930s and the nineteenth century which Benjamin intimates: "The small hat tipped forward over the forehead, a style we owe to the Manet exhibition, demonstrates quite simply our new readiness to confront the end of the previous century" (AP 72, TM) (Das in die Stirn gerückte Hütchen, das wir der Manet-Ausstellung zu verdanken haben, beweist nichts anderes als daß wir eine neue Bereitschaft haben, uns mit dem Ende des vorigen Jahrhunderts auseinanderzusetzen [PW 122]).

There was indeed a prominent Manet exhibition in Paris about that time: in 1932, on the occasion of what would have been the painter's hundredth birthday, a show of his works was staged at the Musée de l'Orangerie in the Tuileries Gardens. Paul Valéry, at this point already a member of the Academie française, was enlisted to write the preface for the catalog. Towards the end of the ten-page piece, Valéry turns to a single painting included in the show, and dedicates several paragraphs to a sustained contemplation of it: an 1872 portrait which Manet painted of his fellow artist Berthe Morisot (Fig. 4.1).

Valéry opens with an assessment of the painting's blunt color impact: "Above all, black" (Avant toute chose, le Noir); he closes with the realization that the appeal and affect which the painting exerts is the result of a structural feature that complements the first impression of monolithic darkness with a system of juxtapositions and opposites:[1]

> For the moment I can say that the portrait of which I am speaking is a poem. Through the strange harmony of colors, through the dissonance of their forces; through the opposition of the elusive and ephemeral detail of a hairstyle from days gone by [coiffure de jadis] with the *je ne sais quoi* of a quite tragic expression of the figure, Manet makes his work ... resonate with the firmness of his art.
>
> *Je puis dire à moment que le portrait dont je parle est poème. Par l'harmonie étrange des couleurs, par la dissonance de leurs forces; par l'opposition du détail futile et éphémère d'une coiffure de jadis avec je ne sais quoi d'assez tragique dans l'expression de la figure, Manet fait résonner son œuvre ... à la fermeté de son art.*[2]

What Valéry here calls the firmness of Manet's art—presumably an assertion of its lasting character—thus correlates with the "ephemeral detail of a hairstyle of bygone days" marking its subject's belonging to an aesthetic past that is no longer *au courant*. The construction of this opposition between the transitory and even evanescent and the long-term solidity, perhaps even "timeless" appeal of Manet's art here clearly sounds a Baudelairean note in its combination of the ephemeral and the eternal. And so does the mention of "the black of a hat that forms part of a mourning garb" (le noir d'un chapeau de deuil), which recalls the "grand deuil" in which Baudelaire's fashionable passerby encountered the subject from whose perspective the sonnet "A une passante" is articulated (see chapter 3).

And then there is Valéry's description of the artfully casual, convoluted, and also stiff and propped-up black pattern that surrounds the painted face. He declares that "[t]he full might of these black tones" (La toute puissance de ces noires) is intricately bound up with "the bizarre silhouette of the hat that used to be 'of the latest fashion' and 'young'" (la bizarre silhouette du chapeau qui fut 'à la dernière mode' et 'jeune').[3] The image of Berthe Morisot, dating to 1872 and exhibited 60 years later at the Orangerie thus manifests in 1932 a rather complex pattern of forms and aesthetics values/valuations in time: the arc of the sitter's hat strikes the viewer as bizarre, prompting him to note that at the time of this image's making, that shape will have looked young, fresh, and in style, and implying it no longer does. The painting registers a form that has gone out of fashion; it communicates its outdatedness.

There is an irony to Valéry's assessment, because—as Grund relates to Benjamin—it is precisely in the area of millinery that a return of nineteenth-century styles into fashion became palpable, one example being the influence of the Manet show. And, surveying the fashion collections of the later 1930s, this idea indeed does not seem far-fetched. It is quite visible, in particular—again—in the work of Schiaparelli. A number of hats she confectioned for her collections indeed did approach the shapes of millinery that could be observed in Manet's paintings; such a connection seems at least plausible if we compare, for instance, the representation of female millinery on canvases such as *Au Père Duthuile*, or *Argenteuil*—which were included in the Orangerie show—and a number of indeed rather miniscule headpieces, more like fascinators, with which Schiaparelli completed several outfits that channeled nineteenth-century riding habits.⁴ The parallel is even more tangible in cases such as a black ostrich feather and tulle creation combined with a black and blue velvet jacket emulating a tartan pattern in her Fall 1939 collection, and the Morisot portrait, both of which not only share the rather extravagant silhouette that Valéry found remarkable in the case of the portrait.⁵ Both also display the characteristic positioning—a trend, we might say—of tilting the headgear into a forward slant, so that its brim covers the wearer's forehead. Although in these cases what might have begun as a small accessory would have gained quite considerable volume, hence no longer qualifying as the "small hats" which Benjamin reports Grund mentioning. The effect was particularly strong in the fashion drawings of Bérard, whom Vogue employed to produce illustrations of Schiaparelli's 1938 Circus collection, on the occasion of which the draughtsman produced lightly brushed imagery whose starkly contrasting black and white tones and the visual construction of figures and headgear from a stacked system of blotches could be seen as approximating Manet's oil sketches of Berthe Morisot.⁶

The fashionable engagement with the nineteenth century was driven home most explicitly in Schiaparelli's aptly termed Belle Epoque collection, her penultimate show before the outbreak of World War II, created on the occasion of the 50th anniversary of the Eiffel Tower's construction—a monument that had, of course, been erected for a World Fair, like the one that Paris had celebrated in 1937 when the *Pavillon de l'Élégance* was put on display, and which showcased the constructive possibilities of steel, an engineering feat of the nineteenth century (Fig. 4.2).

In her collection, Schiaparelli not only replicated the silhouettes and looks of late nineteenth-century Paris, only shunning the original metal-wire infrastructure that held up the crinoline. She also brought back the famed *cul de Paris*—the bustle—and skirt shapes that approached the extensions of nineteenth-century models. *Vogue Paris* had detected the first signs of interest in the *pouf de 1880* in Schiaparelli's (as well as Patou's) dresses as early as 1934, but in real Schiaparelli style, the 1939 collection succinctly bundled this tendency into an overall look.⁷

True to her principle of using garments as a medium for the articulation and projection of witty images and references, Schiaparelli here incorporated— as a print on one gown—the curvy silhouette of a Belle Epoque lady, or at least

Figure 4.2 François Kollar: Three Models from Elsa Schiaparelli's Spring-Summer 1939 Collection (1939). Kunstbibliothek der Staatlichen Museen zu Berlin. © Mediathèque de l'architecture et du patrimoine, Charenton le Pont.

one image of a Belle Epoque lady (Fig. 4.3). The pattern is in all likelihood based on a drawing by Vertès showing Mae West, whose hourglass shape Schiaparelli herself had helped model into that of a late nineteenth-century bombshell when designing the Hollywood star's costumes for *Every Day's a Holiday* two years earlier (see chapter 2).[8]

Schiaparelli's work here presents us with another version of the fashion/cinema loop that is bent to serve her operative principle of projecting and/or inscribing concise, metamorphic imagery onto the medium of the dress, visually approximating it to a piece of furniture (the drawer suit) or the

Figure 4.3 Maison Schiaparelli, design sketch (collection spring–summer 1939). Paris, Musée des Arts décroatifs—collection UFAC. Copyright MAD, Paris / Christophe Delliäre.

substitute of a body part (the hat as a stand-in for the sexual organ), or exaggerating the female silhouette to such an extent that it became the equivalent of a tailor's dummy, the extravagant shape of Mae West, which also figured as a perfume bottle, or, as in the present case, the recourse to the nineteenth century. In each case, the cinematic screen and the medium of the dress are conceived as mutually reinforcing factors, beyond any questions of elegance or movement.[9] (Stylistically, Schiaparelli's contributions to the costumes of Robert Bresson's first film, the 1945 *Les Dames du Bois de Boulogne*, proved that, if necessary, the rhetorical extravagances of her signature hard-edge chic could also be toned down and produce effects that were indeed close to the ideal of elegance, an aesthetic space she shared in Bresson's film with Vionnet's fellow classicist Alix, alias Mme Grès, who also contributed costumes. The work of both designers had been picked by the director for his actresses, and both bodies of fashion work had been cineaesthetically edited down, as it were—Grès looking less romantically "Grecian" to a nearly equal degree as Schiaparelli looked less strange, as if both had been subjected to Bresson's in/famous directing method, by which his cast would produce the desired mode of inexpressive delivery.)

Schiaparelli's fashionable reappropriation of her cinematically amplified work, and the concomitant appropriation of Belle Epoque styles, would come full circle in another contemporary film, as well as in the form of a cinematic afterthought in a production 15 years after the Eiffel anniversary collection. The contemporary piece is, again, a work by Marcel L'Herbier, who in 1939 directed a short promotional film commissioned by the Chambre syndicale de la couture to be screened at that year's World Fair in New York. Far from L'Herbier's highly stylized visual language and geometrically patterned sets that characterized *L'Argent*, in which Brigitte Helm modeled the affluent sinuousness of Jacques Manuel's film-fitted Louiseboulanger gowns (see chapter 2), *La Mode rêvée* switches between the public spaces of Paris—streets, the Tuileries Gardens, the Louvre—and shots from the interiors of fashion salons. The film transcends a realist agenda and synchronizes with the fashion agenda of the moment, through a stylistic proto-fantastical device. An American film star comes to Paris and on a visit to the Louvre falls asleep in front of Watteau's 1717 canvas *Embarkation for Cythera*. The film engages in a dream logic and, through superimposition replacing the personnel of the rococo bucolic scene with real actors, has a group of young actresses "climbing out of the painting" and escaping onto the streets and salons of Paris, where they rush, roam, and shop, dressed in wide, historic gowns. These blend into a larger retro-aesthetic panorama with the productions of the couturiers of 1939 who, like Schiaparelli, were mining the historical depths—her contribution being a cigar-shaped evening ensemble that also harked back to turn of the century styles. The second, later elaboration of a Belle Epoque aesthetic came in 1952, when both Schiaparelli and her peer, fashion illustrator Marcel Vertès, who in the late 1930s had drawn a number of Schiaparelli's nineteenth-century inspired looks for the fashion press, collaborated on John Huston's *Moulin Rouge*. The main historic figure of reference here is not Manet but Toulouse-Lautrec whose illustrations and posters for the *Moulin Rouge* cabaret quickly turned into an idiom of the Bohème's nightlife, and whose biography as a voluntary outcast from the *juste milieu* Huston's film plots into a model narrative of a troubled artist's subjectivity. Here, the aesthetic connection to the Belle Epoque is even stronger: Vertès's costumes, for which he won an Academy Award, could be seen as actual textile executions, designed for the camera, of the stylistic values and parameters of his fashion sketches which, as of the late 1930s, had taken more than a few formal hints from Toulouse-Lautrec's graphics and prints.

Mixed among these are Schiaparelli's costumes for Zsa Zsa Gabor, who plays the part of the Moulin Rouge's star singer Jane Avril. Her wardrobe edges the nineteenth-century reference out of the realm of filmic costume into genuine celluloid-based neo-Belle Epoque creations. Busty chests and wide skirts of the period are matched with masses of yellow feather decorations, as boas and millinery elements. Pink satin gowns are complemented with asymmetrically placed over-the-shoulder shocking pink tulle embellishments that touch upon the shape of fairy wings. And the graphic planar reduction of Toulouse-Lautrec's images is turned into elements of dresses, bodices, wide-brimmed hats with pom-poms and shawls which turn the burlesque Gabor into a veritable flower of the nineteenth century (Fig. 4.4a-c).[10]

Figure 4.4a-c Zsa Zsa Gabor in John Huston's "Moulin Rouge," costumes by Schiaparelli (1952), filmstills. United Artists / British Lion Films.

The general Belle Epoque recourse which began in the late 1930s finally included the vestimentary epitome of late nineteenth-century styles of feminine dress, at least as periscoped through its rejection in the fashions of the early twentieth century: the corset. This was immortalized in photographer Horst's black and white shot of an otherwise undressed model's upper body, the back turned toward the viewer, wearing a boned corset manufactured by Detoile for the couture house of Mainbocher, dating to 1939 (Fig. 4.5).

This icon of twentieth-century fashion photography encapsulates the straightforward return of the "wasp waist," which at the time was immediately identified as a resurgence of Victorian-era stylistics.[11] Making the cover of

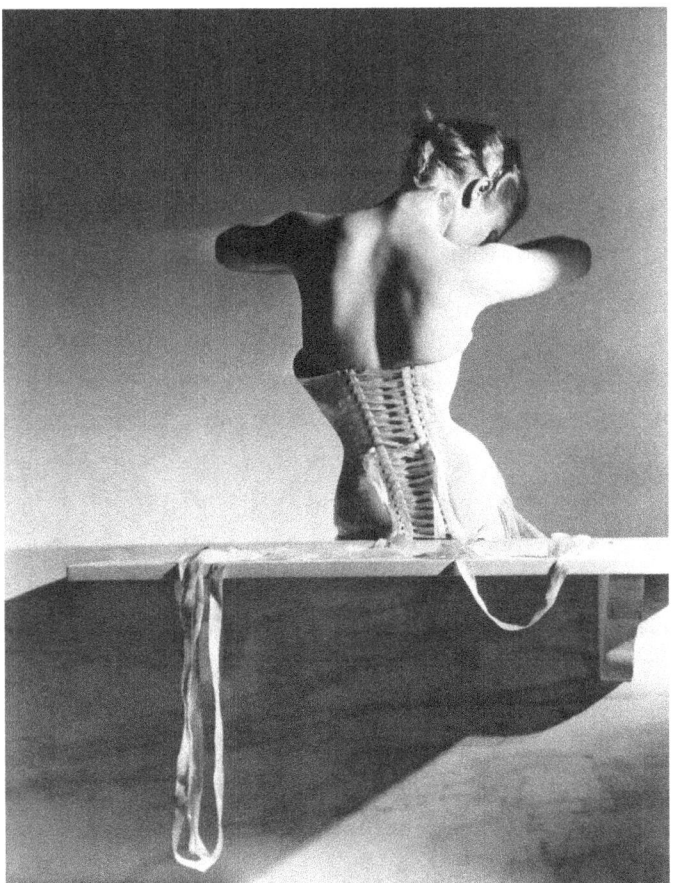

Figure 4.5 Horst P. Horst: Model in corset by Detoile for Mainbocher (1939). © Condé Nast/Getty Images.

LIFE Magazine that very year, *Vogue* declared the corset as the "key to new Paris silhouettes,"[12] the point being that the key was obviously not new at all.

Striking a note in fashion history

Benjamin talks about the "corset as the torso's arcade" (AP 492) (Das Korsett als Passage des Rumpfes [PW 614]), and thus succinctly gathers the historico-temporal focus of his own work, the architectural formation that stands at its center, and the fashion emblem of the Belle Epoque into a single frame: when Benjamin returns to the *Arcades*, fashion returns to the corset. We have a similar effect looking at Schiaparelli's Belle Epoque collection, which suggests a strange parallel between the tendencies of Paris fashion in the late 1930s and the historical objective of Benjamin's work: the Paris of the nineteenth century.

The dialectical image, plotted in analogy to the tiger's leap into the past, with its particular temporal and historical localization in the *Arcades Project*, was thus not just modeled on the general structures of fashion's chronotechnics. Through its implication with a retrieval and working through of the formations of the nineteenth century—formations which the early twentieth century had discarded—the *Arcades Project* parallels the concrete collective stylistic historico-temporal politics of its own moment. For a historical moment—its historical moment, perhaps—the dialectical image shared not just the structures of fashion, but fashion's present and its reach into the past. It was embedded in the real temporality of styles.

This parallel is astonishing enough in that it demonstrates the extent to which Benjamin's thought was indeed in close exchange with fashion's historical and systemic realities. However, rather than stopping short here and contemplating this congruence, we can further qualify this observation and unfold its implications. Firstly, the late 1930s return in Paris fashion to the styles of the Belle Epoque—which can, indeed, be observed not just in the work of Schiaparelli, but also in that of her peers—is not the only recourse to that historic moment. As of ca. 1934, there was a wave of empire dresses, which remodeled the very high-waisted and flowing column dresses that had historically preceded the corset and the crinoline—i.e., the looks of the various *Républiques*, during the reign of the Directoire.[13] Rather than an isolated reach into one moment in the history of style, at least the second part of that decade thus remodeled a certain arc in nineteenth-century fashion, to the point of rearticulating what had initially been a return in itself: the crinoline and corset under the rule of Emperor Louis Philippe had restaged in the field of women's couture, the looks of the Ancien Régime.[14] Or, as a line from *Harper's Bazaar* in 1938 suggested, these were stylistic options that were available to the customer at nearly the same time: "If you don't want to be 1830 or 1860 and if you don't like the tight molded line, then you can be a Directoire lady in this pale blue chiffon dress with pink pailletted flowers around the décolletage and the skirt slit up in front to show the crêpe de Chine slip. Directoire dresses are

Figure 4.6 *Femina* (June 1939). Kunstbibliothek der Staatlichen Museen zu Berlin.

enchanting this season."[15] If one look didn't suit, another was available, as long as one struck a "note in fashion history."[16] Or, in the words of a 1939 title line in *Femina*, fashion was "A la recherche des Modes perdues. Ampleurs retrouvées" (Fig. 4.6).[17]

Morphology in history: Time as ground

Looking at these examples, it is perhaps safe to say that, beyond the surprising concrete parallels on the level of manifest content—the return to the Belle Epoque in the *Arcades Project* and the styles of the very late 1930s Paris fashion—there is a structural parallel here of a different sort from the one that we observed earlier: it is not just the mere fact that the rearticulation of past styles in fashion—the tiger's leap—functions as one model for the mechanisms of the dialectical image. Rather it is, both more specifically and more generally, the view that the temporality of fashion is to be understood according to such a "retro-ist" modeling of time; a position which subtends Benjamin's attempt to demonstrate the logics of the dialectical image by turning to fashion's tiger's leap. (In chapter 1 we saw already that even among Benjamin's sources such a view wasn't inevitable, an example being Simmel's work, for whom such historical rearticulations didn't figure.)

There are two implications for our understanding of Benjamin's thought here. First, we are in the position to return to the question of morphology which, in chapter 2, we had broached on the occasion of Focillon's observations regarding the temporal developments of *lignes*, i.e., silhouettes and styles. At that point we already noted that a Benjaminian morphological concept—at least as seen from the perspective of a theory of fashion—differs from Focillon's and related models (we could name Simondon's currently quite influential work on the grounds of significant parallels to *La Vie des Formes*) on central counts. We noted that Benjamin's morphology was set apart in that it does not rely on the concept of a milieu, in the sense of a spatial environment as a ground against which forms are profiled. At this point, and considering the model of the tiger's leap, we can now further modify this assessment.

Contrasting Benjamin's approach with morphologies such as Focillon's (and Simondon's) we could say that theirs also exemplify a different model of temporality, which in turn informs the corresponding conceptualizations of milieus. For them, the milieu serves as a ground against which to profile the figure of form. That configuration was also characterized by a certain temporality. We saw that the milieu was understood as a zone of potentiality from which future forms could be developed or solicited. If the milieu as ground thus amounted to a stratum of latent forms, this latency was marked by a certain temporal unidirectionality: the temporality of these forms consisted in them not yet having been actualized.

In his fashion theory, Benjamin also thinks about coming forms, yet, as we saw, this future-oriented axis is, again, most strongly articulated through its pastward slant: if the tiger's leap is the main operation for the generation of fashions, its overall reservoir would be those styles that had once been formed, that had been lost and forgotten and had not been redeemed. Perhaps we thus could indeed locate an element in his theory (and morphology) which by analogy at least excercises a function similar to that of the category of the spatial milieu as ground. However, in the Benjaminian model, this milieu would not be spatial; it would be temporal, charged with those forms that have disappeared and are awaiting their eventual re-actualization.[18]

And there is another connection to morphological thought in Benjamin's work, a connection that is arguably more central to his thinking, and it takes the form of a reference to the writings of Goethe. This second morphological axis pertains to the structural comparison of the times of fashion and history. It is encapsulated in the following comparison from the convolute on epistemology: "The dialectical image is that form of the historical object which satisfies Goethe's requirements for the object of analysis: to exhibit a genuine synthesis. It is the urphenomenon of history" (AP 474, TM) (Das dialektische Bild ist diejenige Form des historischen Gegenstands, die Goethes Anforderung an den Gegenstand einer Analyse genügt: eine echte Synthese aufzuweisen. Es ist das Urphänomen der Geschichte) [PW 592]).[19]

The parallel is partly surprising, because one important element of Benjamin's thought, at least as mediated by his Frankfurt readers, was the objection to the dogmas of intuitive viewing and understanding, the concept of an organic continuum between sensory perception and cognitive grasping of ideal structures which in German thought was referred to as *Anschaulichkeit*, which had one of its origins in Goethe's morphology, articulated, for instance, in the poet's insistence on the possibility of instantaneous and immediate deciphering of the laws of transformation that regulated the changes of form in nature.[20] In contrast to Focillon, Benjamin here does not establish the comparison with the fashionable transformations of silhouettes (see chapter 2). This would entail a parallel between the unfolding of the styles of fashion and the unfolding of vegetal forms from leaf to plant, as envisioned by Goethe—a parallel which Benjamin clearly did not intend. Rather, Benjamin's parallel between dialectical image and Urphänomen is, again, situated on the level of a model; it is an epistemological parallel, i.e., a model of time rather than a phenomenon in time.[21] Radically simplifying the terms of Goethe's complex theory of forms (natural and beyond) for the purposes of this comparison—a body of thought and writings which, as Eva Geulen has demonstrated, is in its development anything but static, but rather subjected to a transformative process itself—we could still establish the following provisional analogy:[22] the Goethean Urphänomen is to the metamorphic development of plants as the dialectical image, and its temporalized operationalizing of (fashion's) difference in the tiger's leap, is to history. This is to say that what comes to visibility in the dialectical image is not a metamorphic flux, but the intervention and temporal hiatuses and discontinuities in history. The congruencies between Goethe's and Benjamin's frameworks are not phenomenal but structural: the positing of the possibility of an instantaneous, intuitive grasp of occurrences and regularities that extend over time.

Benjamin opens yet another trajectory between his and Goethe's undertaking which allows for a final situating operation of his thought vis-à-vis the field of fashion. Again, in convolute N, Benjamin situated his inquiry into the formation of the arcades as follows:

> Marx points out the causal nexus [Kausalzusammenhang] between economy and culture. For us, what matters is the expressive nexus [Ausdruckszusammenhang]. It is not the economic genesis of culture that will be presented, but the expression of the economy in its culture. At issue, in other words, is the attempt to grasp an economic process as perceptible [anschauliches] ur-phenomenon, from out of which emerge all manifestations of life of the arcades (and, accordingly, in the nineteenth century).
>
> AP 460, TM

Marx stellt den Kausalzusammenhang zwischen Wirtschaft und Kultur dar. Hier kommt es auf Ausdruckszusammenhang an. Nicht die wirtschaftliche Entstehung der Kultur sondern den Ausdruck der Wirtschaft in ihrer Kultur ist darzustellen. Es handelt sich mit anderen Worten um den Versuch, einen wirtschaftlichen Prozess als anschauliches Urphänomen zu erfassen, aus welchem alle Lebenserscheinungen der Passagen (und insoweit des 19ten Jahrhunderts) hervorgehen.

PW 573/574

These—i.e., the manifestations of the life of the arcades—Benjamin intended to track "from their beginning to their decline" (AP 462) (von ihrem Aufgang bis zu ihrem Untergang [PW 577]).

We should pause here, because Benjamin's description of the manifestation of the life of the arcades as ur-phenomenon which brings to visibility an economic process introduces a second trajectory in addition to his earlier identification of the ur-phenomenon and the dialectical image. The latter is constellational and it requires the articulation across a historico-temporal caesura. This was the idea of the temporal kernel—the *Zeitkern*—at the heart of the dialectical image, which marks its constellational structure: rather than occupying a single temporal place, it is relational. While processual (i.e., indicating a development over time), the development of the arcades does not fulfill this criterion, unless we would complete Benjamin's argument by adding that the demise of the arcades (i.e., their entering the stage of obsolescence), which was indeed the condition in which Benjamin, like the Surrealists, claimed to encounter them in his own present, would implicitly add the caesura which is the otherwise indispensable element for the constitution of dialectical images.[23]

Turning to the concept of an expressive nexus (Ausdruckszusammenhang), Benjamin's intention was to address the fundamental importance of economic facts and relations while avoiding the hoary issue of determinism which haunted orthodox Marxian interpretations of culture that adhered to a strict base/superstructure dogma.[24] In those approaches, culture and its forms are seen as mere outgrowths of an all-determining economic force. By shifting to the notion of *Ausdruckscharakter* (expressive character), Benjamin circumvented a model based on *Kausalzusammenhang* (causal nexus). His research, he writes, deals ... with the expressive character [Ausdruckscharakter] of the earliest industrial products, the earliest industrial architecture, the earliest machines, but also the earliest department stores, advertisements, etc.

AP 460

mit dem Ausdruckscharakter der frühesten Industrieerzeugnisse, der frühesten Industriebauten, der frühesten Maschinen aber auch der frühesten Warenhäuser, Reklamen etc.

PW 574

Or, as he puts it in another fragment, the point lies in treating economic facts (wirtschaftliche Fakten) not as *Ursachen* (causes), but as *Urphänomene* (AP 462, PW 577). Benjamin thus repositioned his own methodology in the study of the nineteenth century and the study of Marxism itself, which he intended to read as a doctrine—in its expressive character in relation to the nineteenth century. The idea was to "show in what respects Marxism, too, shares the expressive character of the material products contemporary with it" (zeigen, in welchen Zügen auch der Marxismus den Ausdruckscharakter der ihm gleichzeitigen materiellen Erzeugnisse teilt [AP 460, PW 574]).

The tiger's leap as expression of the economy (Benjamin's fashion ideology)

In 1929 the European and North American financial markets crashed, pulling vast sectors of their respective economies down with them, leading to what in North America became known as the Great Depression which there, as well as in Europe, caused unprecedented waves of impoverishment across vast sectors of society. Although not monocausally linked these developments contributed to the rise of totalitarian regimes such as National Socialism in Germany. While obviously far from the existential threats suffered by many, the fashion economy was also impacted. This impact took a form which at first might seem counter-intuitive. During the comparably affluent second half of the 1920s, a marketing model had taken hold in a number of fashion houses which addressed a much wider customer base than the traditional pre-First World War houses had. As mentioned above (see chapter 2), Jean Patou and his peers—such as Coco Chanel, and even Schiaparelli in her earliest lines—had been producing with an eye to more casual, more wearable, and even sportswear purposes. Chanel's dresses famously allowed their wearer to navigate day- and nighttime occasions, also inflicting less physical constriction upon her movements.[25] The tendency is exemplified in Patou's "athletic" designs, and in his, Chanel's, and other designers' opening of boutiques for beachwear, for instance in Deauville. Benjamin included a quote from Louis Sonolet's *La vie parisienne sous le second empire* in the *Arcades Project* that tracked the earliest developments in this direction, dating back into the nineteenth century: "It was bathing in the sea ... that struck the first blow against the solemn and cumbersome crinoline" (AP 70) (Les bains de mer ... donnèrent le premier coup à la solenelle et encombrante crinoline [PW 119]). The crinoline (and the corset) wouldn't survive that shift. The emblem of that fashion moment and also one of the prime commodities in terms of the businesses of fashion houses was, if not the flapper dress, then *knitwear* (e.g., sweaters), an unlikely medium for Schiaparelli to make her debut in, but so she did, developing the first illustrational patterns—tropical fish—on women's pullovers. Patou had preceded her in working geometrical patterns that spelled out his monograms into the sweater's weave. This segment of production and retail was gravely hit during the economic crisis that ensued after 1929. These forms of textile commodities that were situated between the very high end and a mass consumer market lost their buyers—ostensibly a better-off, upper middle-class customer in Europe and North America, rather than the exquisitely wealthy.[26]

Yet the industry didn't collapse entirely. Fashion historians have observed (an observation, by the way, which is still confirmed in today's reiterating, or perhaps seamlessly blending, moments of crisis) that the contraction hurt the more costly, more laboriously produced, "luxury" sector less than the sector of wider affordability. In other words, while a broad spectrum of potential customers was no longer in the position to afford the wares of Paris or their licenses, the extraordinarily wealthy still could and did. As a matter of fact, it could be argued that the ultimate institutionalization of the manufacturing and marketing of extraordinarily expensive garments occurred only in response to this serious economic aggravation. It was only after the crash that the Chambre Syndicale established an official calendar that listed the fashion shows of its members, reducing the sizes of collections from approximately

400 to 100 pieces. Only the products of listed houses had the right to figure as "couture," meaning *haute couture*, whereas others received a lesser classification as "moyenne couture."[27] The commercial response to the downturn thus consisted in a forced delimitation of numbers, a strategy of pre-emptive rarefaction.

This contraction toward the more narrow sectors of the rich showed, and it is difficult not to perceive the shift on the pages of those magazines which were still being sold to a wider readership, such as *Vogue* or *Harper's Bazaar* or *Für die Frau*.[28] The development of ever-more glamorous fantasies offsets the large-scale massive economic deprivation that is unfolding at that moment.[29] The effect of this contraction could be called a recouturization of the practice and business of fashion, an aesthetic focus on more ambitiously constructed, more laboriously furnished, and more socially exclusive modes of making and wearing a dress. This is obvious in the very development which Helen Grund and her colleagues observed in 1929, the very year of the economic collapse. For not only did the re-emergence of the more elaborately constructed women's dress imply a resurgence of gender-dimorphous silhouettes; the shift from the easy outfits of the 1920s coincided with and was executed as a return to more elaborate constructions, dresses, and gowns, which registered in more elevated, more exclusive, and more excluding social codes.[30] These are, of course, also part and parcel of Grund's advocacy for the value of elegance, which may be perfectly realized in a manner of tying one's scarf, but which also—as a technique and value that first appeared in the select circles practicing elegant diction (see chapter 3)—implies a narrowing down of the social contexts in which it is practiced. Such a contraction coincides with social distinction, and more often than not implies exclusion along its lines. This fact was explicitly commented upon as early as 1929 when Martine Rénier, the editor-in-chief of *Femina*, described the incumbent shift in fashionable silhouettes as a "return of grand elegance" (Le Retour à la grande élégance), claiming that the emergence of the long skirt "ends the era of the multipurpose ensemble and of department store elegance, which allowed starry-eyed young girls who work in the couture industry and the *grandes dames* to adore the same little more or less well-tailored, more or less identical sheath. It returns us to rare luxury, which is the only true luxury" (termine cette ère de l'ensemble omnibus et de cette élégance de bon marché, qui faisait que cettes midinettes ou grandes dames revêtaient le même petit fourreau plus ou moins bien taillé, mais de forme identique. Elle nous ramène au luxe rare qui seul est le véritable luxe).³¹ (L'Herbier's *La mode rêvée*, with its intercuts of adoring, giggling, and gushing employees of the couture houses clad in apron-like dresses, and their dreamy, aloof, and slightly amused customers, all played by professional fashion models, who change from neo-rococo gowns into contemporary couture garments, gives a concrete image of this relationship.)

We could go on: the distinction between the animation of material, as we saw it in Vionnet, and matter's "obdurate" rendering in the intricate strategies of Schiaparelli, are far more reliant on craftsmanship, elaborate cutting, and sewing, as well as on the selection of garments, than the (proto-)industrial manufacturing of, say, a patterned sweater, for which the machineries of weaving, if tooled the right way, could be employed. Their articulation relies very much on the conditions of a recouturized fashion practice. And, finally, the specific orchestration of the very historico-temporal recourse which establishes the parallel between 1930s Paris couture and the programmatics of the *Arcades Project* also relies on these conditions. Even if there were no identical replicas, the sartorial refabrication of *cul de Paris* and the corset would have been nearly impossible to achieve on the basis of a more mass market-oriented fabrication mode. Beyond this specific example, the very historical rearticulation that Benjamin had in mind, or before his eyes, when he conceived of fashion's tiger's leap into the past, would have been bound to such sartorial prowess, flexibility, and variability which a more classically "tailored" model of fashion offered, in contrast to the more limited industrial fabrications that became established in the 1920s.

Put differently, at the historical moment at which Benjamin develops the relation between what he terms the dialectical image, and its part modeling through the chronotechnics of fashion, the execution of these chronotechnics relies on a sartorial, industrial, and material assemblage that had been reconfigured after the incision of a major economic crisis. Hadn't it been for the parallel contraction of the fashion industry and the narrowing down of its customer base to the very wealthy, the type of historical recourse that Grund and Benjamin were witnessing, and which Benjamin noted in the *Arcades Project*, could not have been articulated in the manner in which it was.

As explained above, Benjamin pondered in which ways the dialectical image—as an equivalent to the Goethean *Urphänomen* in historical time—could be considered an expression—an *Ausdruck*—of economic conditions, rather than positing cultural formations, including the epistemic formation of Marxism, as results of economic causes. While he didn't develop the thought for his reader, we are now able to recognize a certain—surely unintentional—parallel in his own writings. For to center as strongly as Benjamin did in his theoretical works on the historico-temporal recourses of fashion, and to turn this one aspect into one of the core threads of his fashion thought, was certainly not to entirely miss the mark. Fashion indeed does offer the option of a non-linear rearticulation of past styles across a temporal caesura, but not all fashion(s) rely on this option for the production of fashionable difference.

Looking at the fashion panorama of his moment—that is, the moment of him working on the *Arcades Project*, and the styles that his source Helen Grund was writing about—Benjamin could certainly be forgiven for focusing as strongly as he did on fashion's backward slant. The mood of the decade was indeed retrospective. What Benjamin seems to have failed to realize, however (or at least, what he didn't develop for his readers), was the fact that his own concept of fashion as an engine of historico-temporal recursion was to an extent an expression of the economic conditions of his and fashion's particular moment in history. After the financial crash and the drastically uneven redistribution of wealth, of an ever-growing division between the affluently rich and the increasingly drastic impoverishment of vast parts of society, fashion as an industry (i.e., in its economic articulation) developed into an arena for the upper classes (again). The gowns, the salons, the chateaus, down to the many socialites as models (a substantial number of which seem to have been princesses, heiresses, and other aristocrats) represented a distinct break with what, for instance, one of Grund's readers in the 1920s would have found on the pages of the magazine she had purchased. Gone was the emphasis on Patou's tennis players, the American girls, or even the reports on women in the Soviet army, as *Für die Frau* had printed them. It was within this new climate that the refined returns to the Belle Epoque could be sartorially produced and critically appreciated and reinforce the view of fashion as working, if not linearly, then still along the vector of history.

This is another angle on the question—discussed in chapter 1—of the interrelation between fashion's tiger's leap and its situatedness in an arena in which "the ruling class" gives commands. From this angle, however, the question is less if and to what extent the historico-temporal recourses and rearticulations of the past can be a model for the grand operation of revolution "under the open skies of history." More modestly, but still pertinently, the point is that any approach—Benjamin's included—formulated at the historical instant in question (after 1929), which straightforwardly identifies fashion with and reduces fashion to the operation of the tiger's leap, overlooks that the tiger at that point only leaps for the very wealthy. Not because fashion *tout court* exists for the ruling class, but because this particular concept of fashion, in all its complexity, is—if exclusively put—in actuality expressive of massive economic exclusion. The ground against which the figure of fashion came to be completely identified with the elegant rearticulation of forgotten moments was real deprivation.

Benjamin's identification of the tiger's leap as a fashion operation that can be harnessed for a modeling of time, and that, qua its temporal recursions, also opens one way of thinking about the possibility of redeeming lost elements of the past is, of course, among his central intellectual achievements. Yet, in claiming its exemplarity, Benjamin also reduces the complexities and contingencies under which fashion—understood as systemic, aesthetic, and historical practice—could present the tiger's leap as its chief maneuver. At the moment of Benjamin's writing—a moment which, as we saw, Benjamin did take as the point of origin for his own project—this narrowing down occurred under the condition of economic deprivation and injustice, conditions which Benjamin's theory of the tiger's leap, for better or worse, expresses.

These conditions did not *cause* Benjamin to model the theory of the dialectical image to a degree along fashion's tiger's leap into the past; they are not its *Ursachen*. But this very act of modeling certainly *expresses* these conditions: this nexus is not causal but expressive (not a *Kausalzusammenhang* but an *Ausdruckszusammenhang*). We are thus left with a peculiar intersection of the structural and the actual articulations of Benjamin's elaboration of fashion as a chronotechnic and as a model. Its most general aspect coincides with the particular salience of the (fashion) historical moment of its articulation. Fashion's leap into the past thus turns out not only to be framed by fashion's specific leap into its own history—1930s recouturized design practice as informed by and rearticulating the Belle Epoque. Benjamin's general theorization of fashion's capacity for such historical recursion in its systematic and content aspects also expresses the conditions of the moment of its own articulation—in economy, in fashion, in its history, and in history at large.

Notes

Fashion-forward Benjamin: A brief introduction

1 See chapter 3 for an exploration of matters of movement, gait, stance etc., as they were present in the fashion context of Benjamin's writings.
2 Benjamin thus anticipates and pre-empts our contemporary Latourian critiques of simplified conceptualizations of historical ruptures, in particular as they have crystallized around the notion of modernity, without succumbing to the all-too-easy dismissal of temporal disjunctures and discontinuities that we frequently encounter here.
3 Friedrich Kittler, *Gramophone, Film, Typewriter* (Stanford: Stanford University Press, 1999), xxxix.

1 On some systematic aspects of Benjamin's Fashion Theory

1 Among the sources quoted by Benjamin in the *Arcades Project*, Georg Simmel's writing represents such a position. In his *Philosophy of Fashion* (Philosophie der Mode) Simmel calls the "life conditions of fashion" (Lebensbedingungen der Mode) a "universal phenomenon in the history of our species" (durchgängige Erscheinung in der Geschichte unserer Gattung) (PoF 188, PdM 11). A similar position is espoused at a later point in twentieth-century sociology in René König's frequently underestimated essay collection *À la Mode. On the Social Psychology of Fashion*, introd. Tom Wolfe (New York: Continuum, Seabury Press, 1973). See ibid., 29, 36, 66, 68, 70. Scholarship in the recent field of evolutionary aesthetics—by default—also assumes the continued existence of fashion, or related phenomena, not just in human culture, but even in pre- or proto-anthropological systems. See, for instance, Winfried Menninghaus, "Caprices of Fashion in Culture and Biology. Charles Darwin's Aesthetics of Ornament", in *Philosophical Perspectives on Fashion*, ed. Giovanni Matteucci, Stefano Marino (London, Oxford, New York: Bloomsbury, 2017). See in particular chapter 4, "The Time of Fashion," 143–144. Menninghaus's central reference point is Darwin's 1871 *The Descent of Man, and Selection In Relation to Sex*, whose positions regarding the "fashionable" redistribution of body ornaments across the individuals of animal species were

adapted by his son George Darwin and turned inside out, so to speak, when, in his 1872 article "Development in Dress" he argued that the development of sartorial fashions could also be understood according to the laws of evolution established in his father's work (George H. Darwin, "Development in Dress", *Macmillan Magazine* 26 [1872]).

2   Cf. Elizabeth Wilson, *Adorned in Dreams. Fashion and Modernity.* rev. ed. (London, New York: I.B. Tauris, 2003), 16–18, where she discusses the emergence of different cuts for men's and women's fashion, and 26, where she discusses, with reference to the work of Jacob Burckhardt, the hypothesis of fashion's first flourishing in the Italian city states of the Renaissance. Barbara Vinken develops the incision of the French Revolution and the emergence of a bourgeois dress code (and its subsequent deconstructions), however, with a crucial difference, in that she speaks of 1789 as a "revolution in fashion," not the revolution from which fashion emerges. See her *Fashion Zeitgeist. Trends and Cycles in the Fashion System* (Oxford, New York: Berg, 2005), 10.

3   The first approach is Gilles Lipovetsky's in *The Empire of Fashion. Dressing Modern Democracy*. Pref. Richard Sennett (Princeton: Princeton University Press, 1994). "Fashion does not belong to all ages or to all civilizations: it has an identifiable starting point in history. Instead of seeing fashion as a phenomenon consubstantial with human life and society, I view it as an exceptional process inseparable from the origin and development of the modern West" (ibid., 16). The second approach is developed by the Luhmannian sociologist Elena Esposito in her *Die Verbindlichkeit des Vorübergehenden. Paradoxien der Mode* (Frankfurt am Main: Suhrkamp), 2004; and in a strongly abbreviated manner in her article "The Fascination of Contingency. Fashion and Modern Society", in *Philosophical Perspectives on Fashion,* ed. Giovanni Matteuci, Stefano Marino (London, Oxford, New York: Bloomsbury, 2017), 75. "Fashion is a typically modern phenomenon—in the sense that it only exists in modern society, and in the sense that it expresses in a concentrated way the essence of modernity."

4   A particularly straightforward proposal for such a division is Gabriel Tarde's distinction between types of mimetic behavior ("imitation") oriented toward custom, and others oriented toward fashion. Cf. the chapter "Custom and Fashion" in his *The Laws of Imitation* (New York: Holt, 1903), 244–365.

5   Bruno Latour, *We Have Never Been Modern* (New York, London: Harvester Wheatsheaf, 1993), 10. Cf. ibid., 76 for this related vestimentary model: "ancestral folklores are like the 'centenary' Scottish kilt, invented out of whole cloth at the beginning of the nineteenth century ... 'Peoples without history' were invented by those who thought theirs was radically new. In practice, the former innovate constantly; the latter are forced to pass and repass indefinitely through the same

rituals of revolutions, epistemological breaks, and quarrel of the Classics against the Moderns. One is not born traditional; one chooses to become traditional by constant innovation. The idea of an identical repetition of the past and that of a radical rupture with any past are two symmetrical results of a single conception of time. We cannot return to the past, to tradition, to repetition, because these great immobile domains are the inverted image of the earth that is no longer promised to us today: progress, permanent revolution, modernization, forward flight."

Symptomatically, the subject of fashion seems to at least implicitly mark a point of irresolution within Latour's project and its self-professed genealogies. In *Reassembling the Social* Latour clearly positions his enterprise in the intellectual trajectory of Tarde's (and against Durkheim's) sociology. Cf. Bruno Latour, *Reassembling the Social. An Introduction to Actor-Network-Theory* (Oxford, London: Oxford University Press, 2005), 13–16, and in his article "Gabriel Tarde and the End of the Social" he aligns himself with Tarde's view that all scales of the social behave according to equal laws: "The macro is but a slight extension of the micro" (in *The Social in Question. New Bearings in History and the Social Sciences*, ed. Patrick Joyce [London: Routledge, 2002]). Here, 123. In other words, Latour turns to Tarde for a model of how to avoid categorical breaks and qualitative leaps within the material assemblages from which, in his view, social, epistemic, etc traffic emerges. In his critique of what he regards as "critical sociology" "the social" is one such entity, and its arch-proponent in Latour's view is Tarde's anatgonist Durkheim. It seems quite clear that the division between "traditional" and "modern" societies and culture, as formations without or with fashion, institutes such a qualitative break—extended into the historical dimension—which Latour opposes. Ironically, the question of fashion—or, put differently, the opposition of fashion versus custom—marks exactly a point in Tarde's work in which such a qualitative break persists. See footnote 4, above.

6   As per the opening chapter of Baudelaire's essay *Le peintre de la vie moderne*: "Le beau, la mode et le bonheur." Cf. Charles Baudelaire, *Critique d'art suivi par critique musicale,* ed. Claude Pichois (Paris: Gallimard, 1992). The exploration of this chronological coexistence has also inspired central studies in the visual disciplines, such as Mark Wigley, *White Walls, Designer Dresses. The Fashioning of Modern Architecture* (Cambridge, Mass. and London: The MIT Press, 1995); Nancy Troy, *Couture Culture. A Study in Modern Art and Fashion* (Cambridge, Mass. and London: The MIT Press, 2003), or Caroline Evans, *The Mechanical Smile. Modernism and the First Fashion Shows in France and America 1900–1929* (London, New Haven: Yale University Press, 2013). A comprehensive study of the interconnection between fashion and modernity as negotiated in the field of (Germanophone) literature is Julia Bertschik's *Mode und Moderne. Kleidung als*

Spiegel des Zeitgeistes in der deutschsprachigen Literatur 1770–1945 (Vienna, Cologne, Weimar: Böhlau, 2005).

7 *Le Grand Robert de la langue française*, ed. Alain Rey, vol. 4. (Paris: Robert, 2001), 1540.

8 Ibid., 1546–1547.

9 Ibid., 1540–1541. Cf. also Esposito: *Verbindlichkeit des Vergänglichen*, 49–50, 53, who connects the seventeenth-century emergence of the notion of fashion from the theory of modes to what in Luhmannian systems theory is referred to as a shift to a regime of contingency. In her own manner, she thus reintroduces the idea of a systemic passage to the theory of fashion, indicating that what she calls "the dissolution of the ontological compactness of the middle ages" corresponds with the ascendance of fashion, and an overall shift toward contingency (ibid., 54). Cf. ibid., 55: "The characteristics of Baroque semantics originate in the dissolution of the compact disposition of ontology and in the violent entry of contingency into the dimensions of the social and of time" Cf. Esposito: *The Fascination of Contingency*, 176.

10 *Grand Robert*, 1551.

11 One example for such a modeling function could be found in the field of science studies, and in particular in the notion of epistemic objects, as developed by Hans Jörg Rheinberger. Cf. Hans Jörg Rheinberger, *Toward a History of Epistemic Things. Synthesizing Proteins in the Test Tube* (Stanford: Stanford University Press, 1997). Rheinberger understands by "epistemic objects" or "epistemic things" entities, not necessarily things in the narrow sense of the term, but also structures, functions, relations, in and through which scientific research is articulated, also pointing to Serres's concept of the veil as a hybrid between sign and object. As such, the concept seems indeed applicable to Benjamin's treatment of fashion as an object of inquiry. The parallel ends where Rheinberger—as a historian of the natural sciences—introduces the concept of the technical thing, for instance the apparative assemblages of the laboratory, which frames and stabilizes epistemic objects. Or, in our present case we would need to inquire into the specific medial and (techno-)cultural assemblages that enable the observation of fashion: for Benjamin, and for others. This would require a radically twisted application of Rheinberger's idea, implying some severe conceptual bending. Such an endeavor would also need to reconcile Benjamin's writings on fashion with his serious engagements with the sciences and scientific epistemology, as elaborated, for instance, in the volume Kyung-Ho Cha, ed., *Aura und Experiment. Naturwissenschaft und Technik bei Walter Benjamin* (Vienna: Turia und Kant, 2017). Whether such a parallel is indeed tenable lies beyond the scope of the present study and would thus need to discussed on a separate occasion.

12 Looking at the field of post-media archaeological thinking, we find the concept of operationalization, for instance, in Siegert's concept of cultural techniques as "operationalizing distinctions in the real. They generate the forms in the shape of perceptible unities of distinctions" (Bernhard Siegert, *Cultural Techniques. Grids, Filters, Doors, and Other Articulations of the Real* [New York: Fordham University Press: 2015], 14. Siegert mentions a model that is close to the topic of fashion, namely Marcel Mauss's elaborations of so-called "techniques of the body" (cf. ibid.). Siegert sets his concept apart from Mauss's in that cultural techniques require an element of recursion. Fashion, it seems, would not only exemplify a "technique of the body," at times literally so—for instance, where it requires the adoption of modes of movement (see chapter 3 in this volume, in particular those sections dedicated to the problem of walking, and heed fashion historian Caroline Evans's insight that models can be considered "technicians of the walk"). Through its collective implementation and persistent modification along an ongoing, renegotiated distinction between "before" and "after," "in" and "out" fashion also displays the required element of recursiveness. Another way in which operationalization is employed in recent humanities and cultural studies would also seem—albeit distantly—compatible with our present concerns. In the field of empirical, in particular digital humanities, operationalization refers to the transmission of a concept through quantification into an analysis of the world. Cf. Franco Moretti, "Operationalizing: or, the function of measurement in modern literary theory", *New Left Review* 84 (2013). Cf. 103. One could make the argument that fashion allows its students, such as Benjamin, to operationalize time, to get a handle on it.

13 An approach that combines both figures in a symptomatic manner is, again, Gilles Lipovetsky's reactionary stance in his *The Empire of Fashion*, according to which the rupture of modernity inaugurates a regime of terrorizing evanescence. Cf. Lipovetsky, *Empire of Fashion,* passim.

14 Cf. Esposito: *Verbindlichkeit des Vorübergehenden*, where she writes: "Once the univocity of the objective dimension (Sachdimension) has been given up, nothing can stop the intrusion of the dimension of time. Reflexivity is now oriented toward the difference of before and after, and it is imperative to indicate at what point of time a certain observational perspective is being articulated.... Fashion ... ties the indeterminacy of the social dimension to the dimension of time and vice versa and effectively neutralizes both" 26–27.

15 Vinken's scholarship has in particular taught us to read the grand couture dress, the iconic embodiment of *la mode de cent ans*, from Worth (contemporary to Baudelaire, Mallarmé, Manet, and Zola) to Saint Laurent, including its analytical dissections in the post-fashion decades of the 1980s and 1990s, as anamnestic

rearticulations of the chopping of the aristocracy. Whereas other approaches cast the (French) revolution as a monolithic cut in history, this incision which for them "generates" fashion is here treated in and through fashion, in its temporal dimension. See Vinken, *Fashion Zeitgeist*, 3–76.

16 Andrew Benjamin, *Style and Time. Essays on the Politics of Appearance* (Evanston: Northwestern University Press, 2006), 25.

17 Barbara Vinken: *Fashion Zeitgeist*, 42–44.

18 Theodor Adorno, *Ästhetische Theorie* (Frankfurt am Main: Suhrkamp, 1973), 265. Theodor Adorno: *Aesthetic Theory*, transl. Robert Hullot-Kentor (London, New York: Continuum, 2002), 192 (TM). Cf. ibid., 468 in the German edition on fashion's "indiscrete betrayals" (Adorno: *Aesthetic Theory*, 316).

19 Susan Buck-Morss, *The Dialectics of Seeing. Walter Benjamin and the Arcades Project* (Cambridge, Mass. and London: The MIT Press, 1989), 97.

20 Ibid.

21 Eiland's and Jephcot's English translation renders Benjamin's quote from Leopardi here as fashion calling out for "Madam Death," not "Sir Death," and thus aligns both with Charles Edward's translation, as well as with Leopardi's original, which has "Moda: Madama Morte, Madama Morte" and thus complies with the Italian substantive *morte*'s grammatical gender. While faithful to the original text, this rendering loses the negotiation of the relation between two sexes that is, allegorically, inscribed into the German version, in which "death" is masculine (der Tod). Part of the point of Benjamin's appropriation of Leopardi's dialogue is that it recasts the relation of male and female sex/gender as a relation between death and fashion. For the implications of this constellation, see chapter 2 in this volume.

22 Buck-Morss: *Dialectics of Seeing*, 97.

23 Ibid., 97–98.

24 Just as Benjamin does not cast tradition as a stratum of continuity, he operates on other occasions in a similarly counterintuitive manner. An entry in the *Arcades Project* makes an argument which takes a stance against the inventory of *idées reçues* on the subject of fashion: "Fashions are a collective medicament for the ravages of oblivion. The more short-lived a period, the more it is oriented toward fashion" (PW 80, TM) (Moden sind ein Medikament, das die verhängnsivollen Wirkungen des Vergessens, im kollektiven Maßstab, kompensieren soll. Je kurzlebiger eine Zeit, desto mehr ist sie an der Mode ausgerichtet [PW, 131]). For instance, Buck-Morss writes in response to this passage that "the effect on collective historical memory of satisfying the thirst for novelty through fashion" leads to "obliviousness to even the most recent past" (Buck-Morss: *Dialectics of*

Seeing, 98). There is of course no disputing that Benjamin did diagnose a lack of working through of his own present's past—hence the *Arcades Project*—but to blame the absence of memory on fashion, as Buck-Morss does, amounts to a near reversal of Benjamin's sense here: (the effects of) forgetting are compensated for, not caused by fashion. If anything, fashion is (an imperfect) *aide mémoire*, not an agent of amnesia.

25 This even holds for an occasional variation of Benjamin's speculative dialectical reversal of his categorizing of tradition as discontinuous, evinced in a fragment in which he sketches the "materialist dialectician's" standpoint according to which "discontinuity is the regulative idea of the tradition of the ruling classes (i.e., in the first instance, the bourgeoisie), while "continuity is the regulative idea of the tradition of the oppressed (i.e., in the first instance the proletariat)." Benjamin goes on to flesh out this proposition by declaring that

> [t]he proletariat lives more slowly than the bourgeois class. The examples of its champions, the insights of its leaders do not grow old. Or, at any rate, they grow old much more slowly than the epochs and great personages of the bourgeois class. The waves of fashion break against the compact mass of the oppressed.
>
> AP 364, TM

> *Das Proletariat lebt langsamer als die Bürgerklasse. Die Beispiele seiner Kämpfer, die Erkenntnisse seiner Führer veralten nicht. Sie veralten jedenfalls sehr viel langsamer als die Epochen und die grossen Führer der Bürgerklasse. Die Wellen der Mode brechen sich an der kompakten Masse der Unterdrückten.*
>
> PW, 459

The movements of the ruling class, he contends

> have a modish quality to them.... For not only must they, like the ideas of the latter, adapt each time to the situation of societal struggle, but they must glorify the situation as fundamentally harmonious. Such a business is managed only eccentrically and erratically. It is modish in the fullest sense of the word.
>
> AP 364, TM

> *einen modischen Einschlag an sich: Denn sie haben sich nicht nur, wie die Ideen der letztern, der jeweiligen gesellschaftlichen Kampfsituation anzupassen, sondern sie als eine im Grunde harmonische Situation zu verklären. Bei diesem Geschäft muss exzentrisch und sprunghaft verfahren werden. Es ist im vollsten Sinne des Wortes ein modisches.*
>
> PW 459–460

The identification of the proletariat as a historico-social formation whose developmental "slowness" turns it into a rock against which crash the waves of fashion may at first sight be reminiscent of the position that declares "tradition" to be immune from fashion, but upon closer analysis this is not the case: Benjamin here operates with a model of parallel temporalities that develop in coexistent (i.e., synchronous) socio-political formations. The time of the proletariat is continuous; that of the bourgeoisie is modishly discontinuous—i.e., fashion is not figured as a "rupture" within the continuum of tradition as a monolithic block, because quite obviously the proletariat and the bourgeoisie share the same historical moment. In addition, Benjamin clarifies that both discontinuity and continuity, a) refer to regulative ideas rather than empirical data and b) both relate to the category of tradition—i.e., rather than univocally qualifying tradition *as* continuous, Benjamin here offers two inflections *of* tradition: one discontinuous, the other continuous. Both open up from the perspective of the materialist dialectician.

26 Buck-Morss: *Dialectics of Seeing*, 82.
27 Lipovetsky: *Empire of Fashion*, 20, 24.
28 Ibid., 20, 23.
29 Ibid., 23. Obviously there are ample examples of non-reactionary fashion sociologies that operate under completely different premises. See, for instance, König, *A la Mode*, 49: "What applies to the elementary postures applies equally to all natural body adornments. The Romans already experienced changing fashions not only in the wearing of a beard, but also in the varying shapes of beard. Sometimes the vogue was the clean-shaven face of the ephebe, at others the curled beard of the Farnese Hercules, or the austere schoolmaster of the Stoic"—all fashionable changes the existence of which Lipovetsky would have to deny.
30 Buck-Morss: *Dialectics of Seeing*, 99.
31 The original German makes this clearer than the English translation. The grammatical gender of *Agentin* is feminine (to accord with the grammatical gender of *Mode*, which is also feminine). "Quintessence" is related to its determining category through a genitive article, *dessen* (whose), which is gendered *neutrum* or masculine, clearly relating it—and with it the category of the new—to consciousness, which in German also has a grammatically neutral gender (*das Bewußtsein*).
32 If one were to look for shared avenues in the works of Benjamin and contemporaneous thinkers, this could be one point of departure for a common concern with Tarde's sociology, which seems otherwise quite incompatible with Benjamin's thought. We would need to heed Deleuze's admonition in *Difference and Repetition* that Tarde, with his focus on agglomerations of multitudes of small to miniscule acts of imitation, inaugurates a "micro-sociology"—an insight quite in line with Benjamin's insistence on the smallness of fashion changes. See Gilles Deleuze, *Difference and Repetition* (New York: Columbia University Press, 1994),

314. See also Christian Borch, "Gabriel Tarde (1843–1904)", in *The Oxford Handbook of Process Philosophy and Organization Studies*, ed. Jeny Helin, Tor Hernes, Daniel Hjorth et al. (Oxford: Oxford University Press, 2017), 191. Another convergence between Benjamin's and Tarde's ideas would seem to open up where, as mentioned above, Benjamin emphasizes the centrality of "misunderstandings" in the spread of fashions (see above), which would correspond to the proto-differentialist stance of Tarde, who, as Éric Alliez points out, underlines the transformative processes that take place in imitation.
Cf. Éric Alliez, "The Difference and Repetition of Gabriel Tarde", *Distinktion. Scandinavian Journal of Social Theory* vol. 5, no. 2 (2004), 50. Cf. Borch: "Tarde", 190.

33 There are several published versions of Simmel's text on fashion, the most visible being *Philosophie der Mode*. Simmel included this essay as a chapter simply titled "Die Mode" in his 1911 collection *Philosophische Kultur. Gesammelte Essais*. Cf. Georg Simmel: *Philosophische Kultur. Gesammelte Essais*, in idem, *Gesamtausgabe* vol. 14, eds. Rüdiger Kramme, Otthein Rammstedt (Frankfurt am Main: Suhrkamp, 1996), 159–459. Here, 186–218. This version is excerpted by Benjamin in the *Arcades Project*. There are also two shorter pieces: one the 1895 short "Zur Psychologie der Mode. Sociologische Studie" (On the Psychology of Fashion), which anticipates the argument of the later, more developed piece. See Georg Simmel, "Zur Psychologie der Mode. Sociologische Studie", in idem, *Gesamtausgabe* vol. 5, ed. Heinz-Jürgen Dahme, David Frisby (Frankfurt am Main: Suhrkamp, 1992). The 1908 "Die Frau und die Mode," which appeared in Herwarth Walden's periodical *Das Magazin*, is a nearly identical excerpt of a number of pages from *Philosophie der Mode*. Cf. Georg Simmel, "Die Frau und die Mode", in idem, *Gesamtausgabe* vol. 8, ed. Alessandro Cavalli, Volkhard Krech (Frankfurt am Main: Suhrkamp, 1993); and the editors' comments, ibid., 438.

34 In the field of social theory, Simmel's work has indeed been classified accordingly as "formal sociology." Cf., for instance, Talcot Parsons, "Simmel and the Methodological Problems of Formal Sociology", in *The American Sociologist* 29, no. 2 (Summer 1998): 31–50; or Larry Ray, ed., *Formal Sociology. The Sociology of Georg Simmel* (Aldershot, Vermont: Elgar, 1991), xiii. For a discussion of Simmel's aesthetic writings in the context of other theories of form which prevailed in late nineteenth- and early twentieth-century Germany, see Malika Maskarinec, *The Forces of Form in German Modernism* (Evanston: Northwestern University Press, 2018).

35 Cf., for instance, the argument regarding the ontological status of fictions and their characters in Kendall Walton, *Mimesis as Make-Belief. On the Foundations of the*

Representational Arts (Cambridge, Mass. and London: Harvard University Press, 1990), 385–430.

36 Bernhard Siegert, "Öffnen, Schliessen, Zerstreuen, Verdichten. Die operativen Ontologien der Kulturtechnik", *Zeitschrift für Medien- und Kulturforschung* 8, no. 2 (2017): 95–114. Here, 99, 96.

37 The formulation is Geoffrey Winthrop-Young's and is quoted in Siegert: "Öffnen, Schliessen", 100.

38 Fashion would, for instance, also fulfill Siegert's criterion for cultural techniques of having the potential for self-reference or a "pragmatics of recursion," which he develops, along with fellow cultural historian Thomas Macho, in response to the systems theoretical notion of second-order observation as second-order techniques. See Siegert, *Cultural Techniques*, 12. See Esposito's remark that, from the perspective of systems theory, fashions cannot be thought but in relation to second-order observation (Esposito, *Verbindlichkeit des Vergänglichen*, 30).

39 Siegert, *Cultural Techniques*, 9. For a substantial critique of the program of operative ontologies from the perspective of a non-ontologically oriented philosophy of technology, see Petra Gehring, "'Operative Ontologien' Technikmaterialismus als prima philosophia?", in *Zeitschrift für Medien- und Kulturforschung*, 8, no. 2 (2017): 143–155. Gehring fundamentally questions the necessity of slanting a materialist study of techniques and technologies as an ontology in the first place. Gertrud Koch's observation that the "operative fabrication of temporary ontologies is part of a performative action which draws contextual distinctions" would seem to indicate, once again, a potential connection to Simmel's analysis of fashion, with its strangely pure implementation of categorically temporalized entities—fashions—through the ongoing, i.e., temporalized, re/negotiation of demarcations and boundaries, from which spring contextual distinctions. See Gertrud Koch, "Operative Ontologien. Ein Versuch, einen klaren Begriff zu verunreinigen", *Zeitschrift für Medien- und Kulturforschung* 8, no. 2 (2017): 187–212. Here, 188.

40 While limiting her perspective to one such mode—contingency—Esposito underlines categorically: "Fashion ... is first of all the recognition and dissemination of a modal notion" (Esposito, "Fascination of Contingency", 176).

41 Georg Simmel, "The Picture Frame. An Aesthetic Study", transl. Mark Ritter, *Theory, Culture & Society* 11 (1994): 11–17. Here, 11 (TM) Georg Simmel, "Der Bildrahmen. Ein ästhetischer Versuch", in idem, *Gesamtausgabe* 7.1, ed. Rüdiger Kramme, Angela Rammstedt, Otthein Rammstedt (Frankfurt am Main: Suhrkamp, 1995).

42 It is impossible to do translational justice to the full range of Benjamin's original German notion *sprunghaft* without exploding the coherence of his sentences

through an expansive explanatory commentary. First, *sprunghaft* here encodes a reference to the figure of the tiger's leap into the past, i.e., the idea of a temporal "jump" into the past across a temporal hiatus. *Sprunghaft*, second, is here defined in opposition to progression and means "sudden," "abrupt," "instantaneous." *Sprunghaft*, finally, could also be translated as "erratic," "inconsistent," "desultory," as which it figures in Benjamin's schematic description of "bourgeois" rule as "modish" and "erratic." See above.

43 Peter Fenves, *The Messianic Reduction. Walter Benjamin and the Shape of Time* (Stanford: Stanford University Press, 2011), 242.

44 The materials in question were published by Ng, with coeditor Rochelle Tobias, in *Modern Language Notes,* 127.3 (2012).

45 Julia Ng, "Acts of Time. Cohen and Benjamin on Mathematics and History", *Paradigmi. Rivista di critica filosofia. Special Issue on Critical Idealism and Messianism. From Hermann Cohen to Walter Benjamin and Beyond* (2017): 41–60. Here quoted via https://philpapers.org/archive/NGAOT-3.pdf, 5.

46 Fenves: *Messianic Reduction*, 4. Fenves also points to an early fragment from 1918 in which Benjamin states that: "In general history is a unidirectional course" (Allgemein ist Geschichte ein einsinniger Verlauf [GS VI, 93]). Cf. Fenves: *Messianic Reduction*, 233.

47 Fenves, *Messianic Reduction*, 111; cf. ibid., 16.

48 The question remains why Benjamin—if in his late works he indeed did have recourse to his early conversations with Scholem—still writes of the "differentials of time," if, as Fenves cogently argues, the earlier models of time consist in non-differentiable functions. Another point of conjunction between Benjamin's late and very early reflections on these matters could lie in the notion of the continuum and discontinuum, which, as we saw above, he employed for modeling questions of tradition and the temporality of history in the context of the *Theses on the Concept of History*. Julia Ng has suggested to understand this late Benjaminian notion of the continuum of history in reference to another theorem, namely as a mathematical continuum. Fenves points out that among Benjamin and Scholem's early conversation topics might have been the Cantor set: an equivalent to "the complete set of points on the linear continuum, even though there are an infinite number of gaps on the corresponding line" (Fenves, *Messianic Reduction*, 110)—a discontinuum.

49 We could also pit Simmel's and Benjamin's time/fashion theories against each other on another level: Simmel observes time in the formation of fashions, and fashions as the processing of time; Benjamin observes how fashion breaks down time. Simmel is a formalist, Benjamin a functionalist thinker of the time/fashion nexus. This pairing of Simmel and Benjamin, as suggested by their treatment of

fashion, does not lack a certain irony, given that—as Fenves has also convincingly pointed out—Benjamin's first engagement with the concept of historical time occurred within the context of a reading of Simmel's works on historical time, of which Benjamin was dismissive. Fenves, *Messianic Reduction*, 14, 116 .

50 Werner Hamacher, "'Now': Walter Benjamin on Historical Time", in *Walter Benjamin and History*, ed. Andrew Benjamin (London, New York: Continuum, 2005), 47.

51 Although not fully formulated, Benjamin hints at a similar insight when he quotes from Simmel's *Philosophie des Geldes* (Philosophy of Money) and its theorization of a "concurrent differentiation" (Differenzierung im Nebeneinander), which he juxtaposes with a mode of differentiation that he calls "consecutive" (im Nacheinander), referring to the latter as "fashion" (AP 226/7) (Mode [PW 299]). The key point here lies in the recognition that concurrent differentiation is a) included in the deployment of fashion and b) has a temporal dimension. In other words, unlike in structuralism, the synchronous dimension in fashion does not amount to a field of extra-temporal relations between differences, but rather is the product and the furthering of their temporal articulation.

52 In *Philosophy of Fashion*, Simmel accordingly defines the specific profiling of individual fashions as a "change in contents which gives to fashions of today an individual stamp compared with those of yesterday and of tomorrow" (PoF 189) (Wechsel der Inhalte, der die Mode von heute individuell prägt gegenüber der von gestern und von morgen [PdM 11]), the point being that the structuring division runs between two adjacent segments of time (today/yesterday, tomorrow/today, at which point "today" will have acquired the status of a new yesterday, and what is at a given point referred to as "tomorrow" will count as a new "today").

53 Latour, *We Have Never Been Modern*, 76.

54 The *Handexemplar* has an almost identical formulation (BG 42).

55 Such an idea is espoused, for instance, in Ulrich Lehman, *Tigersprung. Fashion in Modernity* (Cambridge, Mass. and London: The MIT Press, 2000), in which the author chastises the *Passagenwerk*'s editor, Rolf Tiedemann, for opting to publish Benjamin's convolutes under the title of a *Werk* (a work, an œuvre), alleging that this "derobe[s] the project of its transitoriness—a quality within the structure itself that reflects the most important parts of the contents, namely Benjamin's aim to analyze the ephemeral, the ambiguous within the history of Paris as the capital of the nineteenth century." Notwithstanding that ephemerality and ambiguity are two different and unconnected phenomena, Lehmann asserts: "Benjamin's *Arcades Project* was meant to appear like a fabric—a fabric constantly in the making, woven from notes, materials, excerpts, and theoretical patterns.... It was meant to remain a progressing assemblage of texts, and its fragmentary and

ambiguous character, its discontinuity, was an inherent part of its potential" (216). Lehmann fails to give evidence for this claim. Citing the "fleeting" character of the Proustian memoir, Lehmann seeks to corroborate his argument: "Within this context, and in a vein perhaps instrumental for understanding his *Arcades Project*, Benjamin continues to lament the 'difficulty of finding a place for the publication of my ephemeral, although perhaps not at all superficial considerations.' Here he sides clearly with the French author's sentiment" (210). Such a use of the concept of the ephemeral is misplaced in relation to Benjamin's work, as becomes clear when one turns to the full passage from which Lehmann extracts his quote: "Besides translations I am currently occupied with criticism; yet, the stronger it appeals to me to account for contemporary topics, in particular the books of the Parisian Surrealists, the more acutely I feel the difficulty of finding a place for my ephemeral but perhaps not superficial reflections. I have had to slightly lower the hopes which I had put into the publication of the 'Literary World.'" – "Neben der Übersetzung beschäftigt mich Kritisches; aber je grösser der Reiz ist, über einige aktuelle Gegenstände, besonders Bücher der pariser Surréalisten, mir Rechenschaft zu geben, desto empfindlicher wird die Schwierigkeit fühlbar, ephemere und doch vielleicht nicht oberflächliche Überlegungen irgendwo unterzubringen. Hoffnungen, die ich auf das Erscheinen der 'Literarischen Welt' in diesem Sinne setzte, muss ich ein wenig herabstimmen" (Walter Benjamin, *Gesammelte Briefe* III [1925–1930], ed. Christoph Gödde, Henri Lonitz [Frankfurt am Main: Suhrkamp, 1997], 105). It is clear that Benjamin here uses the expression "ephemeral" to describe his texts for magazines and newspapers—i.e., the products of his work as a critic. The *Literarische Welt* was one of the publications that printed these essays. In other words, not only does the passage which Lehmann cites pre-date even the beginning of Benjamin's work on the *Arcades*, let alone his serious engagement with the project during the 1930s, by several years (the letter is from 1925), the letter also does not refer to "the ephemeral" in the sense in which Lehmann understands it—i.e., as an alleged quality of a pseudo-Proustian "memory." Rather, "ephemeral" here describes short pieces of journalistic prose; it refers to the formal and medial conditions of criticism that are published in magazines. Formally and in terms of content these are entirely unrelated to the *Arcades Project*.

56 Hamacher, "Now", 59.
57 Irving Wohlfahrt, "Et cetera? Der Historiker als Lumpensammler", in *Passagen. Walter Benjamins Urgeschichte des XIX. Jahrhunderts,* ed. Norbert Bolz, Bernd Witte (Munich: Fink, 1984), 83.
58 Josef Fürnkäs, *Surrealismus als Erkenntnis. Walter Benjamin—Weimarer Einbahnstraße und Pariser Passagen* (Stuttgart: Metzler, 1988), 316, 170.

59 Michael Jennings, "The Will to Apokatastasis. Media, Experience, and Eschatology in Walter Benjamin's Late Theological Politics", in *Walter Benjamin and Theology*, ed. Colby Dickinson, Stéphane Symons (New York: Fordham University Press, 2016), 102.

2 The contingent primacy of sex(es)

1. See Manfred Flügge, "Die wilde Helena", in Helen Hessel, *Ich schreibe aus Paris. Über die Mode, das Leben und die Liebe,* ed. Mila Ganeva (Nimbus: Wädenswil, 2014), 355. Mila Ganeva discusses Helen Grund's writing in the context of Weimar fashion journalism. Cf. Mila Ganeva, *Women in Weimar Fashion. Discourses and Displays in German Culture, 1918-1933* (Rochester: Camden House, 2008), 84–110. Cf. the chapter dedicated to Grund in Julia Bertschik, *Mode und Moderne*, 274–282.
2. See Mila Ganeva, *Women in Weimar Fashion*, 87; Bertschik, *Mode und Moderne*, 182. At a later point Grund would, albeit covertly and indirectly, achieve international literary and cinematic fame—the ménage à trois which she and her husband led with French writer, critic, and Duchamp interlocutor Henri Pierre Roché serving as material for the latter's 1953 novel *Jules et Jim* and the eponymous 1962 film by Truffaut, in which the character based on Grund would be played by Jeanne Moreau.
3. *Für die Frau*, February 1929, 12.
4. Ibid.
5. *Für die Frau*, April 1929, 12.
6. Ibid., 10.
7. *Für die Frau*, July 1929, 13.
8. Ibid., 11.
9. *Für die Frau*, November 1929, 9.
10. *Für die Frau*, March 1930, 9.
11. On the *élegance sportive* in Patou's designs of the era, cf. Johanna Zanon, "Quand la couture célèbre le corps féminin: Jean Patou (1919–1920)", Thèse pour le diplôme d'archiviste paléographe, École nationale des chartes, Paris, 2012, 443–446. In her *thèse*, Zanon provides a meticulously detailed study of the organizational, commercial, as well as aesthetic strategies of the *maison* and its founder, relying throughout on previously unearthed archival material.
12. *Für die Frau*, May 1930, 8.
13. *Harper's Bazaar UK*, I.1, October 1929, 18.
14. Ibid., 31.
15. Ibid., *Harper's Bazaar UK,* I.2, October 1929, 22.

16 *Vogue UK*, November 13, 1929, 60. *Vogue*, January 4, 1930, 50–53.
17 *Vogue UK*, 1, 1930, 47.
18 *Harper's Bazaar UK*, I.1, October 1929, 31. Cf. Martine Rénier in *Femina*: "Une grande nouvelle vous attend au début de ce printemps: vous avez à nouveaux des formes, ô femmes élégantes! vous avez une taille à sa place" (*Femina*, April 1929, 3).
19 *Harper's Bazaar UK*, I.1, October 1929, 31. "Et voici donc que la ligne 'ajustée' reparaît après une éclipse de tant d'années! Car il est une vérité indiscutable qui ressort de toutes les collections nouvelles vues ce temps-ci: la taille est revenue à sa place presque partout et le corsage suit à peu près la ligne du corps" (*Femina*, March 1929, 3).
20 *Vogue*, quoted in Meredith Etherington-Smith, *Patou* (London, Melbourne, Sydney: Hutchinson, 1983), 113, 115. In 1931 *Vogue Paris* summarily declared, "Le tailleur occupera une place de choix dans la mode, non seulement par lui-même mais par son influence. Sa netteté, sa sobriété serviront de règle et de mesure pour de nombreux modèles" (*Vogue Paris*, August 1931, 15). Cf. the following assessments: "la nouvelle silhouette tire parti des lignes naturelles; si elle en modifie l'apparence elle ne les comprime ni les déforme. Nous aurons, c'est un fait, la taille plus mince" (*Vogue Paris*, October 1931, 31). One issue later, *Vogue Paris* declared "le corps de la femme" to be the common denominator of the central recent developments in fashion: "Évidemment, on pourrait avancer que toutes les vêtements ont toujours été faits pour être portés sur un corps, mais á certaines époques le rôle de cette armature était secondaire, tandis qu'il est redevenu primordial. Actuellement, ce qu'il y a de plus important dans la robe, c'est la femme. L'emplacement de la taille qui pendant longtemps avait été une ligne idéale, une suggestion, et même pourrait-on dire: un souvenir historique—est de nouveau une réalité précise. . . . Le mot de 'taille' n'est plus un vain mot. On a éliminé tout détail qui tendrait à altérer la ligne véritable du corps, au lieu de l'accuser. Les courbes naturelles, la place, et surtout l'étroitesse de la taille, la longueur des jambes, sont nettement et également accentuées le jour et le soir" (*Vogue Paris*, November 1931, 15).
21 *Vogue*, quoted in Etherington-Smith: *Patou*, 113. Cf. also fashion scholar Guillaume Garnier's assessment that the determining event of the decade consisted in the lengthening of the skirt. Garnier also qualifies the uniqueness of Patou's position by pointing to earlier tendencies in the collections of Hartnell and parallel developments at Lelong (Garnier, "Quelques couturiers", 9). See also Rénier in *Femina*, March 1929, 3.
22 *Femina*, April 1929, 3. About half a year later, Rénier declares, "On a vraiment applaudi, que dis-je? acclamé sa collection d'automne et je crois que 1929

comptera dans l'histoire du costume." Patou's biographer, Etherington-Smith, points out that the transformation did not occur quite as unprecedentedly as the tone of the reviews of 1929/1930 might indicate. During several seasons of 1927 and 1928 he had already begun slightly altering and twisting the silhouette to move away from the geometric layout of the more orthodox flapper dresses, as a matter of fact also mentioning these alterations in interviews. Cf. Etherington-Smith, *Patou*, 103. She also points out that, between 1924 and 1929, Patou had been designing costumes for stage dancers (among his clients were Josephine Baker and the Dolly Sisters)—dance dresses—in which he kept the waistline distinctly defined and accentuated. What occurred in 1929 was, to an extent, the displacement and refinement of these cuts that were engineered to be viewed from the distance of the theater audience to the close proximity of the fashion house, its salon runway, and ultimately the immediate social gatherings of the fashion customer. Cf. ibid., 108–109. See also Emmanuelle Polle, *Jean Patou. A Fashionable Life* (Paris: Flammarion, 2013), 42–43. Cf. also fashion historian Patricia Mears's assessment that the beginnings of the "long and sinuous silhouette of the period" and its various constitutive elements "articulated (but not exaggerated) shoulder, fitted torso, natural waistline, narrow hip, and elongated hemline" can be located around 1927. Patricia Mears, "The Arc of Modernity I. Women's Couture in the 1930s", in *Elegance in an Age of Crisis. Fashions of the 1930s*, ed. idem, G. Bruce Boyer (New Haven, London: New York, Yale University Press/Fashion Institute of Technology, 2014), 62.

23 Cf. Peter Wollen, *Raiding the Icebox. Reflections on Twentieth-Century Culture* (London, New York: Verso, 2008); and Caroline Evans, *Mechanical Smile*, 3. On the relations between the *Maison Patou* and various female athletes, cf. Zanon: "Patou", 313.

24 Evans has researched this case in her article "Jean Patou's American Mannequins. Early Fashion Shows and Modernism", *Modernism/Modernity*, 15, no. 2 (2008): 243–263. See also Polle, *Jean Patou*, 232–257. On the company's overall multimedia publicity strategy, see Zanon: "Patou", 293–324. And, on the case of the American girls, as well as Patou's overall "Americanism" during the second half of the 1920s, ibid., 332–334. On one attempt by Patou to master the immediate economic implications—i.e., the ongoing commercial relation between the French producers, their American customers (as well as illegal copyists abroad—a fact that greatly chagrined Patou's colleague Vionnet; see chapter 3), namely the foundation of the short-lived subsidiary line *Jane Paris*—see Véronique Pouillard, Johanna Zanon, "Wholesale Couture. Jean Patou's Line Jane Paris", forthcoming in *Dress. The Journal of the Costume Society of America.*

25 Cf. the short biography of Manuel in Caroline Evans, Marketa Uhlirova, ed., *Marcel L'Herbier: Dossier* (London: Fashion in Film, www.fashioninfilm.com, 2014), 58.
26 At least by Manuel's account, Boulanger was far from happy to execute what, in 1927, when filming for *L'Argent* took place, for her—in his words—amounted to "destroying the current 'line'." Cf. Jacques Manuel, "Esquisse d'une historie du costume de cinéma", *La revue du cinéma,* no. 19–20 (1949): 3–63. Here, 36–40. This section is excerpted and translated in Evans, Uhlirova, *Marcel L'Herbier*, 25. See also Guillaume Garnier, "Quelques couturiers, quelques modes", in *Paris Couture Années Trente* (Paris: Musée de la mode et du costume, Palais Galiera, 1987), 9.
27 SW 3, 117; GS I.2, 461.
28 Manuel: "Esquisse", 4; Evans, Uhlirova: *Marcel L'Herbier*, 10–11.
29 Ibid., 11.
30 For the identification of the color of Helm's gown see Mireille Beaulieu, Moving Human Décor. Marcel L'Herbier, Fashion, and Cinéma Total in Evans, Uhlirova, *Marcel L'Herbier*, 18.
31 Evans: *Mechanical Smile*, 233.
32 One notable exception from this overall disregard is Howard Eiland's and Michael Jennings's *Walter Benjamin: A Critical Life* (Cambridge, Mass. and London: The Belknap Press/Harvard University Press, 2014), 498.
33 Walter Benjamin, *Gesammelte Briefe*, v, ed. Christoph Gödde, Henri Lonitz (Frankfurt am Main: Suhrkamp, 1999), 133.
34 Ibid.
35 See Eiland, Jennings: *Walter Benjamin*, 285–286
36 Walter Benjamin, *Gesammelte Briefe*, v, 155–156. See "…und immer nur Handschuhe. Das Leben von Gretel Adorno", *Neues Deutschland. Sozialistische Tageszeitung*, 20.12.2014, accessed at https://www.neues-deutschland.de/artikel/956137.und-immer-nur-handschuhe.html.
37 Theodor W. Adorno, *Briefe und Briefwechsel* vol. 1, ed. Henri Lonitz (Frankfurt am Main: Suhrkamp, 1994), 147.
38 Thorstein Veblen, *The Theory of the Leisure Class. An Economic Study in the Evolution of Institutions* (New York: Macmillan, 1899). Barbara Vinken points to Simmel's recognition of the function of the *demi monde* in the creation of fashion, which evidently contradicts trickle-down assumptions that Benjamin—who likewise acknowledges the function of bohemia for the generation of fashion—shared with him. Vinken, *Fashion Zeitgeist*, 14. See also Esposito: *Verbindlichkeit des Vorübergehenden*, 22, where she expands this critique, contra Bourdieu, to the point of fashion marking exactly an instance in which taste consistently does *not*

correlate with class identity. See also Herbert Blumer, "Fashion. From Class Differentiation to Collective Selection", in *The Sociological Quarterly*, 10, no. 3 (1969): 275–291; and Robinson, who introduced the lateral version of a "trickle-across" model in Dwight E. Robinson, "The Rules of Fashion Cycles", in *Harvard Business Review* (November–December 1958). Contemporary fashion theory has also coined the expression of "bubble-up" movements for the adoption of the styles of economically and politically underprivileged or deprived social subgroups, and there are of course ample examples for such tendencies: The crucial point, however, is that fashion as a temporalized processing of difference can operationalize such difference regardless of its social situatedness or "point of origin," to the point that said point of origin need not correlate to any existing social fault line.

39 For a bibliography of Grund's publications, to the extent that they are known, see Helen Hessel, *Ich schreibe aus Paris. Über die Mode, das Leben und die Liebe*, ed. Mila Ganeva (Wädenswil: Nimbus, 2014), 367–374.

40 Winfried Menninghaus has emphasized that Darwin considered all sorts of cultural fashions, including body ornaments and dress styles, as extensions of and substitutes for "the sexually selected caprices ... of the natural bodies of sexual organisms." Cf. Winfried Menninghaus, "Biology à la Mode. Charles Darwin's Aesthetics of 'Ornament'", in *History and Philosophy of the Life Sciences*, 31, no. 2 (2009): 271–272. In "Caprices of Fashion," Menninghaus further points to a potential relation between Darwin and Benjamin, in that the former, with an eye to the fashions of his own historical present, theorized "the sexual ornaments of natural bodies" through a visual inventory which in turn became the anchoring point for Benjamin's dialectical image work in the *Arcades Project* (Menninghaus: "Caprices of Fashion", 144).

41 George H. Darwin: "Development in Dress", 410.

42 Cf. Ernest Jones, "Early Development of Female Sexuality (1927)", in idem, *Papers on Psychoanalysis* (London: Baillière, 1950). See also the entry "Aphanisis" in *International Dictionary of Psychoanalysis* vol. 1, ed. Alain de Mijolla (Detroit, New York, San Francisco, etc: Thomson Gale, 2005), 105.

43 Tristan Tzara, "D'un certain Automatisme du Goût", *Minotaure*, no. 3/4 (1933): 81–84. Benjamin was familiar with this publication. At other points in the *Arcades Project*, he excerpted from segments of Stéphane Mallarmé's 1874 monoauthored, short-lived, fashion journal, *La dernière mode*, which had been republished in *Minotaure*'s 1935 winter issue.

44 Cf. Blum: *Shocking!*, 127.

45 Cf. Tzara: "Automatisme", 82.

46 Ibid.

47 Ibid. Tzara's construction is indeed not entirely without precedent and overall less eccentric than it would seem, given Darwin's connection between cultural and biological "caprices of fashion" and sexual selection. (Cf. footnote 40). What marks Tzara's position—and marks it as Surreal—is its strange literalism, i.e., the assumption that millinery, not just structurally but qua resemblance, substitutes and extends genital organs, hence generating the unsettlingly graphic effect of human—in this case female—bodies on which sexual organs "wander," shift positions, etc.
48 Tzara: "Automatisme", 82.
49 Ibid.
50 Ibid.
51 Ibid.
52 Ibid.
53 Cf. Etherington-Smith: Patou, 116.
54 Cf. *Shocking Life. The Autobiography of Elsa Schiaparelli* (London: V&A Publications, 2007), 88–89.
55 Helen Grund, "Vom Wesen der Mode" (Munich: Meisterschule für Mode, 1935)., 12.
56 Cf. James C. Fluegel, *The Psychology of Clothes,* ed. Leonard and Virginia Woolf (London: The Hogarth Press and the Institute of Psycho-Analysis, 1930).
57 *Vogue UK*, September 4, 1929, 34. In her history of Paris fashion, Valerie Steele cautions that with the perspective of greater hindsight sometimes even protagonists of the historical moment of the 1920s and 1930s such as Cecil Beaton might emphasize the continuities, rather than the differences between the periods, hence also relativizing the described "feminization" of women's couture. Cf. Valerie Steele, *Paris Fashion. A Cultural History* (New York, Oxford: Oxford University Press, 1988), 266. Given the fundamentally differential character of fashion, such changes in opinion are hardly surprising. What in 1931 might have seemed a watershed moment, might from the perspective of 1961 or even 1971 seem much more of a continuum.
58 While not to be regarded as determining the course of fashion, it is highly informative to consider the wider cultural and historical context against which this newly accentuated opposition of two sexes emerges. For France, one could turn to the scholarship of cultural historian Mary Lou Roberts and her study *Civilization without Sexes. Reconstructing Gender in Postwar France (1917–1927)* (Chicago: University of Chicago Press, 1994).
59 Sigrid Weigel has investigated a related genealogy in Benjamin's writings by which the whore comes to function as an allegory of modernity. See Sigrid Weigel,

Entstellte Ähnlichkeit. Walter Benjamins theoretische Schreibweise (Frankfurt am Main: Fischer, 1997), 130–146.

60 Susan Buck-Morss, "The Flaneur, the Sandwichman and the Whore: The Politics of Loitering", in *New German Critique*, 39 (Fall 1986): 119.

61 Ibid., 120.

62 Buck-Morss: *Dialectics of Seeing*, 121.

63 On a structural level, these operations thus participate in the overall sociological obfuscation of women's labor in modernity, as well as in the sociological literature studying the problem of labor in modernity, which Janet Wolff has analyzed. See Janet Wolff, "The Invisible Flâneuse: Women and the Literature of Modernity", in *The Problems of Modernity. Adorno and Benjamin*, ed. Andrew Benjamin (London, New York: Routledge, 1989). See also Anne Friedberg's expansion of these concerns into an analysis of the gendering of observation and *flânerie* in nineteenth-century (Parisian) culture, and her point that it is within the architectural *dispositif* of the department store that the possibility of female *flânerie* is first explored (Anne Friedberg, *Window Shopping. Cinema and the Postmodern* [Berkeley, Los Angeles, Oxford: University of California Press, 1993], 32–37). Cf. also Aruna D'Souza, Tom McDonough, eds., *The Invisible Flâneuse. Gender, Public Space and Visual Culture in Nineteenth Century Paris* (Manchester: Manchester University Press, 2006).

64 Cf. Dora Benjamin's letter to Gerschom Scholem in Hans Puttnies, Gary Smith, ed., *Benjaminiana* (Giessen, Anabas Verlag: 1991), 152. For a study of fashion journalism at Ullstein publishers, see Mila Ganeva: *Women in Weimar Fashion*, 50–83.

65 Cf. Die praktische Berlinerin. Das Blatt der Bazar-Schnittmuster. Vol.2 No 2 (January 1927).

66 Foster, Hal. Compulsive Beauty. Cambridge, Mass. and London (The MIT Press) 1993. In particular chapter 5 - Outmoded Spaces.

67 Already George H. Darwin implicitly identified the problem of morphology as underlying the common study of fashion and evolution: "The development of dress presents a strong analogy to that of organisms, as explained by the modern theories of evolution ... We shall see that the truth expressed by the proverb, 'Natura non facit saltum,' is applicable in the one case as in the other; the law of progress holds good in dress, and forms blend into one another with almost complete continuity" (Darwin, "Development in Dress", 411). What the analysis of evolution and fashion shared was an interest in processes of metamorphosis, which, since Goethe, in parallel to the physician Burdach, coined the term "morphology" and initiated this mode of inquiry, had been identified as part and parcel of any morphological study. To study form meant studying its transformation.

68 Henri Focillon, *The Life of Forms in Art,* transl. Charles Hogan, George Kubler (New York: Zone Books, 1989), 85–87. Cf. AP 80. Focillon's translators—his Yale colleague Charles Beecher Hogan and his Yale student George Kubler—classify Focillon's approach as morphological for the Anglophone reader, while also clarifying that here morphology implies the study of metamorphoses: "This . . . is a critique that applies to art the principles of morphology that may be observed in and are manifested by means of metamorphoses." Cf. Charles Beecher Hogan, George Kubler, "Foreword", in *Henri Focillon: The Life of Forms in Art* (New Haven: Yale University Press, 1942), vi. (This foreword isn't included in the Zone re-edition of the text.)
69 Focillon, *Life of Forms,* 85.
70 See, for instance, the subchapter "Technical Invention: Ground and Form in the Living and in Inventive Thought" in Gilbert Simondon, *On the Mode of Existence of Technical Objects* (Minneapolis, Univocal Publishing, 2017), 59–62. In Simondon's approach, a theory of the inventive process of forms relies on the assumption that a milieu, in the sense of a ground, functions as "the common reservoir of the forms' tendencies, well before they exist separately and constitute themselves as an explicit system." In this sense, the relation of ground/milieu to forms "diffuses an influence of the future onto the present, of the virtual onto the actual. For the ground is the system of virtualities, of potentials . . ., whereas forms are the system of actuality" (ibid., 62). These ideas would be perfectly easy to adopt into a theory of fashion, namely where it is concerned with the genesis of new forms, i.e., the reservoir of potential, non-actualized forms. In Benjamin's fashion thought, this future-oriented axis is, again, most strongly articulated through its pastward slant: if the tiger's leap is the main operation for the generation of fashions, its overall ground would be those styles that once had been formed, that had been lost and forgotten, and had not been redeemed. If we were to insist on using the category of milieu, we'd have to turn it into a concept which refers to a doubly temporal milieu: the ground of forms to come is the ground of latent forms to be retrieved. The analogy could be extended into Benjamin's reflections on historical apocatastasis, which operate with the idea of a negative *fonds*/ground for the retrieved positives (see chapter 1 and chapter 4). Historian of science Henning Schmidgen draws a line from Simondon's notion of an interior milieu to Focillon's concept of style. See Henning Schmidgen, "Mode d'existence. Memoirs of a concept", in *Reset Modernity,* ed. Bruno Latour, Christophe Leclerq (Cambridge, Mass. and London, Karlsruhe: MIT Press/ZKM, 2016).
71 Focillon: *Life of Forms,* 154.
72 In his highly influential treatise *The Shape of Time,* Focillon student and historian of pre-Columbian art George Kubler nearly exactly inverts (and confirms) this

logic. In his account, the concept of formal change relates to a sequence of linked solutions for a corresponding problem ("Each class of forms consists of a real difficulty and of real solutions"): George Kubler, *The Shape of Time. Remarks on the History of Things* (New Haven, London: Yale University Press, 1962), 38. Examples for such "gradually altered repetitions of the same trait" given by Kubler are the development of segmented structures with rib vaults in the history of French Gothic cathedral architecture, which, in its manifestation at Mantes cathedral, allowed for a "uniform rhythm of equivalent supports under evenly distributed light," while leaving the volume of the interior intact; ancient Greek vase painting; but also, by analogy, theories of canonicity, such as TS Eliot's view, articulated in his famous essay "Tradition and the Individual Talent," that each (successful) new literary text engenders a reappraisal and restructuring of the extant field of canonical texts (ibid., 35, 37). Fashion, by contrast, is for Kubler not only marked by its brief durations, but also by the fact that it is "the projection of a single image of outward being, resistant to change during its brief life, ephemeral, expendable, receptive only to copying but not to fundamental variation" (ibid., 39). Fashions "belong not to a connected chain of solutions, but they constitute, each fashion in turn, classes of only one member each" (ibid.). Kubler's stance is perhaps best summed up in the following sentence: "A fashion is a duration without substantial change: an apparition, a flicker, forgotten with the round of the seasons. It is like a class, but it differs from a sequence by having no appreciable dimension in time" (ibid.). The point being that, through the layers of his animus against fashion, and in labeling fashion as executing transformations without substance, Kubler almost arrives at the acumen of Simmel's and Focillon's analyses, which both treat fashion as change in its purest manifestation, almost as an intransitive: not change of something, but change by itself. Where Kubler's stance divergences from the ones at the center of this book is, obviously, the question of whether fashion contributes to making time appreciable. Kubler denies this; Benjamin and others answer in the affirmative.

3 In/Elegant materialisms

1 Walter Benjamin-Archiv, call number WBA 227, 5.
2 Helen Grund, "Vom Wesen der Mode" (Munich: Meisterschule für Mode, 1935). Here, 4. In recent years the text has been reprinted in Hessel, *Ich schreibe aus Paris*, 251–272.
3 Bertschik, *Mode und Moderne*, 278.

4 See Ganeva, *Women in Weimar Fashion*, 102, 110, who quotes from the article "Die Sorgen einer Meisterschule" (The Concerns of One Professional School) that appeared in *Das Schwarze Korps* on January 21, 1937. See also Bertschik, *Mode und Moderne*, 279.
5 Ibid.
6 Grund, "Wesen der Mode", 21.
7 Ibid., 5.
8 Ibid., 10.
9 WBA 227, 5.
10 Ibid, 4–5.
11 Grund's employs the term *Stofflichkeit*, which in German, in addition to its more narrow meaning of "materiality," also carries textile connotations (*Stoff* referring both to matter and cloth).
12 WBA 227, 1
13 Grund's attention to and appreciation of the figure of the model are another proof of the frequently overlooked centrality which, as Caroline Evans puts it, the mannequin occupied "in . . . a modernist flow of images, commodities, bodies and styles that circulated in the early twentieth century," and within which the overall production of fashion occurred. Caroline Evans, *The Mechanical Smile*, 3.
14 WBA 227, 1.
15 Ibid., 2.
16 Ibid., 1–2. Grund's account coincides precisely with Evans's observation that French models were known for their gliding walk. Cf. *Mechanical Smile*, 219, as well as Evans's analysis of the semantics of movement in the fashion press on 299.
17 Ibid., 7.
18 In this regard we can observe another impact of the medium of film, which mediated the movement qualities of outfits, the way in which a body would walk in them. Historically coeval with the presentation format of the fashion show (which in its interspersing of the model's walk with a moment of still posing also communicated the fashion shoot), the filmic camera, while arguably far less exhaustively used in its documentary capacity than the photographic camera, provided images that transported and even instituted core kinetic features of fashion. As much was clear even beyond the terrain of fashion, in everyday life, as discussed in a famous lecture by anthropologist Marcel Mauss. Theorizing *techniques of the body* ("all the modes of training, imitation and especially those fundamental fashions that can be called 'modes of life', the *modes*, the *tonus*, the matter, the manners, the way"), Mauss gives the example of the strangely familiar gait of the nurses at a New York City hospital where

he was recovering from an illness, to realize that he recognizes this manner of walking from the cinema where it had been exercised by actresses; later, upon his return to France, the movies had brought that particular mode of movement to the streets of Paris. Cf. Marcel Mauss, "Techniques of the Body", in *Incorporations*, ed. Jonathan Crary, Sanford Kwinter (New York: Zone, 1992), 456.

19 This acknowledgment of the character of fashion as an industry—i.e., as a system in which production, and labor, occurs on all sorts of levels—is again difficult to reconcile with the allegorical alignment of the commodity and the figure of "woman," which we find in Benjamin's writing (see chapter 2). In turn, Grund has little to offer as far as a critical theory of commodification is concerned.

20 In a piece that is roughly contemporaneous with her lecture "On the Essence of Fashion," Grund expands these observations into a series of reflections on the category of *Haltung* (stance), both in the sense of bodily posture and of attitude in and toward the world. *Haltung*, which also qualifies a model, can be trained, Grund holds. Cf. Helen Grund, "Über die Haltung", in Hessel, *Ich schreibe aus Paris*, 273–278.

21 For the German context, i.e. the language in which Grund formulated her concept of elegance, see *Deutsches Wörterbuch von Jacob und Wilhelm Grimm. Neubearbeitung* vol. 7 (Stuttgart, Leipzig: Hirzel, 1993), 1209-1211. Cf. the entry "elegant", according to which the expression has been used since the late fifteenth century in English, in *The Barnhart Dictionary of Etymology*, ed. Robert K. Barnhart (New York: Wilson, 1988), 32. See also the investigation of concepts of elegance done at the Frankfurt Max Planck-Institute for Empirical Aesthetics, published in Winfried Menninghaus, Valentin Wagner, Vanessa Kegel, Christine A. Knoop, Wolf Schlotz: "Beauty, Elegance, Grace, and Sexiness Compared", in: PLoS ONE 14:6 (2019). https://doi.org/10.1371/journal.pone.0218728. For the history of the concept see ibid, 2. The overlaps between Grund's theorization of elegance, which derived from years of observation and exercising critical discernment in relation to fashion, and the findings of Menninghaus et al's empirical study of linguistic conceptualizations of elegance are astonishing. These pertain to general qualities associated with elegance, such as lightness, fluency and simplicity. They relate to the juxtaposition of elegance and grace, whereby the former is associated with a cultural, and the latter with a natural pole, hence matching approximately with the distinction proposed above, according to which "grace" figures as a quasi-transcendental category—a gift, whereas elegance pertains to the realm of techniques. The matches even extend down to the very concrete implementations of fashion history: when asked to identify features of physical build and gait attributed to individuals perceived as elegant, participants in the Frankfurt study named "long legs". One of the central tendencies of Paris 1930s couture was of

course, the development of a silhouette that created an impression of "elongated" legs, in that it raised the waist-line and dropped the hems.

22 WBA 227, 4.
23 Ibid.
24 Ibid.
25 Grund, "Wesen der Mode", 10.
26 Benjamin deemed the entire chapter in the *Le poète assassiné* which Apollinaire dedicated to the subject of fashion "one of the most important texts for elucidating the eccentric, revolutionary, and surrealist possibilities of fashion" (AP 68) ([e]ine der wichtigsten Stellen zur Beleuchtung der exzentrischen, revolutionären und surrealistischen Möglichkeiten der Mode [PW 116–117]).
27 Dilys E. Blum, *Shocking! The Art and Fashion of Elsa Schiaparelli* (New Haven, London: Yale University Press/Philadelphia Museum of Art, 2003), 51.
28 Spyros Papapetros has analyzed a wide variety of examples for such disanimating tendencies in late nineteenth- and early twentieth-century culture, aesthetics, architecture, and art in his *On the Animation of the Inorganic. Art, Architecture, and the Extension of Life* (Chicago, London: The University of Chicago Press, 2012). See in particular chapter 6, "Daphne's Legacy" (ibid., 263–317).
29 Schiaparelli and Antoine extended their project into the depths of art history with their 1935 fancy dress costume for the Vicomtesse Benoist d'Azy on the occasion of the *Bal des tableaux célèbres*, where she appeared as Botticelli's *Birth of Venus*—her wig a massive protrusion of golden torques. Cf. Blum: *Shocking!*, 180.
30 The coat is in the Brooklyn Museum Costume Collection at the Metropolitan Museum's Costume Institute. Accession Number 2009.300.1212. The suit, part of the same collection, is 2009.300.198a, b.
31 Cf. Blum, *Shocking!*, 132.
32 Ibid., 191.
33 Ibid, 165.
34 Ibid.
35 Comparatist Sabine Mainberger points out that Benjamin, in one of the entries to his volume *Denkbilder*, discusses a Biedermeier parlor game in which the participants were presented with lists of semantically unrelated words which they then, respecting their order, had to craft into ad hoc stories, claiming that this echoed the manner in which "the people" (das Volk) also read novels. Mainberger further underlines the proximity of these ideas to Surrealist production practices. Cf. Sabine Mainberger, *Die Kunst des Aufzählens. Elemente zu einer Poetik des Enumerativen* (Berlin, New York: de Gruyter, 2003), 33–35. Cf. ibid., 228–230 for observations on the function of word lists and enumerations in avant-garde manifestos, including Breton's *First Manifesto of Surrealism*.

36 Cf. Peter Bürger, *Der französische Sürrealismus. Studien zur avantgardistischen Literatur* (Frankfurt: Suhrkamp, 1996), 148.
37 Charles Baudelaire, *Les Fleurs du mal, précédées d'une notice par Théophile Gauthier* (Paris: Calmann-Lévy, 1869), 270.
38 SW 4, 324.
39 GS 1.2, 623.
40 SW 4, 324, TM.
41 GS 1.2, 623.
42 AP 79-80, TM; PW 130. On Baudelaire's fashion aesthetics, see Vinken, *Fashion Zeitgeist*, 42-50.
43 In another variant, Benjamin described the wax museum as the site of a "mixing up" (Vermengung) of the ephemeral and the fashionable, testing a perspective in which what counts as "in" is not to be equated with the passing or the fleeting moment (AP 860; PW 1030): "Waxworks: mixture of the ephemeral and the fashionable."
44 Cf. Betty Kirke, *Madeleine Vionnet* (San Francisco: Chronicle Books, 1998), 36, 140-142.
45 On Vionnet's draping technique, see Betty Kirke, "Vionnet: Fashion's Twentieth Century Technician", in *Thresholds* 22 (2001): 78-83. Here, 80. On her usage of crêpe, see *Madeleine Vionnet. Puriste de la mode,* ed. Pamela Golbin (Paris: Les Arts Décoratifs, 2009), 49. Golbin further notes that muslin and crêpe are similar textiles, the latter having a higher thread count and a more elaborate torsion (ibid.). Garnier points out that the bias also served to sculpt the body underneath, by profiling its surfaces in space (Garnier, "Quelques couturiers", 12).
46 *Femina*, February 1931, 15.
47 See Lydia Kamitsis's analysis in her entry "Le style 'antique'", in *L'Art de la couture. Madeleine Vionnet, 1876-1975* (Marseille: Musées de Marseille, Union Française des Arts du Costume, 1991), 66-67. Here, 67.
48 Cf. Blum, *Shocking!*, 64, 185.
49 See, for instance, the review in *Vogue Paris* ("sorte d'imaginaire ville pétrifiée") excerpted in the *Pavillon*'s official round-up booklet: *Le Pavillon de l'Élégance à l'Exposition Internationale des Arts et Techniques 1937* (Paris: Arts et Métiers, 1938), 14; *Vogue Paris*, June 1937, 55. The description as a grotto, ibid. Cf. Hélène Guéné, "Jeanne Lanvin et les grandes expositions", in *Jeanne Lanvin*, ed. Sophie Grossiord (Paris: Galliera, 2015), 261. The same impression was recorded in a review in *Le Figaro*, where it was applied to the pavillon's mannequins: "Voici donc des mannequins en glaise, sans visage sinon

sans tête, d'une ligne un peu hors nature et pétris" (*Le Pavillon de l'Élégance*, 14).

50 Cf. Valérie da Costa, *Robert Couturier* (Paris: Éditions Norma, 2000), 32.

51 Ibid. The only participant in the show who shunned the prerogative was Schiaparelli who, instead, chose to drape her dress on a chair next to a mannequin, which, seated on the ground, remained "nude." Tellingly, the *Figaro* review explains (and approves) of the "heavy" aesthetic of the mannequins by the necessary principal shortcomings of "des mannequins immobiles et rigides"; i.e., the perceived lack of movement and animation can only be countered by additionally emphasizing gravity (Le pavillon de l'Élégance, 14). Cf. even more explicitly the view of Être Belle: "Auprès des mannequins vivants, créateurs du movement, il a fallu imaginer des mannequins qui ne soient plus une pâle reproduction de la femme comme celles qui encombrent les vitrines depuis un demi-siècle.... C'est là une heureuse tentative de renouvellement de l'art du mannequin qui, jusqu'ici, trahissait par son immobilité d'attitudes les créations de la couture" (ibid.).

52 In his memoirs Théodore de Banville calls her "une fille ... d'une très haute taille." As quoted in Beatrice Stith Clark, "Elements of Black Exoticism in the 'Jeanne Duval' poems of *Les Fleurs du mal*", in *CLA Journal* 14, no. 1 (September 1970): 62–74. Here, 62.

53 *Vogue Paris* described the *Pavillon* as taking on a Surrealist air (*Vogue Paris*, June 1937, 55).

54 Cf. Couturier's description of the *Pavillon*'s interior design, which evoked a subterranean world in several ways: "Ce pavillon de l'Élégance avait une structure comme une voûte de métro. Les bas-reliefs représentaient une ville, une ville méditerranée après une catastrophe qui rappelait Pompéi" (da Costa: *Couturier*, 32).

55 In August 1937 *Vogue Paris* illustrated their opening column, "Point de vue de Vogue," with a large number of Wols's pictures. The first systematic account of Wols's fashion photography and its impact can be found in Christine Mehring, *Wols. Photographs* (Cambridge, Mass.: Busch Reisinger Museum, 1999). See also Nina Schleif, "Die Modefotografien in Paris 1937: Ein Blick auf alte und neue Quellen", in *Wols als Photograph. Der gerettete Blick,* ed. Michael Hering (Ostfildern: Hatje Cantz, 2013).

56 Cf. Jacqueline Demornex, *Madeleine Vionnet* (London: Thames and Hudson, 1991), 109.

57 On Ubac's photographic methods within the overall context of the radical formal strategies of the Surrealists cf. Rosalind Krauss, "Corpus Delicti", in October 33 (Summer 1985), 31–72.

58 Schiaparelli's Summer 1937 collection was explicitly titled *Metamorphosis*. On the various aesthetic implementations of the Daphne motif at that point in time, see Papapetros, *On the Animation of the Inorganic*.

59 In these oscillations we can perhaps recognize a shifting between the poles of a matrix from which unilateral vectors of thought were extracted on other occasions, omitting the push and pull in both directions. Think of Caillois's little story of mimicry as a deconstitutive drift of the individual into its surroundings, the collapse into dead matter. Enriched by a theory of the psyche, the article in which Caillois articulated these ideas was titled *Mimétisme et psychasthénie légendaire* (Mimicry and Legendary Psychasthenia) and published in the seventh issue of *Minotaure* in 1935; this text would become one of the launching points for Lacan's reformulation of the Freudian theory of the death drive, accomplished in his *Seminar XI – The Four Fundamental Concepts of Psychoanalysis (1963/64)*. What at that point had solidified into a straightforward theory of the fall into inertia might, if considered within its original context, and even if regarded from the admittedly eccentric perspective of fashion, have only been one half of the equation: a field in which what mattered could be made light and alive, as well as heavy and inanimate. At least as far as the aesthetics and poetics of *la mode* were concerned, this was the case.

60 Georg Simmel, "Aesthetik der Schwere", in *Gesamtausgabe* vol. 7, ed. Rüdiger Kramme, Angela Rammstedt, Otthein Ramstedt (Frankfurt am Main: Suhrkamp, 1995). On Simmel's "Aesthetics of Gravity" in the context of a general theorization of force and form in the German aesthetics and literature of the nineteenth and early twentieth centuries, see Maskarinec, *Forces of Form*, 33–36.

61 SW 4, 259; GS I.2, 488.

62 Walter Benjamin, "What is Epic Theatre?" (first version), transl. Anna Bostock, in idem *Understanding Brecht* (London, New York: Verso) 1998, 1–13, p. 3. Walter Benjamin: "Was ist das epische Theater? Eine Studie zu Brecht", (1), GS 2.2, 521.

63 GS 2.3, 1381. In the artwork essay, Benjamin mentions in passing another example of what he considers "material." He writes that the Dadaists perform a fundamental "degradation" (Entwürdigung) of their "material": "Their poems are 'word salad' containing obscene expressions and every imaginable kind of linguistic refuse. The same is true of their paintings, on which they mounted buttons or train tickets" (SW 3, 119) (Ihre Gedichte sind "Wortsalat", sie enthalten obszöne Wendungen und allen nur vorstellbaren Abfall der Sprache. Nicht anders ihre Gemälde, denen sie Knöpfe oder Fahrscheine aufmontierten [GS I.2, 502]). Although not explicitly, Benjamin here advances an idea of language as material. Already in the case of Dadaist visual montage works, the logics is less clear: are we

supposed to understand "buttons and tickets" as material, in the sense of material scraps, or is the visual production the material that is debased through the application of buttons and scraps?

64 Benjamin: "What is Epic Theatre?", 3 (TM); Benjamin: "Was ist das epische Theater?", GS 2.2, 521.

65 Cf. Mears, "Arc of Modernity," 63–64.

66 Cf. my article "Passage als Modell. Zu Walter Benjamins Architekturtheorie", in *Poetica* 37, no. 3/4 (2005): 429–462 for an extensive analysis of this complex.

67 Rolf Tiedemann writes that "Benjamin's trajectory from the first to the second sketch of the *Passagenwerk* documents his effort to safeguard his work against the demands of historical materialism; in this way, motifs belonging to metaphysics and theology survived undamaged in the physiognomic concept of the epoch's closing stage.... Whether Benjamin's realization of his program was capable of fulfilling its promise, whether his physiognomics lived up to its materialist task, could have been proven only by the actual composition of the *Passagen-Werk* itself." See Rolf Tiedemann, "Dialectics at a Standstill", in Walter Benjamin, *The Arcades Project* (Cambridge, Mass. and London: The Belknap Press/Harvard University Press, 1999), 940–941. In particular with regard to more recent adaptations of Benjamin's thought from the perspective of material culture studies and the field of new materialisms, we would also be well served to heed Alberto Toscano's admonition that, contrary to certain beliefs, the historical materialist position does not rely on a notion of "materiality" or on references to matter, as, for instance, prevails in object studies. Rather, Toscano argues, materialists from Gramsci to Adorno and Sohn-Rethel were concerned with analyzing real, social abstractions. See Alberto Toscano, "Materialism without Matter. Abstraction, Absence and Social Form", in *Textual Practice* 28, no. 7 (2014): 1221–1240.

68 Adorno's reproach focused on Benjamin's notion of an anthropological materialism, which he criticized for turning the human body (Leib) into the measure of concretion (Mass der Konkretion) of an analysis that no longer deemed being called historical. Theodor W. Adorno, *Briefe und Briefwechsel* 1, 192–193. For an in-depth analysis of the controversy between Adorno and Benjamin, see Susan Buck-Morss, *The Origin of Negative Dialectics. Theodor W. Adorno, Walter Benjamin, and the Frankfurt Institute* (Hassocks: Harvester Press, 1977), in particular chapters 9–11. Norbert Bolz and Willem van Reijen argue that Benjamin's epistemology was indeed materialist, but one that substituted the concept of the embodied collective for what they refer to as Marxism's abstract concept of matter. Cf. Norbert Bolz, Willem van Reijen, *Walter Benjamin* (Frankfurt am Main: Campus, 1991), 87.

69 Margaret Cohen has made a case for positioning Benjamin's materialism in relation to the "modern realism" which Breton proclaimed and which inaugurated a tradition of psychoanalytically reformed materialist thought. See her *Profane Illumination. Walter Benjamin and the Paris of the Surrealist Revolution* (Berkeley, Los Angeles: University of California Press, 1995). Sami Khatib has systematically investigated what he calls Benjamin's trans-materialist thought, i.e., a mode of materialist thought that straddles the divisions between Marxism, anthropology, theology, psychoanalysis, and the ideas of nineteenth-century sectarian utopianists. See his "Walter Benjamin's 'trans-materialistischer' Materialismus. Ein Postskriptum zur Adorno-Benjamin-Debatte der 1930er Jahre", in *Walter Benjamins anthropologisches Denken,* ed. Carolin Duttlinger, Ben Morgan, Anthony Phelan (Freiburg: Rombach, 2012).

70 This is not to say that within the overall epistemic horizon of Benjamin's historical moment such connections would have been impossible to draw. Tobias Wilke discusses a number of examples from interwar Germany in his dissertation *Medien der Unmittelbarkeit. Dingkonzepte und Wahrnehmungstechniken 1918– 1939* (Munich: Fink, 2010). In these cases, questions of perception intersect with theoretical accounts of "things," and Wilke attends in particular to the role of the haptic sense in these techno-medial/sensorial configurations. The book closes with a chapter on Benjamin that examines the notoriously double edged notion of the *Taktisches* (the tactical) in Benjamin's late media-theoretical writings, which unfolds both into the realm of a (crypto-military) media *tactic,* as well as into a reconstitution of *tactility.* Whereas the sense of touch figures prominently here, the absence of a *strictu sensu* "thingly" component is telling. Cf. ibid., 189–229. Julia Ng has investigated the frequently overlooked yet sustained implication of Benjamin's interest in a theory of things (Sachen) with a "political philosophy of nature qua *unsustainable* life" i.e., a model that is, as she demonstrates, difficult to reconcile with certain neo-vitalist tendencies in a number of strands of thing theory or new materialism. See Julia Ng, "Each Thing a Thief. Walter Benjamin on the Agency of Objects", in *Philosophy and Rhetoric* 44, no. 4 (2011): 382–402. Here, 385.

71 Cf. John Rajchman's proposition to think the quality of lightness in architecture neither as the result of a subtraction of material, nor as the implementation of an aesthetic and ideology of transparency, but as the result of design processes that *make material light.* See his *Constructions* (Cambridge, Mass. and London: The MIT Press, 1998), 40, 51.

72 Evans: *The Mechanical Smile,* 2: "The Paris trade ... exported not goods but ideas, in the form of model dresses and the right to reproduce them" and 11: "As an

export trade the French garment trade was unusual: it sold not wholesale garments but designs, in the form of model dresses, and the rights to reproduce them." For an analysis of the respective legal and economic implications and frameworks in two major national fashion markets of the decade, see Véronique Pouillard, "Design Piracy in the Fashion Industries of Paris and New York in the Interwar Years", in *The Business History Review* 85, no. 2 (Summer 2011): 319–344.

73 See Christine Senailles, "Lutter contre la copie", in *Madeleine Vionnet. Les Années d'Innovation, 1919-1939* (Lyon: Musée des Tissus, 1994).

74 Cf. Lynne Cooke, "Madeleine Vionnet. Exhibition review", in *The Burlington Magazine* 152, no. 1284 (March 2010): 197–198. Here, 197. Caroline Evans mentions the institution of the mirrored corner copyright shot by Vionnet in her article "The Ontology of the Fashion Model", in *AA Files* 63 (2011). Here, 64. Evans also points out that both model dress and the mannequin occupy positions on a sliding scale of fashion prototypes (ibid., 66–67). We could add that the example of Vionnet's work further serves to demonstrate that the obfuscation of a dress's materiality—as is the case in the elegant designs which she pioneered—does not coincide with the attempts at protecting its specific material articulation. The copyright shot and other techniques result from the insight that it is the specific execution of dress qua dress, which enables the vanishing of its material concreteness in elegant movement, that needs to be protected against copying, which Vionnet perceived as theft. See also Senailles, "Lutter contre la copie". Every six months Vionnet had an album of copyright shots produced that documented her collection of the previous half year. In the advertisements in magazines such as *Vogue* and *L'Illustration* she warned of the legal recriminations against copying, as well as explaining where to buy original Vionnets and how to verify the authenticity of a garment by correctly identifying her label. For an analysis of the intricacies and latent contradictions of Vionnet's approach—preventing copying while relying on the practice of licensing; i.e., the attempt at establishing a controlled system of reproduction and circulation, from which to extract royalties—cf. Troy: *Couture Culture*, 327–337, in particular 331. Troy also discusses Vionnet's practice as an exemplar of wider tendencies of artistic production and monetization of her historical moment.

75 Brecht develops the concept of *gestus*—in which gesture and stance intersect—in the "Kleines Organon für das Theater," a text written in 1948 that attempts to summarize his theoretical and production of the previous decades. See Bertolt Brecht, "Kleines Organon für das Theater", in idem *Schriften* vol. 23, ed. Werner Hecht, Jan Knopf, et al. (Berlin, Weimar, Frankfurt am Main: Aufbau Verlag,

Suhrkamp, 1993). On *gestus* and stance (Haltung), see ibid., 89. On *gestisches Material*, ibid., 91. On distancing and the alienation (V-Effekt) regarding gesture see his "Hervorbringung des V-Effekt", in idem, *Schriften* vol. 22, ed. Werner Hecht, Jan Knopf, et al. (Berlin, Weimar, Frankfurt am Main: Aufbau Verlag, Suhrkamp, 1993).

76 See chapter 1, fashion and/as mode.

77 In this, Benjamin's (and Grund's) approach anticipates certain of our own contemporary positions, while also providing alternatives to them. For instance, in his article "Materials against Materiality," anthropologist Tim Ingold argues against the assumption of pre-established, given properties that would inhere materials, and forms that could readily be projected onto them, instead insisting on a perspective that sees the forms of things emerging out of the continued negotiations between these materials and their surrounding mediums from which they are separated and connected through surfaces. See Tim Ingold, "Materials Against Materiality", in *Archaeological Dialogues* 14, no. 1 (2007): 1–16. One crucial difference that sets Benjamin's and Grund's approaches apart from Ingold's work, but also other projects that are contemporaneous to their own writing and have in recent years gained a certain prominence again, is that their thinking of the category of form doesn't seem to rely on a concept of "environment" or "milieu" in a spatial sense. Benjamin's work, however, does allow for a perspective according to which time could be seen as a milieu for the generation of the forms of fashion. See chapters 2 and 4, sections on morphology.

78 This is exemplified, for instance, in the work of Jane Bennett who points to precursors from Democrit and Spinoza to Deleuze. See her *Vibrant Matter. A Political Ecology of Things* (Durham, NC, London: Duke University Press, 2010).

79 Benjamin's non-recuperability for the project of new materialism is also already indicated by his critical stance toward Bergson—a reference figure for new materialist thought—whose positions in *Matière et Mémoire* Benjamin rejected.

80 Or if so, only very remotely. Historian of science Henning Schmidgen points out that Étienne Souriau, whose *The Different Modes of Existence*, along with Simondon's *On the Modes of Existence of Technical Objects* anticipated Latour's recent *Inquiry into the Modes of Existence*, did in fact take note of Benjamin's artwork essay in his 1951 *Passé, présent, avenir du problème de l'esthétique industrielle*, the introductory text for a special issue of the journal *Revue d'esthétique*, which he edited. Schmidgen, *Mode d'existence*, 321. A parallel track is also given in Simondon's and Benjamin's shared interest in Focillon's morphology (see above). In *Passé, présent, avenir*, Souriau makes use of Focillon's concept of style for the purpose of his own morphology of industrial forms. Cf. ibid.

4 The tiger's leap and the expression of history

1. Paul Valéry, "Triomphe de Manet", in *Manet 1832-1883. Préface de Paul Valery. Introduction de Paul Jamot*. (Paris: Musée de l'Orangerie, 1932–2ieme edition corrigée), xiv.
2. Ibid., xvi.
3. Valéry, xv. Carol Armstrong comments on the interest in "the ephemera of fashion" which Valéry's analysis here displays. Cf. Carol Armstrong, *Manet Manette*. New Haven, London: Yale University Press: 2001, 175.
4. Blum, *Shocking!*, 185.
5. Cf. the documentation in Blum, *Shocking!*, 220–222.
6. Cf. Cédric Edon and Franck Sagne, eds. *Schiaparelli and the Artists*. New York, Rizzoli: 2017, 126.
7. *Vogue Paris*, October 1934, 27.
8. Cf. Blum: *Shocking!*, 203. Blum identifies Jean Peltier as the designer of the printed satin fabric and speculates that the pattern may be based on an illustration showing West in *Every Day's a Holiday* that was published in *Harper's Bazaar* in 1937. Already that very year Schiaparelli had based a number of Edwardian-style evening capes in her April collection on her costumes for Mae West (ibid., 116).
9. Writer and critic Anne Hollander has argued in a similar vein that the preference for neo-classical black and white tones of the decade can also be seen as a feedback effect from the silvery movie screens onto the parquet of the fashion houses, a draining of color from the register of fashion. As quoted in Mears, 68.
10. On Schiaparelli's general employment of Belle Epoque cuts, cf. Mears: "Arc of Modernity", 83.
11. While pushed to a height of visibility at the end of the 1930s, corseting techniques had actually been gradually reintroduced during the decade on a number of less violent, less visible levels, for instance through elastic body-shaping spanks. See Valerie Steele, *The Corset. A Cultural History* (New Haven, London: Yale University Press, 2001), 154–156. On the return of the wasp waist, ibid., 156.
12. Cf. Susanna Brown, "Mainbocher Corset, 1939", in *Horst. Photographer of Style* (London, New York Victoria & Albert Museum, Rizzoli, 2014), 76. The impact of the corseted silhouette would unfold fully only after the war with the arrival of Dior's new look, which, as he explicitly stated, was in parts inspired by the Belle Epoque fashions his mother wore. Cf. Mears: "Arc of Modernity", 62.
13. Cf., for instance, the various references to the re-emerging Directoire styles in subsequent issues of *Vogue Paris* in 1934: April, 31; July, 39; August, 24.
14. Naomi Lubrich, *Die Feder des Schriftstellers. Mode im Roman des französischen Realismus* (Bielefeld: Aisthesis, 2015), 11.

15 *Harper's Bazaar UK*, May 1938, 34.
16 Ibid. Cf. *Vogue Paris*'s earlier assessment: "Partout ce rappel d'autrefois accentue le goût d'aujourd'hui", October 1934, 27.
17 *Femina*, January 1939, 20.
18 Peter Fenves has described the interrelation of history and time in Benjamin's thought as one between unidirectionality vs. non-directionality, and how, in relation to Benjamin's early studies of Cohen, there is way of thinking about the anti-mythical character of his idea as a strange adaptation and transformation of the phenomenological principle of *époché* in relation to time and history and, in the last consequence, to the idea of messianism (see chapter 1). This *époché*, or as Fenves terms it, *messianic reduction*, would consist in neutralizing the linear character of history, associated with the deployment of mythical guilt, in order to profile the pure flow of time. It is certainly a far step from the grand designs of messianism to the intricate and frequently minute operations of fashion, but perhaps there is indeed a certain parallel to be encountered here. It is under the premise of fashion's temporal recursions, its rearticulations of the past (i.e., its no longer unidirectional character) that we could begin to think of Benjamin's conceptualizations of fashion as allowing him another modeling of such a profiling of time. While the tiger's leaps rearticulate the discontininuous, the lost, such discontinuity could be seen as entries of the non-directional character of time onto the unidirectional axis of history, fashion here serving once again as a model of time.
19 Already Anselm Haverkamp points to the proximity between the theory of dialectical image and Goethe's theory of the *Urphänomen*. See his *Figura Cryptica. Theorie der literarischen Latenz* (Frankfurt am Main: Suhrkamp, 2002), 64. Cornelia Zumbusch provides a sustained and highly detailed analysis of the interrelation of Benjamin's appropriation of the Goethean concept of the *Urphänomen* as it plays out in Benjamin's later works in her chapter "Theorie aus Fakten: Benjamin, Warburg und Goethes symbolische Wissenschaften" in her *Wissenschaft in Bildern. Symbol und dialektisches Bild in Aby Warburgs Mnemosyne-Atlas und Walter Benjamins Passagen-Werk* (Berlin: Akademie Verlag, 2004). See 306–322. Both Zumbusch and Haverkamp further underline that, beyond the question of morphology, this strand extends to Goethe's (and Benjamin's) theories of the symbol.
20 The sections of Goethe's morphology that beg this comparison pertain to the metamorphosis of plants.
21 Cf. Cornelia Zumbusch's remark that the motivation for Benjamin's appropriation of Goethe's developmental theories for the purposes of his own concept of the dialectical image is epistemological. Zumbusch: *Wissenschaft in Bildern*, 318.
22 Cf. Eva Geulen, *Aus dem Leben der Form. Goethes Morphologie und die Nager* (Berlin: August Verlag, 2016). On the metamorphic, transformative content of

Goethe's theory of form, in relation to its material and intellectual transformations over the long course of its development, see in particular the chapter "Schwanken", 65–76. Geulen concludes her book with an analysis of yet another connection between Benjamin's thought and Goethe's morphology, namely Benjamin's early treatment of the Goethean notion of the *Urphänomen* in his dissertation on the concept of art criticism in German Romanticism. Geulen points out that, at that point, Benjamin still contrasted a Goethean approach, which he located on the level of *Gehalt* (substance, content) with the early Romantics' theory of form, which combined unity and infinity (*Einheit* and *Unendlichkeit*) in the notion of the idea, and which identified infinite becoming as the source of art—the "schöpferische … Bewegung im Formenmedium" (creative movement within the medium of forms). Cf. ibid., 148–152. The quotation is Benjamin's, ibid., 150. While clearly beyond the scope of the present study, it is perhaps still interesting to note that in his dissertation, as Geulen points out, Benjamin criticizes the Romantics for failing to articulate a notion of the content (Gehalt) of art, which appears as a refraction (Brechung), rather than in a medium, taking on the state of a "begrenztes, harmonisches Diskontinuum" (a circumscribed, harmonic discontinuum), ibid., 148. The term "discontinuum" anticipates Benjamin's late reflections on history as a continuum and tradition as a discontinuum, which stand in the context of the idea of fashion as the tiger's leap into the past (see chapter 1).

23 The conflict between an approach that recognizes the ur-phenomenon in the unfolding of a historical formation at a specific instant in historical time, and the second approach which insists on the temporally disjunct, constellational nature of the dialectical image (the ur-phenomenon) could potentially be broken down into two different approaches: one that inquires into the articulation of economic processes, the other that inquires into the articulation of history. Both can perhaps be reconciled through a perspective offered by Eli Friedlander, who insists that Benjamin considers "the transformations that the historical phenomenon undergoes insofar as it is considered in view of its realization in the present." Eli Friedlander, *Walter Benjamin. A Philosophical Portrait* (Cambridge, Mass. and London: Harvard University Press, 2012), 66.

24 Hal Foster has made the related point that the Benjaminian notion of the démodé, the outmoded, may indeed be deciphered as addressing issues pertaining to the modes of production. Cf. Foster, Compulsive Beauty, 159. We could add that the *modal* understanding of fashion, a concept of fashion as a practice of materialization, would indeed resonate with this idea. Cf. chapter 3.

25 Caroline Evans conveys the related observation that the American fashion press dubbed the little black dress the "Chanel Ford" (*Mechanical Smile*, 131). What expresses a proximity to a general aesthetics of movement and automation, as well

as to industrial seriality, also speaks to the idea of ubiquity and mobility behind Chanel's designs. A woman in a little black dress "goes to places."

26 Etherington-Smith reports that the immediate effect of the 1929 crash consisted in a complete abstention of American buyers from the shows at the beginning of 1930, while houses actually registered a slight uptick in private clientele (Etherington-Smith, *Patou*, 118–119). On the impact of the economic downturn, cf. Mears: "Arc of Modernity", 62, 71 and Evans, *Mechanical Smile*, 257 on the collapse of French exports.

27 Evans: *Mechanical Smile*, 257.

28 Just as today, the vast majority of the readers of magazines would not have been the actual customer base for the designs showcased on their pages. However, even allowing for the mediating function that the publication of sewing patterns in these magazines held, providing the less well-heeled reader with opportunities for manufacturing their own versions of the garments they saw photographed, the gulf between the realm of couturized fashion and their own vestimentary reality became ever wider: a gown, the emblem garment of the late 1930s, is nearly impossible to execute "at home," whereas costumes would have indeed made for much easier home production.

29 Garnier points to fashion critic Louis Chéronnet as articulating this antinomy between the economical and social crisis and the overabundance of decorated and refined interiors and the corresponding fashions right away. Garnier: "Quelques couturiers", 46.

30 Cf. Etherington-Smith's account: "By the winter of 1930, the number of foreigners visiting Paris twice a year for clothes dwindled almost to nothing as a result of the Depression, and the couture business was flung back on its original resources. These quietly elegant private European clients, such as Elsie de Wolfe and Mrs Harrison Williams, now became the backbone of the couture business once again, and this had an effect on fashion direction. Designs made to be widely copied must be relatively simple. Clothes for private clients, who are prepared to spend time having them fitted to perfection, and to their individual taste, however, can be much more complex. Couture, in the early years of the thirties, survived simply through much more complicated dressmaking. Two-dimensional simplicity – 'one size fits all' – had given way to elaborate, sinuous dresses cut in bias shapes, pieced together on the individual client.... Precise, echoing the lines of the body, and needing several fittings to achieve the second-skin effect" (*Patou*, 122).

31 *Femina*, October 1929, 3–4. On the pejorative implications of the term *midinette*, as well as a socio-historical profile for this figure, cf. Anaïs Albert, "Les midinettes parisiennes à la Belle Épqoue: bon goût ou mauvais genre?", *Histoire, Économie et Société* 32, no. 3 (September 2013): 61–74.

Bibliography

Adorno, Theodor W. *Aesthetic Theory*, transl. Robert Hullot-Kentor. London, New York: Continuum, 2002.

Adorno, Theodor W. *Ästhetische Theorie*. Frankfurt am Main: Suhrkamp, 1973.

Adorno, Theodor W. *Briefe und Briefwechsel*, vol. 1, ed. Henri Lonitz. Frankfurt am Main: Suhrkamp, 1994.

Albert, Anaïs. "Les midinettes parisiennes à la Belle Époque: bon goût ou mauvais genre?", *Histoire, Économie et Société* 32, no. 3 (September 2013): 61–74.

Alliez, Éric. "The Difference and Repetition of Gabriel Tarde", *Distinktion. Scandinavian Journal of Social Theory* vol. 5, no. 2 (2004): 49–54.

Armstrong, Carol. *Manet Manette*. New Haven, London: Yale University Press, 2001.

Barnhart, Robert K., ed. *The Barnhart Dictionary of Etymology*. New York: Wilson, 1988.

Baudelaire, Charles. *Critique d'art suivi par critique musicale*, ed. Claude Pichois. Paris: Gallimard, 1992.

Baudelaire, Charles. *Les Fleurs du mal, précédées d'une notice par Théophile Gauthier*. Paris: Calmann-Lévy, 1869.

Beaulieu, Mireille. "Moving Human Décor. Marcel L'Herbier, Fashion, and Cinéma Total", in Evans, Caroline and Marketa Uhlirova, eds. *Marcel L'Herbier: Dossier*. London: Fashion in FIlm, www.fashioninfilm.com, 2014.

Beecher Hogan, Charles and George Kubler, "Foreword", in Henri Focillon, *The Life of Forms in Art*. New Haven: Yale University Press, 1942.

Benjamin, Andrew. *Style and Time. Essays on the Politics of Appearance*. Evanston: Northwestern University Press, 2006.

Benjamin, Walter. *The Arcades Project*, transl. Howard Eiland and Kevin McLaughlin, on the basis of the German volume, ed. Rolf Tiedemann. Cambridge, Mass. and London: The Belknap Press/Harvard University Press, 1999.

Benjamin, Walter. "On the Concept of History", transl. Edmund Jephcott, in idem *Selected Writings* vol. 4, ed. Howard Eiland and Michael Jennings. Cambridge, Mass. and London: The Belknap Press/Harvard University Press, 2006: 389–411.

Benjamin, Walter. *Gesammelte Briefe*, ed. Christoph Gödde and Henri Lonitz. Frankfurt am Main: Suhrkamp, 1996–2000.

Benjamin, Walter. *Gesammelte Schriften*, ed. Rolf Tiedemann, Hermann Schweppenhäuser et al. vol. i–vii. Frankfurt am Main: Suhrkamp, 1974–1991.

Benjamin, Walter. *Das Passagenwerk*, ed. Rolf Tiedemann. Frankfurt am Main: Suhrkamp, 1983.

Benjamin, Walter. *Selected Writings*, ed. Howard Eiland, Michael Jennings et al. vol. 1–4. Cambridge, Mass. and London: The Belknap Press/Harvard University Press, 1996–2005.

Benjamin, Walter. "What is Epic Theatre?" (First Version), transl. Anna Bostock, in idem *Understanding Brecht*. London, New York: Verso, 1998: 1–13.

Benjamin, Walter. *Werke und Nachlaß. Kritische Gesamtausgabe*, vol. 19. *Über den Begriff der Geschichte*, ed. Gérard Raulet. Berlin: Suhrkamp, 2010.

Benjamin, Walter. *The Work of Art in the Age of Technological Reproducibility, and Other Writings on Media*, ed. Michael Jennings, Brigid Doherty and Thomas Levin. Cambridge, Mass. and London: The Belknap Press/Harvard University Press, 2008.

Bennett, Jane. *Vibrant Matter. A Political Ecology of Things*. Durham, NC, London: Duke University Press, 2010.

Bertschik, Julia. *Mode und Moderne. Kleidung als Spiegel des Zeitgeistes in der deutschsprachigen Literatur 1770–1945*. Vienna, Cologne, Weimar: Böhlau, 2005.

Blum, Dilys E. *Shocking! The Art and Fashion of Elsa Schiaparelli*. New Haven, London: Yale University Press/Philadelphia Museum of Art, 2003.

Blumer, Herbert. "Fashion. From Class Differentiation to Collective Selection", in *The Sociological Quarterly* 10, no. 3 (1969): 275–291.

Bolz, Norbert and Willem van Reijen. *Walter Benjamin*. Frankfurt am Main: Campus, 1991.

Borch, Christian. "Gabriel Tarde (1843–1904)", in *The Oxford Handbook of Process Philosophy and Organization Studies*, ed. Jeny Helin, Tor Hernes, Daniel Hjorth et al. Oxford: Oxford University Press, 2017: 185–201.

Brecht, Bertolt. "Hervorbringung des V-Effekt", in idem *Schriften* vol. 22, ed. Werner Hecht, Jan Knopf et al. Berlin, Weimar, Frankfurt am Main: Aufbau Verlag, Suhrkamp, 1993: 355–356.

Brecht, Bertolt. "Kleines Organon für das Theater", in idem *Schriften* vol. 23, ed. Werner Hecht, Jan Knopf et al. Berlin, Weimar, Frankfurt am Main: Aufbau Verlag, Suhrkamp, 1993: 65–97

Brown, Susanna. "Mainbocher Corset, 1939", in *Horst. Photographer of Style*. London, New York: Victoria & Albert Museum, Rizzoli, 2014: 76.

Buck-Morss, Susan. *The Dialectics of Seeing. Walter Benjamin and the Arcades Project*. Cambridge, Mass. and London: The MIT Press, 1989.

Buck-Morss, Susan. "The Flaneur, the Sandwichman and the Whore: The Politics of Loitering", in *New German Critique* 39 (Fall 1986): 99–140.

Buck-Morss, Susan. *The Origin of Negative Dialectics. Theodor W. Adorno, Walter Benjamin, and the Frankfurt Institute*. Hassocks: Harvester Press, 1977.

Bürger, Peter. *Der französische Sürrealismus. Studien zur avantgardistischen Literatur*. Frankfurt: Suhrkamp, 1996.
Cha, Kyung-Ho, ed. *Aura und Experiment. Naturwissenschaft und Technik bei Walter Benjamin*. Vienna: Turia und Kant, 2017.
Cohen, Margaret. *Profane Illumination. Walter Benjamin and the Paris of the Surrealist Revolution*. Berkeley, Los Angeles: University of California Press, 1995.
Cooke, Lynne. "Madeleine Vionnet. Exhibition review", in *The Burlington Magazine* 152, no. 1284 (March 2010): 197–198.
da Costa, Valérie. *Robert Couturier*. Paris: Éditions Norma, 2000.
Darwin, George H. "Development in Dress", *Macmillan Magazine* 26 (1872): 410–416
Deleuze, Gilles. *Difference and Repetition*. New York: Columbia University Press, 1994.
Demornex, Jacqueline. *Madeleine Vionnet*. London: Thames and Hudson, 1991.
Deutsches Wörterbuch von Jacob und Wilhelm Grimm. Neubearbeitung, vol. 7. Stuttgart, Leipzig: Hirzel, 1993.
D'Souza, Aruna and Tom McDonough, eds. *The Invisible Flâneuse. Gender, Public Space and Visual Culture in Nineteenth Century Paris*. Manchester: Manchester University Press: 2006.
Edon, Cédric and Franck Sagne, eds. *Schiaparelli and the Artists*. New York, Rizzoli: 2017.
Eiland, Howard and Michael Jennings. *Walter Benjamin: A Critical Life*. Cambridge, Mass. and London: The Belknap Press/Harvard University Press, 2014.
Ekardt, Philipp. "Passage als Modell. Zu Walter Benjamins Architekturtheorie", in *Poetica* 37, no. 3/4 (2005): 429–462.
Esposito, Elena. *Die Verbindlichkeit des Vorübergehenden. Paradoxien der Mode*. Frankfurt am Main: Suhrkamp, 2004.
Esposito, Elena. "The Fascination of Contingency. Fashion and Modern Society", in *Philosophical Perspectives on Fashion*, ed. Giovanni Matteuci, Stefano Marino. London, Oxford, New York: Bloomsbury, 2017: 175–190.
Etherington-Smith, Meredith. *Patou*. London, Melbourne, Sydney: Hutchinson, 1983.
Evans, Caroline. "Jean Patou's American Mannequins. Early Fashion Shows and Modernism", *Modernism/Modernity* 15, no. 2 (2008): 243–263.
Evans, Caroline. *The Mechanical Smile. Modernism and the First Fashion Shows in France and America 1900–1929*. London, New Haven: Yale University Press, 2013.
Evans, Caroline. "The Ontology of the Fashion Model", in *AA Files* 63 (2011): 56–69.
Evans, Caroline and Marketa Uhlirova, eds. *Marcel L'Herbier: Dossier*. London: Fashion in Film, www.fashioninfilm.com, 2014.
Femina. 1901–1954.
Fenves, Peter. *The Messianic Reduction. Walter Benjamin and the Shape of Time*. Stanford: Stanford University Press, 2011.

Fluegel, James C. *The Psychology of Clothes*, ed. Leonard and Virginia Woolf. London: The Hogarth Press and the Institute of Psycho-Analysis, 1930.

Flügge, Manfred. "Die wilde Helena", in Helen Hessel, *Ich schreibe aus Paris. Über die Mode, das Leben und die Liebe*, ed. Mila Ganeva. Nimbus: Wädenswil, 2014: 353–359.

Focillon, Henri. *The Life of Forms in Art*, transl. Charles Hogan and George Kubler. New York: Zone Books, 1989.

Foster, Hal. *Compulsive Beauty*. Cambridge, Mass. and London: The MIT Press, 1993.

Friedberg, Anne. *Window Shopping. Cinema and the Postmodern*. Berkeley, Los Angeles, Oxford: University of California Press, 1993.

Friedlander, Eli. *Walter Benjamin. A Philosophical Portrait*. Cambridge, Mass. and London: Harvard University Press, 2012.

Für die Frau. Mode und Gesellschaft. 1926–1937.

Fürnkäs, Josef. *Surrealismus als Erkenntnis. Walter Benjamin—Weimarer Einbahnstraße und Pariser Passagen*. Stuttgart: Metzler, 1988.

Ganeva, Mila. *Women in Weimar Fashion. Discourses and Displays in German Culture, 1918–1933*. Rochester: Camden House, 2008.

Garnier, Guillaume. "Quelques couturiers, quelques modes", in *Paris Couture Années Trente*. Paris: Musée de la mode et du costume, Palais Galliera, 1987: 9–74.

Gehring, Petra. "'Operative Ontologien'. Technikmaterialismus als prima philosophia?", *Zeitschrift für Medien- und Kulturforschung* 8, no. 2 (2017): 143–155.

Geulen, Eva. *Aus dem Leben der Form. Goethes Morphologie und die Nager*. Berlin: August Verlag, 2016.

Golbin, Pamela, ed. *Madeleine Vionnet. Puriste de la mode*. Paris: Les Arts Décoratifs, 2009.

Grund, Helen. *Vom Wesen der Mode*. Munich: Meisterschule für Mode, 1935.

Grund, Helen. "Über die Haltung", in Helen Hessel [Helen Grund], *Ich schreibe aus Paris. Über die Mode, das Leben und die Liebe*, ed. Mila Ganeva. Wädenswil: Nimbus, 2014: 273–278.

Grund, Helen. Untitled and undated typescript. Walter Benjamin-Archiv, call number WBA 227.

Guéné, Hélène. "Jeanne Lanvin et les grandes expositions", in *Jeanne Lanvin*, ed. Sophie Grossiord. Paris: Galliera, 2015: 255–262.

Hamacher, Werner. "'Now': Walter Benjamin on Historical Time", in *Walter Benjamin and History*, ed. Andrew Benjamin. London, New York: Continuum, 2005: 38–68.

Harper's Bazaar UK. Since 1929.

Haverkamp, Anselm. *Figura Cryptica. Theorie der literarischen Latenz*. Frankfurt am Main: Suhrkamp, 2002.

Hessel, Helen [Helen Grund]. *Ich schreibe aus Paris. Über die Mode, das Leben und die Liebe*, ed. Mila Ganeva. Wädenswil: Nimbus, 2014.

Ingold, Tim. "Materials Against Materiality", in *Archaeological Dialogues* 14, no. 1 (2007): 1–16.

Jennings, Michael. "The Will to Apokastasis. Media, Experience, and Eschatology in Walter Benjamin's Late Theological Politics", in *Walter Benjamin and Theology*, ed. Colby Dickinson, Stéphane Symons. New York: Fordham University Press, 2016: 93–109.

Jones, Ernest. "Early Development of Female Sexuality (1927)", in idem *Papers on Psychoanalysis*. London: Baillière, 1950.

Kamitsis, Lydia. "Le style 'antique'", in *L'Art de la couture. Madeleine Vionnet, 1876–1975*. Marseille: Musées de Marseille, Union Française des Arts du Costume, 1991: 66–67.

Khatib, Sami. "Walter Benjamins 'trans-materialistischer' Materialismus. Ein Postskriptum zur Adorno-Benjamin-Debatte der 1930er Jahre", in *Walter Benjamins anthropologisches Denken*, ed. Carolin Duttlinger, Ben Morgan and Anthony Phelan. Freiburg: Rombach, 2012: 149–178.

Kirke, Betty. *Madeleine Vionnet*. San Francisco: Chronicle Books, 1998.

Kirke, Betty. "Vionnet: Fashion's Twentieth Century Technician", in *Thresholds* 22 (2001): 78–83.

Kittler, Friedrich. *Gramophone, Film, Typewriter*. Stanford: Stanford University Press, 1999.

Koch, Gertrud. "Operative Ontologien. Ein Versuch, einen klaren Begriff zu verunreinigen", *Zeitschrift für Medien- und Kulturforschung* 8, no. 2 (2017): 187–212.

König, René. *À la mode. On the Social Psychology of Fashion*, introd. Tom Wolfe. New York: Continuum, Seabury Press, 1973.

Krauss, Rosalind. "Corpus Delicti", October 33 (Summer 1985): 31–72.

Kubler, George. *The Shape of Time. Remarks on the History of Things*. New Haven, London: Yale University Press, 1962.

Latour, Bruno. *Reassembling the Social. An Introduction to Actor-Network-Theory*. Oxford, London: Oxford University Press, 2005.

Latour, Bruno. "Gabriel Tarde and the End of the Social", in *The Social in Question. New Bearings in History and the Social Sciences*, ed. Patrick Joyce. London: Routledge, 2002: 117–132.

Latour, Bruno. *We Have Never Been Modern*. New York, London: Harvester Wheatsheaf, 1993.

Lehman, Ulrich. *Tigersprung. Fashion in Modernity*. Cambridge, Mass. and London: The MIT Press, 2000.

Lipovetsky, Gilles. *The Empire of Fashion. Dressing Modern Democracy*, pref. Richard Sennett. Princeton: Princeton University Press, 1994.

Lubrich, Naomi. *Die Feder des Schriftstellers. Mode im Roman des französischen Realismus*. Bielefeld: Aisthesis, 2015.

Mainberger, Sabine. *Die Kunst des Aufzählens. Elemente zu einer Poetik des Enumerativen*. Berlin, New York: de Gruyter, 2003.

Manuel, Jacques. "Esquisse d'une historie du costume de cinéma", *La revue du cinéma*, no. 19–20 (1949): 3–63.

Maskarinec, Malika. *The Forces of Form in German Modernism*. Evanston: Northwestern University Press, 2018.

Mauss, Marcel: "Techniques of the Body", in *Incorporations*, ed. Jonathan Crary and Sanford Kwinter. New York: Zone, 1992: 455–477.

Mears, Patricia. "The Arc of Modernity I. Women's Couture in the 1930s", in *Elegance in an Age of Crisis. Fashions of the 1930s*, ed. idem G. Bruce Boyer. New Haven, London: New York, Yale University Press/Fashion Institute of Technology, 2014: 61–121.

Mehring, Christine. *Wols. Photographs*. Cambridge, Mass.: Busch Reisinger Museum, 1999.

Menninghaus, Winfried. "Biology à la Mode. Charles Darwin's Aesthetics of "Ornament", in *History and Philosophy of the Life Sciences* 31, no. 2 (2009): 263–278.

Menninghaus, Winfried. "Caprices of Fashion in Culture and Biology. Charles Darwin's Aesthetics of Ornament", in *Philosophical Perspectives on Fashion*, ed. Giovanni Matteucci, Stefano Marino. London, Oxford, New York: Bloomsbury, 2017: 137–150.

Menninghaus, Winfried, and Valentin Wagner, Vanessa Kegel, Christine A. Knoop, Wolf Schlotz. "Beauty, Elegance, Grace, and Sexiness Compared", in: PLoS ONE 14:6 (2019). https://doi.org/10.1371/journal.pone.0218728.

de Mijolla, Alain, ed. *International Dictionary of Psychoanalysis*. Detroit, New York, San Francisco et al.: Thomson Gale, 2005.

Modern Language Notes 127.3 (2012).

Moretti, Franco. "Operationalizing: or, the function of measurement in modern literary theory", *New Left Review* 84 (2013): 103–119.

Ng, Julia. "Acts of Time. Cohen and Benjamin on Mathematics and History", *Paradigmi. Rivista di critica filosofia. Special Issue on Critical Idealism and Messianism. From Hermann Cohen to Walter Benjamin and Beyond* (2017): 41–60.

Ng, Julia. "Each Thing a Thief. Walter Benjamin on the Agency of Objects", in *Philosophy and Rhetoric* 44, no. 4 (2011): 382–402.

Papapetros, Spyros. *On the Animation of the Inorganic. Art, Architecture, and the Extension of Life*. Chicago, London: The University of Chicago Press, 2012.

Parsons, Talcot. "Simmel and the Methodological Problems of Formal Sociology", *The American Sociologist* 29, no. 2 (Summer 1998): 31–50.

Le Pavillon de l'Élégance à l'Exposition Internationale des Arts et Techniques 1937. Paris: Arts et Métiers, 1938.

Polle, Emmanuelle. *Jean Patou. A Fashionable Life*. Paris: Flammarion, 2013.

Pouillard, Véronique. "Design Piracy in the Fashion Industries of Paris and New York in the Interwar Years" in *The Business History Review* 85, no. 2 (Summer 2011): 319–344.

Pouillard, Véronique and Johanna Zanon. "Wholesale Couture. Jean Patou's Line Jane Paris", forthcoming in *Dress. The Journal of the Costume Society of America*.

Die praktische Berlinerin. Das Blatt der Bazaar-Schnittmuster.

Puttnies, Hans and Gary Smith, eds. *Benjaminiana*. Giessen, Anabas Verlag: 1991.

Rajchman, John. *Constructions*. Cambridge, Mass. and London: The MIT Press, 1998.

Ray, Larry, ed. *Formal Sociology. The Sociology of Georg Simmel*. Aldershot, Vermont: Elgar, 1991.

Rey, Alain, ed. *Le Grand Robert de la langue française*. Paris: Robert, 2001.

Rheinberger, Hans Jörg. *Toward a History of Epistemic Things. Synthesizing Proteins in the Test Tube*. Stanford: Stanford University Press, 1997.

Roberts, Mary Lou. *Civilization without Sexes. Reconstructing Gender in Postwar France (1917–1927)*. Chicago: University of Chicago Press, 1994.

Robinson, Dwight E. "The Rules of Fashion Cycles", in *Harvard Business Review* (November–December 1958).

Schleif, Nina. "Die Modefotografien in Paris 1937. Ein Blick auf alte und neue Quellen", in *Wols als Photograph. Der gerettete Blick*, ed. Michael Hering, 38–49. Ostfildern: Hatje Cantz, 2013.

Schmidgen, Henning. "Mode d'existence. Memoirs of a concept", in *Reset modernity*, ed. Bruno Latour and Christophe Leclerq. Cambridge, Mass. and London, Karlsruhe: MIT Press/ZKM, 2016: 320–327.

Senailles, Christine. "Lutter contre la copie", in *Madeleine Vionnet. Les Années d'Innovation. 1919–1939*. Lyon: Musée des Tissus, 1994: 18–21.

Shocking Life. The Autobiography of Elsa Schiaparelli. London: V&A Publications, 2007.

Siegert, Bernhard. *Cultural Techniques. Grids, Filters, Doors, and Other Articulations of the Real*. New York: Fordham University Press, 2015.

Siegert, Bernhard. "Öffnen, Schliessen, Zerstreuen, Verdichten. Die operativen Ontologien der Kulturtechnik", *Zeitschrift für Medien- und Kulturtechnik*, 8, no. 2 (2017): 95–114.

Simmel, Georg. "Aesthetik der Schwere", in *Gesamtausgabe* vol. 7, ed. Rüdiger Kramme, Angela Rammstedt and Otthein Ramstedt. Frankfurt am Main: Suhrkamp, 1995.

Simmel, Georg. "Der Bildrahmen. Ein ästhetischer Versuch", in idem *Gesamtausgabe* 7.1, ed. Rüdiger Kramme, Angela Rammstedt and Otthein Rammstedt. Frankfurt am Main: Suhrkamp, 1995: 101–108.

Simmel, Georg. "Die Frau und die Mode", in idem *Gesamtausgabe* vol. 8, ed. Alessandro Cavalli, Volkhard Krech. Frankfurt am Main: Suhrkamp, 1993: 344–347.

Simmel, Georg. "Philosophie der Mode", in idem *Gesamtausgabe* vol. 10, ed. Michael Behr, Volkhard Krech, Gert Schmidt. Frankfurt am Main: Suhrkamp, 1995: 7–37.

Simmel, Georg. "Philosophy of Fashion", transl. David Frisby and Mark Ritter, in *Simmel on Culture. Selected Writings*, ed. David Frisby, Mike Featherstone. London, Thousand Oaks: Sage, 1997: 187–206.

Simmel, Georg. "The Picture Frame. An Aesthetic Study", transl. Mark Ritter, *Theory, Culture & Society* 11 (1994): 11–17.

Simmel, Georg. "Zur Psychologie der Mode. Sociologische Studie", in idem *Gesamtausgabe* vol. 5, ed. Heinz-Jürgen Dahme, David Frisby. Frankfurt am Main: Suhrkamp, 1992: 105–111.

Simondon, Gilbert. *On the Mode of Existence of Technical Objects*. Minneapolis: Univocal Publishing, 2017.

Steele, Valerie. *The Corset. A Cultural History*. New Haven, London: Yale University Press, 2001.

Steele, Valerie. *Paris Fashion. A Cultural History*. New York, Oxford: Oxford University Press, 1988.

Stith Clark, Beatrice. "Elements of Black Exoticism in the 'Jeanne Duval' poems of *Les Fleurs du mal*", in *CLA Journal* 14, no. 1 (September 1970): 62–74.

Tarde, Gabriel. *The Laws of Imitation*. New York: Holt, 1903.

Tiedemann, Rolf. "Dialectics at a Standstill", in Walter Benjamin, *The Arcades Project*. Cambridge, Mass. and London: The Belknap Press/Harvard University Press, 1999: 929–945.

Toscano, Alberto. "Materialism without Matter. Abstraction, Absence and Social Form", in *Textual Practice* 28, no. 7 (2014): 1221–1240.

Troy, Nancy. *Couture Culture. A Study in Modern Art and Fashion*. Cambridge, Mass. and London: The MIT Press, 2003.

Tzara, Tristan. "D'un certain Automatisme du Goût", in *Minotaure*, no. 3/4 (1933): 81–84.

"... und immer nur Handschuhe. Das Leben von Gretel Adorno", *Neues Deutschland. Sozialistische Tageszeitung*. 20.12.2014. Accessed at https://www.neues-deutschland.de/artikel/956137.und-immer-nur-handschuhe.html.

Valéry, Paul. "Triomphe de Manet", in *Manet 1832–1883. Préface de Paul Valéry. Introduction de Paul Jamot*. (Paris: Musée de l'Orangerie, 1932 – 2ieme edition corrigée): v–xvi.

Veblen, Thorstein. *The Theory of the Leisure Class. An Economic Study in the Evolution of Institutions*. New York: Macmillan, 1899.

Vinken, Barbara. *Fashion Zeitgeist. Trends and Cycles in the Fashion System*. Oxford, New York: Berg, 2005.

Vogue. Since 1892.

Vogue Paris. Since 1920.

Vogue UK. Since 1916.

Walton, Kendall. *Mimesis as Make-Belief. On the Foundations of the Representational Arts*. Cambridge, Mass. and London: Harvard University Press, 1990.

Weigel, Sigrid. *Entstellte Ähnlichkeit. Walter Benjamins theoretische Schreibweise*. Frankfurt am Main: Fischer, 1997.

Wigley, Mark. *White Walls, Designer Dresses. The Fashioning of Modern Architecture*. Cambridge, Mass. and London: The MIT Press, 1995.

Wilke, Tobias. *Medien der Unmittelbarkeit. Dingkonzepte und Wahrnehmungstechniken 1918–1939*. Munich: Fink, 2010.

Wilson, Elizabeth. *Adorned in Dreams. Fashion and Modernity*, rev. ed. London, New York: I.B. Tauris, 2003.

Wohlfahrt, Irving. "Et cetera? Der Historiker als Lumpensammler", in *Passagen. Walter Benjamins Urgeschichte des XIX. Jahrhunderts*, ed. Norbert Bolz, Bernd Witte. Munich: Fink, 1984: 70–95.

Wolff, Janet. "The Invisible Flâneuse: Women and the Literature of Modernity", in *The Problems of Modernity. Adorno and Benjamin*, ed. Andrew Benjamin. London, New York: Routledge, 1989: 141–156.

Wollen, Peter. *Raiding the Icebox. Reflections on Twentieth-Century Culture*. London, New York: Verso, 2008.

Zanon, Johanna. "Quand la couture célèbre le corps féminin. Jean Patou (1919–1920)". Thèse pour le diplôme d'archiviste paléographe, École nationale des chartes, Paris, 2012.

Zumbusch, Cornelia. *Wissenschaft in Bildern. Symbol und dialektisches Bild in Aby Warburgs Mnemosyne-Atlas und Walter Benjamins Passagen-Werk*. Berlin: Akademie Verlag, 2004.

Index

(N.B.: As the core document of Benjamin's fashion theory, the Arcades Project is referred to throughout the book and not individually indexed. The same holds for its author. If the index does comprise a separate entry for 'fashion', this exists mostly for its subentries, which provide the reader with a few additional points that complement the structure established through the sequence of chapters and subchapters.)

actor-network theory 7, 34, 160
Adorno, Theodor 19, 76, 154
Aesthetic Theory (Adorno) 19
Alix 136, 142, 152, 169
androgynous looks of the 1920s 4, 28, 89, 94, 115
animation
　of garments 107–10
　of matter 135, 149
Anschaulichkeit 177
Antoine (hairdresser) 118, 120, 126
aphanisis 82
apocatastasis 48
　historical 52–6, 132
Apollinaire, Guillaume 78, 116-117, 126–128, 131, 149, 150
artistic property rights 155–156
Ausdruckscharakter (expressive character) 179–180

bas-reliefs 144
Baudelaire, Charles 112, 131, 149, 155
　"À une passante" 19, 128–30, 150
　"La géante" 139
beach outfits 62
Beaton, Cecil 65, 121, 125
beautiful, the 107–8, 110
being
　in fashion (Simmel) 31–2
　temporalized (fashion as) 33
Belle Époque 4, 5, 28, 173, 184, 186
　in the *Arcades Project* 176
　Schiaparelli's collection 167–8, 170, 171, 174
Benjamin, Andrew 19

Benjamin, Dora (née Kellner) 99, 100
Bennett, Jane 218
Bérard, Christian 167
Bernard, Augusta 99
bias cut 136–8, 153
bicycling costumes 95
Blumenberg, Hans 52
Boulanger, Louise 3, 67–68, 73, 99
Brecht, Bertolt 151–152, 156–159
Bresson, Robert 169–170
Breton, André 96, 133
Buck-Morss, Susan 8, 20, 22, 26–27, 97
Building in France (Giedion) 153–154

camera shots 10, 157
capitalist modernity 20
Chanel, Coco 18, 66, 95, 99, 180–1
chronotechnics 7, 18, 21–2, 50, 55, 163, 174, 183, 185
Cocteau, Jean 146
Cohen, Herman 38
commodification 97–99, 130, 210
commodity form 27
contemporary fashion 94
　and the previous century 164
corsets 4, 11, 173–5, 181, 183
Couturier, Robert 139, 140, 142
couturiers, inspiration of 164
crêpe 60, 137, 144
crinoline 83–4, 88, 175, 181
cultural techniques 7, 34, 191, 196

Dame à l'éventail (painting) 140
Darwin, Charles 80–81, 87, 205
Darwin, George H. 81, 188, 206

Das Schwarze Korps 107
death 20–22, 96, 97
   and fashion 21
demarcations (or boundaries) 32, 33
démodé 41, 43, 44, 54, 100
designers 3 (*see also* Boulanger, Louise; Chanel, Coco; Patou, Jean; Schiaparelli, Elsa; Vionnet, Madeleine)
"Development in Dress" (Darwin) 81, 188, 206
dialectical image 37, 39–40, 176, 177, 178, 179, 183, 185
   definition of 37
   and expression of economic conditions 184
   and implications for theory 131–132
   and tiger's leap 174, 176
   and ur-phenomenon 178–179, 184
   Zeitkern (temporal kernel) and 48, 132, 179
Dialectics of Seeing, The (Buck-Morss) 8, 20, 22
Dialogue between Fashion and Death (Leopardi) 21
Die praktische Berlinerin: Das Blatt der Bazar-Schnittmuster (The Capable Berlin Woman: The Magazine of Bazar Cutting Patterns) 99
dresses 60, 109, 155
   empire 136, 174
   flapper 60, 66, 116, 181
Duval, Jeanne 139

Eiland, Howard 11
elegance 4, 28, 110, 111, 128, 131–135, 142, 149, 155, 159, 169, 182
   in *Arcades Project* 116–17
   definition of 109
   in dress and modeling 3
   and the fashion industry 114–16
   Grund's theory of immanence of 113–14
Epstein, Jean 68
Esposito, Elena 19, 34, 188, 190, 191, 196, 203
Evans, Caroline 9, 12, 71, 112, 155, 189, 191, 209, 217, 221
eveningwear 116

Every Day's a Holiday (film) 89, 92, 168, 219
expressive nexus 178, 179

false consciousness 27
fashion forms
   inert 4, 134, 150
   obdurate 4, 105, 107, 134, 149, 150, 152, 155, 159, 183
   persistence of 149–51
fashion(s)
   1920s 4, 60, 62, 78, 89, 92, 94, 115, 116, 155, 182
   1930s 1, 3, 4, 67, 73, 84, 94, 116, 134, 149, 152, 174
   datability of 8, 15, 16
   discrete temporal origin 15
   evolutionary genealogy of 80
   functionality of 7
   "generational" effects of 82
   as model and as chronotechnics 18–20
   modernity of 15–18
   "in" and "out" 36
   of the past or of distant places 44, 112
   permanence of 30
   and revolution 45–46, 48–52, 185
   sexual etiology of 9
   systemic origin 15
   temporality of 40–43, 45, 128–34
   transience of 21, 30, 130–131
   vestimentary 6, 134
fashion shows 63, 71, 73, 75, 112, 133, 181
fashion work 45, 98–102
Femina 66–67, 73, 89, 115, 138, 142, 176, 182
Fenves, Peter 8, 38
filmic shots 157
First International Surrealist Exposition, Paris, 1938 140, 151
flounces 65, 133
Focillon, Henri 2, 102–4, 176, 178, 208, 218
form, fashion as social (Simmel) 32
Frankfurter Zeitung 2, 59, 76, 107
Fuchs, Eduard 78
Für die Frau (For Women) 3, 59, 61, 63, 182, 184
Fürnkäs, Josef 52

Gabor, Zsa Zsa 171
gesture, Brechtian notion of 151, 152, 159

gestus 156, 158–9
Giedion, Sigfried 153–154
Goethe, Johann Wolfgang von 177–78, 184, 206, 220–21
grace 113–114, 210
gracefulness 113
Great Depression 180
Mme Grès *see* Alix
Grund, Helen 3, 59–62, 64–5, 67, 75, 80–84, 87–89, 92, 105, 114, 128, 144, 159–161, 164, 166-167, 182
    animation of garments 107–10
    "On the Essence of Fashion" 3, 76–7, 79, 105–110, 164
    on the fashion system and fashion production 78
    theory of elegance 3, 10, 105, 109–111, 113, 115, 117, 130-132, 134–136, 142, 149–150, 155
    theory of modeling 110–12

Hamacher, Werner 8, 43, 48, 198
hard edge chic 105, 169
Harper's Bazaar 65–66, 135, 142, 175, 182
hats *see* millinery
haute couture 19, 182
Helm, Brigitte 67–68, 71, 73, 170
Hessel, Franz 63, 73, 75
Hessel, Helen *see* Grund, Helen
historical apocatastasis 52–6, 132
history 43–46, 48, 55–56, 132, 176–178, 184
    concepts of 37
    philosophy of 54, 133
    unidirectionality of 38, 39
Horst, Horst P. 136, 173
Howard, Marjorie 65, 66
Huston, John 170–71

image *see* dialectical image
imitation, in fashion 24, 35
intellectual property rights 155–56
iron construction 153, 154

Jennings, Michael 11, 52
Jephcott, Edmund 11
Jhering, Rudolph 30
Jones, Ernest 82

Karplus, Gretel 75–77, 107
Kausalzusammenhang (causal nexus) 179
Kellner, Dora *see* Dora Benjamin
khiton 138
knitwear 181
Kracauer, Siegfried 59
Kubler, George 207, 208

la mode 17, 34, 161
La Mode rêvée (film) 170, 183
Lang, Fritz 71
Lanvin, Jeanne 99, 114–16, 134, 136, 138
L'Argent (film) 67, 71, 73, 170
Latour, Bruno 187, 188–9
Lelong, Lucien 61, 116, 136
le mode 17, 160–161
Lenglen, Suzanne 66
Le poète assassiné (novel) 78, 116–17
Le sang d'un poète (film) 146
Les Dames du Bois de Boulogne (film) 169
L'Herbier, Marcel 67, 73, 170, 183
licensing 155, 156
LIFE Magazine 174
Life of Forms, The (*La Vie des Formes*; Focillon) 2, 102–104, 207
lifetime of fashion 30
ligne 102, 104, 176
line of the 1930s 67
Lipovetsky, Gilles 27, 188, 191, 199
Louiseboulanger gowns 71, 73, 170
Louis Philippe, Emperor 175

Manet exhibition, Paris 1932 165–6
Manuel, Jacques 67–8, 73, 170
Marxism 180, 184
material, non-givenness of 151–6
materialisms 156–61
matter
    animation of 135, 149
    modality of 161
    articulation of 159–160
Mauss, Marcel 6, 191, 209
media, fashion and 30–31
Metamorphoses (Ovid) 146
Metropolis (film) 71
Miller, Lee 99, 146

millinery 83–95, 120, 166
  bonnets 83–4, 88
  designed by Schiaparelli 84–6
  headpieces 166
  shoe hats 120
Minotaure 78, 84–6, 88, 101, 119, 123
modalities 34
mode (i.e., fashion) see la mode
modeling, theory of 110–12
models (runway and fashion) 71, 99, 110–113, 183–184, 191, 204
moderne 17
modernity 17, 20–1
modes 18, 34, 160
modiste 18
modus (mode of being) 17, 160, 218
Morisot, Berthe 165, 166
morphology
  and metamorphosis/transformation 178, 206–207
  in historical time 176–80
  of the silhouette 102–104, 206
Moulin Rouge (film) 170
movement, of dress and models 71, 109–13, 117, 128, 130, 132, 135–8, 144, 153, 169, 191, 210–11, 213, 218
moyenne couture 182

new materialism 160, 215
newness 26–8
Ng, Julia 8, 38

On the Concept of History (Benjamin) 2, 7, 11, 25, 53, 197
  fashion and revolution 49
  time kernel 45, 47
ontic operations 34, 36
ontological differences 34
operationality of fashion 35
operative ontologies 33, 196
out of style 43–45, 100
outmoded 55, 100 *see also* démodé
Ovid, *Metamorphoses* 146

Paris
  tendencies in 1930s couture 3, 134–49
  1937 World Fair 106, 138
Paris Chambre Syndicale de la Couture 139, 170, 181

"pastest" 42, 43
Patou, Jean 3, 60–61, 65–66, 73, 116, 167, 180–181, 184, 202
Pavillon de l'Élégance 4, 105–6, 138, 141, 142, 167
Penthésilées (Ubac) 144
peplon (tunic) 138
photogénie 68
photography 112, 136, 156
prostitution 97–8

Rajchman, John 217
Raulet, Gérard 11
Ray, Man 101, 119, 120, 150
  photos of hats designed by Schiaparelli 84, 85, 86
  portrait of Schiaparelli 126
Reliability of the Transient: Paradoxes of Fashion, The (Esposito) 19, 188, 190, 191, 196, 204
Rénier, Martine 66, 89, 99, 138, 182
retro 40
revolution 48–52
"revolutionary nakedness" 50
ruffles 132, 133
ruffs 133

Schiaparelli, Elsa 3, 4, 10, 88–89, 92, 99, 101, 105, 117, 128, 134–135, 140, 146, 149-153, 155, 170, 183
  1937 summer collection 125
  1938/39 Zodiac collection 124–5
  1938 Circus collection 167
  1939 Music collection 120
  1942 'First Papers of Surrealism' show 102
  advertisement for perfume 'Shocking' 89, 92
  articulation of the dress as "things" 138
  Belle Epoque collection 167–168, 174
  costumes for Les Dames du Bois de Boulogne 169-170
  costumes for Moulin Rouge 170–171
  costumes for Mae West 89, 92, 168
  drawer suits 120–4
  knitwear 181
  millinery 84–6, 166–7
  Rococo appliqué suit jacket 125–126
  wig 118–20

sex, contingent primacy of 78–83
sexualization, fashion and 95
Siegert, Bernhard 191, 196
silhouettes 176
    fashionable transformations of 178
    gender-dimorphous 4, 115, 182
    geometrical 89
    morphology of 102–4
Simmel, Georg 2, 32, 34, 35, 44, 45
    "Aesthetics of Gravity" 150
    Philosophy of Fashion 29, 31, 77, 95
Simondon, Gilbert 103, 176, 207, 218
Simpson, Wallis 125–6
social forms 32
Sonolet, Louis 181
sport 62
sportswear 95, 116
Stone, Sasha 100
studio film 112
Surrealism 96, 100–1, 127, 133, 134
systematic fashion theory 15

Tarde, Gabriel 188–9, 194–5
taste, notion of 107–8
temporal kernel *see Zeitkern*
textiles 114, 134, 149, 150, 152, 153, 155
Theory of Allegory (Fletcher) 22
Tiedemann, Rolf 11
tiger's leap 4–7, 37, 40, 45–50, 55, 56, 131–132
    and the expression of history 163–86
    as expression of the economy 180–6
    and the "ruling class" 185
time 45–8
    differentials and deviations of direction 36–40
    kernel. *see* Zeitkern *(time kernel)*
    measure of 7, 19, 21, 23, 34
    models of 8, 26, 39, 178, 185, 220
    non-directionality of 38, 39, 220
    seeds of 47
    sorting 43–5

tradition 7, 16, 25–26, 189, 192, 193, 194, 197
transitory, the 19, 128, 130, 131, 132, 133, 166
Toscano, Alberto 216
tree bark crêpe 138, 146
"trickle-down" model of fashion 77, 203
Tzara, Tristan 84, 86–8

Ubac, Raoul 144
une mode 17–18
un mode 17
ur-phenomenon 177–180, 184

Valéry, Paul 165–6, 167
Veblen, Thorstein 77
Verlag, Rowohlt 100
Verlag, Suhrkamp 11
Vertès, Marcel 170–171
Vinken, Barbara 9, 19, 188, 191, 203
Vionnet, Madeleine 3, 4, 10, 99, 105, 116, 136–138, 142, 144, 149, 152–153, 155–156, 153, 183, 217
Vischer, Friedrich Theodor 77
Vogue 65, 89, 101, 115, 123, 125, 135, 142, 144, 167, 174, 182
Vogue UK 66, 95
Vogue Paris 142, 167
volants 71, 133
von Harnack, Adolf 53
von Hoyningen-Huene, George 136, 144

wasp waist 173
Weierstraß function 38
West, Mae 3, 89, 92, 168, 169
Wohlfahrt, Irving 52
Wols (Wolfgang Schulze) 142, 144

zebra, stripe pattern 79–80
Zeitkern *(time kernel)* 7, 19, 45–8, 132, 179
Zeitmass 7, 34
Zola, Émile 67

www.ingramcontent.com/pod-product-compliance
Lightning Source LLC
Chambersburg PA
CBHW052032300426
44117CB00012B/1784